ARCO
Panic Plan for
the SAT

7th Edition

Joan Carris with Michael R. Crystal

THOMSON

PETERSON'S

Australia • Canada • Mexico • Singapore • Spain • United Kingdom • United States

Petersons.com/publishing

Check out our Web site at www.petersons.com/publishing to see if there is any new information regarding the test and any revisions or corrections to the content of this book. We've made sure the information in this book is accurate and up-to-date; however, the test format or content may have changed since the time of publication.

For more information, contact Thomson Peterson's, 2000 Lenox Drive, Lawrenceville, NJ 08648; 800-338-3282; or find us on the World Wide Web at www.petersons.com/about.

Editor: Wallie Walker-Hammond; Production Editor: Alysha Bullock; Manufacturing Manager: Ray Golaszewski; Composition Manager: Linda M. Williams.

ISBN 0-7689-1534-1

Printed in Canada

10 9 8 7 6 5 4 3 2 1   07 06 05

Seventh Edition

CONTENTS

Acknowledgments   **v**

Plan of Attack: A Three-Week Study Plan   **vi**

UNIT 1

First . . . Some Vital Must-Know Info   1

Why Is the SAT Changing? What Will Be Different?
What Should I Do?   4

Vital Tips for Test-Taking   7

Current Scores   8

College Applications   9

List of Abbreviations   10

UNIT 2

Presto—A Better Vocabulary   11

What's the Plan?   11

How to Decode an Unknown Word   12

Helpful Prefixes   13

Vocabulary Review: Wonderful Words and Necessary Roots   14

UNIT 3

Critical Reading   33

Success with Reading Passages   33

Success with Sentence Completion Questions   82

UNIT 4

Writing   99

A Review of Grammatical Terms   100

Identifying Sentence Errors   103

Improving Sentences   107

Improving Paragraphs   115

Writing the Essay   127

Glossary: Diction and Idiom   142

UNIT 5

Math Familiarity for an SAT or PSAT   149

The New Test   150

The Two Question Formats   152

Helpful Hints   154

Arithmetic   155

Fractions   165

Exponents and Square Roots   180

Geometry   186

More Geometry   199

Algebra   210

More Algebra   219
Word Problems and Functions   228
Algebraic Applications   237
Probability and Statistics   242
Graphs   251

UNIT 6 **The Practice SAT**   263

Section 1   264
Section 2   265
Section 3   269
Section 4   284
Section 5   290
Section 6   300
Section 7   304
Section 8   315

Answer Section   323

Answers to Practice Critical Reading Questions   324
Answers to Practice Sentence Completions   327
Answers to Practice Writing Questions   330
Answers to Math Questions   336
Computing Your Score   357
Self Evaluation for SAT Practice Test   360
Answers to Practice Test   365

Exercises

Practice Critical Reading 1-7   60
Practice Sentence Completions 1-4   88
Practice Identifying Sentence Errors 1-2   104
Practice Improving Sentences 1-2   108
Practice Improving Paragraphs 1-2   117
Practice Problems in Arithmetic   162
Practice Problems in Fractions   174
Practice Problems in Exponents and Square Roots   183
Practice Problems in Basic Geometry   195
More Practice Problems in Geometry   206
Practice Problems in Algebra   216
More Practice Problems in Algebra   225
Practice Problems in Word Problems and Functions   234
Practice Problems in Algebraic Applications   244
Practice Problems in Graphs   257

ACKNOWLEDGMENTS

In an attempt to gather the most helpful material for student use, we are indebted to the two parent books, *SAT Success* (1982–2000 editions, by Carris and Crystal), and to all prior editions of *Panic Plan for the SAT,* also by Carris and Crystal, for some of the material in this new edition.

A textbook covers many areas—such as definitions and etymology—which can spark differences of scholarly opinion. When confronted with a dilemma, we used the following authorities: *Merriam Webster's Collegiate Dictionary, 11th Edition;* Robert W. L. Smith's *Dictionary of English Word-Roots;* Warriner's *English Grammar and Composition;* Fowler's *Modern English Usage,* © 2000; and *Brewer's Dictionary of Phrase and Fable,* 15th Edition, © 1996.

For permission to reprint passages similar to those on SATs, we thank Continuum Publishing for excerpts from *H. L. Mencken,* by Vincent Kirkpatrick, and from *The Uncollected Wodehouse,* by P. G. Wodehouse.

We are grateful to John Wiley and Sons for excerpts from *The Urban Naturalist,* by Steven D. Garber; from *Animal Behavior* by C. J. Barnard; and from *It Began with a Stone,* by Henry Faul and Carol Faul.

Thanks go to Princeton University Press for excerpts from *Art Forms and Civic Life in the Late Roman Empire,* by H. P. L'Orange, and from *Economics and Sociology,* by Richard Swedberg.

Likewise, thanks to Thames and Hudson for the reprint from *Celtic Mysteries,* by John Sharkey, and to Longman, Inc., for an eight-line excerpt from *Contemporary Africa,* by Morag Bell.

Further reading passages were supplied by folks gone but definitely not forgotten: Benjamin Franklin, from his *Autobiography;* and Guy de Maupassant, author of "The Hole," from which we excerpted a small segment. Thanks to Herman Melville for an excerpt from *Moby-Dick,* and to Theodore Dreiser for a tiny portion of *Sister Carrie.* Owen Fellham and Thomas Henry Huxley wrote essays on education, from which we excerpted small portions, and the reading passages on the Maoris came from *The Journals of Captain Cook* and from *The Encyclopedia Britannica,* 11th Edition.

The biggest thanks are here, for the staff at Peterson's who have always worked so carefully on this book. Along with our warm-hearted new editor, who has a sense of humor (yeeha!), they have all striven to make this the most accessible, clear, and concise text in the field, and we are grateful.

Joan Carris and Michael Crystal

PLAN OF ATTACK:

WEEK ONE

DAY		☑ ASSIGNMENT	PAGES
1	**WRITING**	☐ Unit 1, Must-know Info	1–10
		☐ Unit 2. Vocabulary to end of prefixes..........	11–32
	MATH	☐ About the New Test	150–152
		☐ Arithmetic	155–164
2	**WRITING**	☐ About Writing and Review of Terms...........	99–102
		☐ Vocabulary: Words of Number, Size, Quantity, & Amount	14
		☐ Nice (or at least Neutral) Nouns & Roots	15–16
	MATH	☐ Fractions.......................................	165–179
3	**WRITING**	☐ Identifying Sentence Errors; plus Practices 1 and 2	103–106
		☐ Vocabulary: Words About Human Nature & Roots	16–17
	MATH	☐ Exponents and Square Roots..................	180–185
4	**WRITING**	☐ Improving Sentences, plus Practices 1 and 2 ..	107–114
		☐ Vocabulary: Normally Negative Nouns.........	17–18
		☐ Medical and Psychological Terms, & Roots ...	18
	MATH	☐ Geometry....................................	186–199
5	**WRITING**	☐ Improving Paragraphs, plus Practices 1 and 2	115–127
		☐ Vocabulary: Nice (or at least Neutral) Adjectives & Roots	19–20
	MATH	☐ More Geometry	199–210
6	**WRITING**	☐ Review all worrisome areas/missed problems. Study the Diction and Idiom Glossary	142–148
		☐ Vocabulary: Depressing Verbs & Roots	20–21
	MATH	☐ Algebra	210–218
7	**REST**	☐ We mean that literally. Tired people get lousy test scores.	

A THREE-WEEK STUDY PLAN

WEEK TWO

DAY		☑ ASSIGNMENT	PAGES
8	WRITING	☐ Writing the Essay; Scoring Rubric; Three-Step Essay System	127–132
		☐ Vocabulary: Words From Mythology, Literature, and People's Names	22
		☐ Vocabulary: Words From the Animal World & Roots	22–23
	CRITICAL READING	☐ About Critical Reading; Basic How-To for Reading Passages; Eliminating Wrong Answers; Key Words; Reading for Main Point or Central Theme	33–38
9	WRITING	☐ Write the 1st practice Essay and score	136–137
		☐ Vocabulary: Review vocabulary studied to date.	
	CRITICAL READING	☐ Decoding Attitude and Tone (Mood); Genre Recognition; Reading for Author's Rhetorical Purpose	38–44
10	WRITING	☐ Review 1st essay and score, if not previously done.	
		☐ Vocabulary: Depressing Adjectives & Roots	23–25
	CRITICAL READING	☐ Reading for Facts and Examples; Reading for What Is Suggested or Implied; Vocabulary in Context	45–49
11	WRITING	☐ Write the 2nd practice Essay and score	138–140
		☐ Vocabulary: Words from Science & Roots	25–26
	CRITICAL READING	☐ Reading Paired Passages; Reading Short Paragraphs	50–57
12	WRITING	☐ Review the 2nd essay and score, if not previously done.	
		☐ Vocabulary: Pleasant Verbs & Roots	26–28
	CRITICAL READING	☐ Summary of Know-How for Critical Reading Passages	58
		☐ Timing for Critical Reading Test Passages	58
13	WRITING	☐ Write the 3rd (final) practice Essay and score	140–142
		☐ Vocabulary: Potluck Assortment & Roots	28–29
	CRITICAL READING	☐ Review all of the Critical Reading Unit	33–98

| 14 | TAKE TODAY OFF | ☐ Make some popcorn and watch a movie. | |

WEEK THREE

DAY		☑ ASSIGNMENT	PAGES
15	**CRITICAL READING**	☐ Practice Critical Reading 1	60–65
		☐ Vocabulary: Word Groups Worth Knowing & Roots	30–31
	MATH	☐ More Algebra	219–228
16	**CRITICAL READING**	☐ Practice Critical Reading 2 (paired passages)	65–71
	MATH	☐ Fractions and Word Problems	228–237
17	**CRITICAL READING**	☐ Practice Critical Reading 3 and 4	71–74
		☐ Vocabulary: Review any unknown words and roots.	
	MATH	☐ Algebraic Applications	237–251
18	**CRITICAL READING**	☐ Practice Critical Reading 5, 6, and 7	75–82
	MATH	☐ Graphs	251–262
19	**CRITICAL READING**	☐ Sentence Completion Questions: Know-How and Practice Set 1	82–90
	MATH	☐ Take the Practice Test under *timed* conditions	263–321
20	**CRITICAL READING**	☐ Sentence Completions, Practice Sets 2, 3, and 4	90–97
		☐ Review Diction and Word Usage Glossary	142–148
	MATH	☐ Evaluate Practice SAT results and review the topics that you need most	360–363
21	**REST SOME MORE**	☐ Sharpen those #2 pencils, and relax. You prepared for the test and soon it will be over. What a happy thought.	

UNIT 1

FIRST . . . SOME MUST-KNOW INFO

Read this unit. The next few pages tell you:

- Facts about the new SAT and PSAT
- What to study
- Why, when, how, and even *where* to study
- Vital tips for test-taking
- The name of your future mate.

Okay, so I probably can't do that last one, but I guarantee the others.

The SAT and the PSAT assess your:

- Knowledge in math and the English language
- Logic and reasoning skills
- Vocabulary and reading comprehension
- Attention to absolute accuracy

These are life skills—not fancy extras—not just for the college-bound.

Basic facts about the new SAT:

The New Sat   **Total test time = 3 hrs. 35 min.**

	Time	*Question Type(s)*	*Score*
Critical Reading	70 min.	Reading Comprehension	200–800
	Two 25-minute sections	Passages long and short	
	One 20-minute section	Sentence Completion— multiple choice	

	Time	Question Type(s)	Score
Writing	60 minutes	25-minute written essay	200–800
	35-minute	Grammar and usage—multiple choice	
Math	70 min.	Arithmetic, Algebra I and II, Geometry,	200–800
	Two 25-minute sections	Data Analysis, and Probability—multiple choice and grid-in	
	One 20-minute section	answers	

New total possible = 2400

The new PSAT is like the new SAT, with a few differences:

1. No written essay

2. No advanced math

3. One and a half hours shorter

Basic facts about the new PSAT:

The New PSAT   **Total test Time = 2 hrs. 5 min.**

	Time	Question Type(s)	Score
Critical Reading	50 minutes	Reading Comprehension	20–80
	Two 25-minute sections	Passages long and short	
		Sentence Completions—all multiple-choice	

	Time	Question Type(s)	Score
Math	50 minutes	No 3rd-year College Prep Math	20–80
	Two 25-minute sections	Algebra and Functions; Geometry and Measurement—multiple-choice and 10 grid-ins	
Writing	One 25-minute	Identifying errors in grammar, segment diction, usage, and style—all multiple-choice	20–80
	Improving paragraphs	All multiple-choice	

New total possible = 240

Scoring Note: To convert any PSAT score to an approximate SAT equivalent, add a zero. For example, a PSAT score of 150 = an SAT score of 1500, out of the new total of 2400 points.

Why Is the SAT Changing? What Will Be Different? What Should I Do?

Since its beginning in 1927, the SAT—and the PSAT, of course—has changed about ten times, trying to keep pace with expectations of colleges for their entering freshmen. Also, the world itself changes. You will need skills and knowledge for the working world that weren't necessary for your grandparents.

Critical Reading Questions on the New SAT

- No analogy questions, but sentence completions remain.
- Two 25-minute test sections; one 20-minute section.
- Short and long reading passages (approx. 500−800 words) followed by multiple-choice questions that test reading comprehension.
- Paragraph-length passages also test reading comprehension, and are followed by one or two multiple-choice questions.
- Score for Critical Reading ranges from 200−800.
- It is $\frac{1}{3}$ of the test.

Best advice: This area of the test will feel familiar. See Unit 3, Critical Reading.

The Writing Section on the New SAT

The essay will take 25 minutes of the total 60 minutes allotted. See Unit 4, Writing, to prepare. And, yes, you can prepare! Multiple-choice questions ask you to identify errors in grammar, diction, and usage. You'll also be improving paragraphs by selecting an answer that corrects the same kinds of errors.

Overall scores will range from 200−800.

It is $\frac{1}{3}$ of the test. You'll get a separate essay subscore ranging from 2−12, along with a subscore of 20−80 for the multiple-choice questions testing Standard English.

Best advice: Insist that your English teachers prepare everyone for this new and important segment of the SAT. Read and do the practice material in Unit 4, Writing. Your writing reveals how clearly you are (*or are not*) thinking, so it's critical.

You can LEARN to write well! Clear, interesting essays are not a gift awarded to a precious few, but the result of learning and practicing the writing craft.

Math Questions on the New SAT

- No quantitative comparison questions.
- Two 25-minute sections; one 20-minute section.
- Questions on Algebra I and II (Seventy percent of high school students complete Algebra II. About 75% of college-bound students complete 4 or more years of math.)
- Questions on Geometry and Measurement (Study Unit 5, Math Familiarity, to review the topics covered in the new SAT.)
- Answer Types: Five-choice multiple-choice problems, or grid-in, for which students produce the answers.

Best Advice: Study as much as possible for this 70-minute segment of your test. It promises to be significantly more difficult.

What to Study

Both the "old" and the new SAT test your acquired skills with the English language and your mathematical reasoning skills, in an attempt to measure your readiness for college-level work.

1. *Focus on problem types you do poorly*. If you aren't sure, take a practice test. Get one from your guidance office or take a test in Peterson's *Ultimate New SAT Tool Kit*. Learn your strengths and weaknesses.

2. *Vocabulary*. A strong, basic vocabulary for SATs (and for life) is in this book: Unit 2, Vocabulary. Vital language roots are here, too. Jump to Unit 2 and check it out. SATs and PSATs are especially good at testing how well you understand what you read, which often depends on your vocabulary.

3. *Follow the test-prep schedule* (pages vi–viii) *because schedules work.*

As you progress, you'll discover *exactly* what you need to study the most.

When to Study

How about now? Too soon? Well, then, go to the study plan in the front of this book and think: *When* do you do your best work? Listen to your body clock, and do your test prep faithfully, at the optimum time for you.

How to Study

Be calm. You have a study schedule, remember? Also, help is available at www.petersons.com. There you can read answers to students' questions about the upcoming test changes. Study the sample questions. Choose which material to focus on.

How about a study group? Budding medical and law students depend on them. There are no distractions and no music—total concentration on the test ahead.

Suppose it is Day 1 of Week 1.

Do what the schedule says for that day. Correct any wrong answers to practice questions. Now, pick a practice test from Peterson's *Ultimate New SAT Tool Kit* and work on one section. Work slowly, being careful. Score it and learn from it, and FEEL GOOD, because this really is *how to do it*.

Where to Study

Your mind needs peace so it can absorb what you're feeding it. Choose a remote, quiet place for studying. You want to be efficient, after all, not prove how long you can mess around with this.

Why Study?

Other students like you are preparing for the SAT, and some of them are doing heavy prep. If you don't do *something*, they'll have a real advantage over you. How dumb. You'd better get in there and compete.

Vital Tips for Test Taking

These tips are really common sense, which takes you farther than anything else in life.

- *Learn the question types and their directions.* On test day, you can't waste time reading directions.

- *For each question with answer choices* (not a grid-in), *read all choices.* Cross out the ones that cannot be right. This is the process of elimination. It is the most crucial step on any standardized test.

- *Focus on one question at a time.* Ignore everything else. Even if there is a big sadness in your life, wall it off in your mind. You can't do anything about it during the test anyway, so just work on this question. And the next one, and so on.

- *Guess whenever you've crossed out one or more answers.* Answers generally fall into these categories:

   One is too big, too all-encompassing, too broad.

   One is too small, too narrow, too limited.

   One is wacko—off the wall. Find it and laugh.

   One is close—watch for this one, and avoid it.

   And one is right, specific, and focused. It answers the question.

- *Whenever a question seems to be coming from "left field,"* and you can't eliminate any answers, STOP. Make a check in the margin and come back later. Let your subconscious mind work on it as you move forward.

- *Learn to pace yourself.* Time yourself with old SATs, even if those tests aren't exactly like the one you'll be taking. You need to develop familiarity with a 25–30-minute test segment. Wear a watch to the test.

   First, scan the entire timed segment. Decide what you do best and do it first. Then do your next-best kind of question, and so on.

Are you a slow-but-thorough reader? If so, save a generous number of minutes for the reading passages—usually half the time allowed, maybe more.

- *No lengthy agonizing* on any question! All questions, no matter how difficult or easy, are worth the same number of points. NOTE: You don't have to answer all the questions. You DO have to finish all the ones you can do correctly.

- *Practice outlining and writing a short essay in 25 minutes*, something you'll do on test day. Doing it for the *first time* on that day would be really dopey, don't you think? In Unit 4, you'll see the criteria for a good essay, examples to ponder, and suggested topics for essay practice.

The Night Before the Test

Reviewing the night before a major test is often upsetting. You are bound to find something you don't know, so just forget the whole idea. Instead, go to a party or a movie or a friend's house. Do NOT come home at 3 a.m. Get a good night's sleep and eat a smart breakfast with protein in it—such as eggs.

What to Take to the Test

- Absolute musts: Your No. 2 pencils and ID card.
- Your calculator—one that you're familiar with.
- Your snack—fruit juice or tea, and a sandwich for the break.
- Your time—enough time to record a thoughtful answer for the questions you decide to do. It's not a crime to run out of time before the last few questions in a test segment. They're usually the hardest ones anyway. No one is expected to score a perfect 800 on any segment.

Current Scores

Based on the 1.4 million college-bound seniors who took the SAT in 2003, the average scores are 507 for the verbal (English) half and 519 for math, making a total average score of 1026.

These scores reflect an interesting development back in 1994–95, when the College Board declared that the scores needed "recentering." Before recentering, the verbal scores had been hanging around 424 and the math scores in the high 470s, for a combined average of just over 900.

After recentering, the average score on the SAT I became 500 and the math score also became 500, for an average total of 1,000.

Recent scores, therefore, do not say that we've been doing much better educationally in the last ten years, only that the scores were recentered by the College Board.

Your Scores Go Off to College, and You . . .

You fill out college applications, of course. Dozens of schools can offer you an excellent education, too. Keeping possible majors in mind, convenience of shuttling from home to school, and affordability, find out the average SAT scores of freshmen at the schools you like best. *Apply to those with freshmen SAT scores similar to yours* because you want to be competitive in the classroom right away. If, as time passes, you become radically brilliant and need to transfer to somewhere like MIT or CalTech, you can do that.

College Applications

Give your applications to college a great deal of care and thought. And for goodness' sake, do them yourself. If you can't fill out the application without a lot of help, how can you possibly survive at that school?

Send applications as soon as possible, not at the last minute when you can be lost in the crowd. After your applications have gone in, if you receive some award or make the honor roll for a quarter, ask the guidance office to send notice of that achievement to be filed with your application at each school. You want the selection committees to recognize your name when they see it . . . and for all the right reasons.

What's Apt to Happen to You and Your Test Score . . . and What Isn't

You will most likely go to college, make tons of new friends, and discover something you really love as a life's work. Your test score may have an influence and it may not, but for sure, in a few years *you won't even think about it*.

Above all, don't let anyone tell you that you cannot do college-level work or learn from professional training. Let your guidance counselor, a great teacher or your parents help you get where you need to go.

Remember that you are unique and you are here for a purpose. The world needs the special gifts you bring to it.

List of Abbreviations

AS (Anglo-Saxon)

Gr (Greek)

L (Latin)

Rom (Roman)

lit. (literally)

opp. (opposite)

pl. (plural)

ref. (referring/refers)

usu. (usually)

adj. (adjective)

n. (noun)

v. (verb)

UNIT 2

PRESTO—A BETTER VOCABULARY

 Are you on schedule?

Check the PLAN OF ATTACK on pages vi–viii.

Now is not the time to bemoan a tiny vocabulary. Now is the time to DO something about it. Give some thoughtful minutes to our word lists, and you'll be amazed at how your vocabulary will grow. This unit of your book occupies only twenty-two pages, but if you learn what's here, the impact will be HUGE.

What's the Plan?

You will review thirty words and three roots a day, six days a week for two weeks. Many students before you have done it, so you can, too. The words presented here are critical for the college-level reading material you'll find on the SATs, on the PSATs, and on the ACTs. You'll know many of these vital words, so focus on the ones you don't know.

1. Make flashcards. They work.

2. Get friends and family to help you review.

Learning units (roughly thirty words and three roots) are divided by broken lines as an aid to planning your review. The thirty-one roots offered here are basic to our language. They will unlock the meanings of thousands of English words.

Remember: You want a better vocabulary because it is a *life skill*, not because you are about to take a test. Your language will shape your life.

How to Decode an Unknown Word

Sometimes you won't understand the meaning of an apparently key word in a sentence. Well, it's time to send your mind on a detective mission. It will zip through these six steps in seconds.

1. *Look for a prefix.* (Vital prefixes are on pp. 13–14.) Jot the prefix's meaning in the margin of your test booklet.

2. *Look for a word root.* Add its meaning to your margin note. Suppose the mystery word is *prescient*. *Pre* = ahead of time, before. *Sci* = to know. *Prescient* literally means "knowing ahead of time, having foreknowledge."

3. *Determine the part of speech being tested.* Is it a noun? What is its relationship to other nouns in the sentence? Is it one of a group of nouns? Is it a verb? If so, is it positive or negative in connotation? And so on. Deciding part of speech can be quite helpful.

4. *Is the sentence,* overall, *positive or negative*? Does your unknown word *sound* positive or negative? Your ear often gives you clues.

5. *Try to remember a context* for this mystery word. Have you ever heard it used? If so, where? When? If you can remember *who* used the word, you may get a glimmer of its meaning.

6. *Last, put your clues together and assign a possible meaning/ synonym.* If the sentence makes absolute sense with your definition, you probably deduced the correct meaning.

Helpful Prefixes

Prefixes to Remember

Prefixes That Are Usually Negative

a, an *(not, without, lacking)*   atypical

ab, abs *(from, away)*   abdicate

anti *(against, opposing)*   antisocial

contra *(against, opposing)*   contradict

counter *(against, opposing)*   counteract

de *(away, from, off, down)*   destruct

di, dif, dis *(off, opposing, away, down)*   diverge, dissent

for *(against, away)*   forbid

il, im, in, ir *(into, within, not, opposing)*   illegal, irregular

mal *(bad, badly)*   maladjusted

mis *(amiss, wrongly, bad)*   misfortune

non *(not)*   nonsense

ob, oc, of, op *(over, against, toward)*   obstacle, offense

un *(not, opposing)*   unwilling

Prefixes That Are Usually Positive

bene, bon *(good, well)*   beneficial

co, col, com, con, cor *(with, together)*   cooperate, correlate

eu *(good, well)*   euphemism

pro *(for, in favor of)*   promote

Prefixes of Time, Location, Size, or Amount

ana *(up, back, again)*   anachronism

ante, anti *(before, previous)*   antecedent, anticipate

cata *(down, away)*   catacombs

circum *(around)*   circumnavigate

e, ef, ex *(from, out, away)*   emit, exit

em, en *(in, among, within)*   embrace, enfold

epi *(outside, over, outer)*   epidermis

exter, extra, extro *(outside, beyond)*   external, extrovert

fore *(before)*   foretold

hyp, hypo *(under, beneath)*   hypodermic

inter *(among, between)*   interact

intro, intra *(inwardly, within)*	intramural
magn, meg, mega *(great, large)*	magnify, megaphone
mini *(tiny, miniature)*	miniskirt
neo *(new, latest of a period)*	neophyte
omni *(all)*	omnivorous
pan *(all, every)*	panorama
per *(through)*	permeate
peri *(around, near)*	perimeter
post *(after, following)*	postpone
pre *(before, in time)*	predict
re *(back, backward, again)*	retract
sub, suc, suf, sug, sum, sup, sus *(under, beneath)*	submerge, support
tele *(far, distant)*	telegram
trans *(over, across)*	transpose, transcend

Vocabulary Review: Wonderful Words and Necessary Roots

Certain words repeat—in magazines, in newspapers and books, in college textbooks, and on tests. You need to own these words for life, though, not just because your test date is approaching.

Words of Number, Size, Quantity, and Amount

bountiful—in great supply; abundant

dearth—scarcity or lack; *paucity*

diminutive—tiny; *lilliputian*

disparity—difference, inequality

minuscule or **minute**—tiny (measurement of size or amount)

paucity—scarcity or lack; *dearth*

plethora—a vast amount; great excess

prevalent—widespread, *pervasive;* common to an area

prodigious—arousing awe; extremely large or impressive

profuse—flowing freely; *lavish,* extravagant (profuse praise)

scant, scanty—barely enough, *meager,* insufficient

voluminous—spacious; extremely wide or large (doesn't refer to volume of sound)

— —

Nice (or at Least Neutral) Nouns

acumen—keen perception, *shrewdness, discernment*

altruism—unselfish giving of time, money, support to others

amity—friendship, *accord,* agreement

clemency—mercy (*clement* weather is *mild* weather)

coherence—the quality of logical consistency of parts of a whole, often applied to speech and writing but not limited to them

deference—honor and respect due an older or more experienced person; esteem (v., *to defer*)

diligence—faithful, careful attention to a task (opp. of *sloth, laziness*)

euphony—pleasing, agreeable sound (opp. of *cacophony*)

finesse—skillful, adroit handling or management

levity—lightness of mood, humor

nostalgia—recollection of "the old days" with fondness

penchant—natural tendency; fondness for; *affinity* (for)

philanthropy—lit., love of humankind; refers to charitable giving (person is a *philanthropist)*

propriety—what is proper or customary; *decorum,* politeness

resolution—determination, decision (v., *to resolve*)

respite—a pause, lull, or break; rest from activity

rigor—thoroughness; unyielding or inflexible strictness

sagacity—wisdom, *perception, keenness,* shrewdness (adj., *sage*)

Roots

CAP, CAPT, CEPT, CIP (L)   TAKE or SEIZE

had a ball playing *capture* the flag (take, seize)

a *captious* reviewer (critical, faultfinding)

receptive to ideas (willing to take in, receive)

DUC, DUCT (L)   LEAD, DIRECT

induce her cooperation (urge, encourage strongly)

the most *ductile* metal (easily shaped or molded)

abduct him at night (take away by force)

FAC, FACT, FICT, FECT, -FY (L)   DO, CREATE, MAKE

a *factitious* demand (not real, created artificially)

his *affected* air of unconcern (put on for *effect*)

work of *fiction* (an imagined, created story)
to *falsify* the evidence (misrepresent, to make false)

— —

Our Human Nature

acute—quick to comprehend, sharply intelligent (n., *acuity*)

aesthetic—referring to the sense of beauty

aloof—distant, unsociable, withdrawn, cool

ambivalence—lack of certainty or definiteness; a feeling of simultaneous, opposing attitudes toward a subject

apathy—lack of interest or feeling

audacity—extreme boldness; *chutzpah, nerve* (adj., *audacious*)

capitulate—to yield to pressure, give in, *concede*

civil—polite, well-mannered

conspicuous—noticeable, obvious

desultory—random, haphazard, casual (opp. of *purposeful*)

discriminate—to see clear distinctions or differences

eccentric—significantly odd or unusual; *idiosyncratic*

ephemeral—fleeting, short-lived (opp. of *eternal*)

fallible—capable of error (adj., *fallacious*)

fervor—deep feeling, passion, zeal

grave—extremely serious, solemn (n., *gravity*)

indifferent—neutral, unbiased, *impartial,* even apathetic

laconic—sparing of speech; concise almost to the point of rudeness

neophyte—beginner, *tyro, novice*

orthodox—according to traditional teaching; accepted, customary

pious—extremely, devoutly religious (n., *piety*)

premonition—a forewarning, omen

provincial—lit., from the provinces; *unsophisticated*

resignation—reluctant acceptance of conditions

reticent—untalkative; restrained in behavior; *reserved*

simulate—to approximate; to *assume, feign* (*simulated* = opp. of *genuine*)

solemn—serious and sober, *grave*

stoic—brave in the face of pain or sorrow; *impassive*

tentative—not final; hesitant, unsure

vehement—profoundly intense, passionate (opp. of *tepid*)

willful—strong-minded, stubborn, determined, headstrong

Roots

FER (L)   CARRY, BEAR, YIELD

transference of ideas (carrying across to a receiver)
a correct *inference* (a conclusion or assumption)
defer to her judgment (yield or give way in respect)

GRAPH, GRAM (Gr)   WRITE, WRITING

a *graphic* picture (delineated well, described exactly)
his witty *epigram* (brief, meaningful statement)
a skilled *graphologist* (handwriting expert)

LOG (Gr); LOQU, LOCUT (L)   SPEECH, STUDY, WORD, TALK

remnants of early *theology* (study of religion)
adding a memorable *epilogue* (words at a book's or play's end)
my *loquacious* cousin (extremely talkative, gabby)
lessons in *elocution* (effective speaking)

— —

Normally Negative Nouns

anarchy—absence of government, often resulting in disorder and
   lawlessness
animosity—a feeling of ill will; strong dislike
antagonist—enemy; opposing force (opp. of *protagonist* = *hero*)
apprehension—fear of evil, a foreboding (v., *to apprehend* = *to take
   hold of, physically or mentally*)
arrogance—a feeling of superiority shown by an overbearing manner;
   excess pride
clamor—loud outcry; continuous, insistent noise
complacence—smugness, self-satisfaction
contempt—feeling of hatred or loathing; *disdain,* disrespect
decadence—a state of decline or deterioration
depravity—a state of moral corruption and decay
detriment—harm; injury or damage
discord—lack of harmony or agreement; disagreement (opp. of
   concord and *accord*)
disdain—*contempt,* a feeling of superiority and disrespect
dissent—disagreement (opp. of *assent* and *consent*)
duplicity—deliberate double-dealing, deception

hypocrisy—saying or doing one thing while believing another; dissembling (adj., *hypocritical*)

indigence—poverty, *destitution* (adj., *destitute*) (Don't confuse with *indigenous* = *native.)*

indolence—laziness, idleness, *sloth*

languor—relaxed sleepiness, unwillingness to move (adj., *languid*)

negligence—lack of proper care and attention

parsimony—extreme thrift, often stinginess

trepidation—fear, worry, or *apprehension*

- -

Medical/Psychological Terms

atrophy—to wither or waste away (opp. of *burgeon*)

debility—physical weakness; *infirmity* (v., *to debilitate*)

fester—to *rankle,* irritate, or worry

phobia—extreme, specific fear (usually illogical)

resuscitate—to revive, bring back to life; revitalize

salutary—promoting good health, curative, remedial

therapeutic—beneficial to recovery from illness or a problem

virulent—fast, powerful, often fatal in its progression; poisonous, *malignant,* evil in intent

Roots

MIT, MISS (L)	SEND

a guided *missile* (anything thrown or sent into space)

emitting a delicious odor (giving off, sending out)

remiss in sending thanks (negligent, careless, lax)

PLEX, PLIC, PLY (L)	FOLD or WEAVE

a ruddy *complexion* (color or appearance of the face, once thought to reveal character)

implicated in a crime (pulled or woven in by circumstances)

are you *implying?* (suggesting indirectly)

PON, POS (L)	PLACE or PUT

postpone a decision (put off until a later time)

an *expository* paper (informative, factual)

to *depose* a tyrant (lit., to put down; to remove forcibly)

- -

Nice (or at Least Neutral) Adjectives

arcane—known to a select few; secret, *esoteric,* mysterious

astute—wise, shrewd, *perceptive, perspicacious*

austere—reserved, somber, grave in manner; *unadorned*

benevolent—good-hearted, generous (n., *benevolence*)

blithe—merry, lighthearted; also, casual or heedless

candid—open, honest, frank

convivial—sociable, *gregarious, congenial*

demure—well-behaved, *sedate,* shy, and modest

dispassionate—unbiased, objective, lacking passion, neutral

docile—easy to direct or discipline; *complaisant,* amiable

eloquent—phrased in a moving, forceful manner; verbally skilled
(n., *eloquence*)

elusive—hard to pin down or to understand; tending to escape
description or capture (v., *to elude*)

fastidious—extremely particular or neat; picky

feasible—possible to do ("doable")

frugal—careful about the use of money or goods; economical

impartial—not biased or prejudiced; fair, just

incessant—continuous, unstopping, ceaseless, *unremitting*

lucid—clear and distinct; logical, intelligible

magnanimous—bighearted, generous and forgiving

novel—fresh, new, original, creative (v., *to innovate*)

objective—not biased or prejudiced (opp. of *subjective*)

palatable—acceptable, even pleasurable (to the mind or the taste
buds)

potent—having strength or power; effective

pragmatic—sensible, practical

profound—deep, with serious meaning; showing perception

prudent—wise, sensible, *judicious* (showing good judgment)

subtle—not obvious; *elusive;* also, refined

succinct—brief and to the point; *concise, pithy*

urbane—polished and sophisticated (said of men, manners, prose, and
other arts, but not used for women)

vigilant—watchful, on guard, *wary* (n., *vigil*)

Roots

SPEC, SPIC, SPECT (L)   SEE or LOOK

a *specimen* of his art (visible sample)

thoughtful, *perspicacious* fellow (observant, wise, shrewd)

speculate on the many clues (reflect, wonder, consider)

TEN, TIN, TAIN, TENT (L)   HOLD or CONTAIN

his long-held *tenet* (belief)

the *tenacity* of a bulldog (determination to hold on, *retention,*
   courage)

a monk's *abstinence* (refraining from worldly pleasures)

detain the culprit (hold back, restrain)

TEND, TENS, TENT (L)   STRETCH

a *tendency* toward lengthy speeches (a proneness toward, a natural
   learning)

on the *pretense* of being tired (false show, sham)

a *pretentious* display (showy, falsely grand)

— —

Depressing Verbs

admonish—to warn strongly or show disapproval; *reprove*

blaspheme—to curse (adj., *blasphemous*)

censor—to edit for questionable material; to examine, with the goal of
   deleting material

censure—to criticize harshly, *chastise, castigate*

coerce—to force or compel (someone or something)

condescend—to come down in level; to unbend; to stoop, as, *she
   condescended to reply to my letter*

denounce—to accuse; to inform against; to criticize

deride—to make fun of, to ridicule or scorn (n., *derision*)

desecrate—to profane (foul) anything sacred (opp. of *consecrate*)

disparage—to belittle or downgrade another's accomplishments

dissipate—to use up in a worthless, foolish way; to waste

enervate—to sap, exhaust, weary

exacerbate—to irritate or worsen a situation or condition; to *aggravate,* intensify

hamper—to get in the way of, to *hinder* or obstruct

instigate—to egg on; to *foment* (something bad)

inundate—to overwhelm, as a flood

lampoon—to ridicule, make fun of; to satirize

malign—to slander, *defame,* speak ill of

mar—to damage the appearance or substance of (but not disastrously)

proscribe—to outlaw, *forbid,* prohibit

recant—to renounce (an opinion or belief); to confess error or wrongdoing

refute—to prove wrong by giving evidence to the contrary; to disprove, rebut, deny

reproach—to reprove or show displeasure (with someone)

repudiate—to reject, refuse to accept; to decline

rue—to regret with sorrow; to feel remorse (adj., *rueful*)

squander—to use in silly, extravagant ways; to waste or *dissipate*

sully—to soil or *defile*

thwart—to foil, baffle, or frustrate (someone's attempts)

usurp—to take (a position of authority) by force, often without the right to do so

vilify—to slander, *malign,* defame

Roots

DIC, DICT (L)   SPEAK, SAY, WORDS

an error in *diction* (word choice or usage)

the emperor's stern *edict* (order, forceful command)

a necessary *interdiction* (ruling that prohibits action or stops or impedes an enemy)

FLU, FLUCT (L)   FLOW

impressive *fluency* of our speaker (polished flow of words)

superfluous addition of lace (extra, extravagant, wasteful)

a *fluctuating* temperature (moving, not stable)

GEN (Gr and L)   CAUSE, KIND, BIRTH, RACE

regenerate your enthusiasm (give new life to)

a noble *progenitor* in our family (forefather, ancestor)

talk that *engenders* arguments (gives rise to, causes)

an *indigenous* species (native to the area, local)

Words from Mythology, Literature, and People's Names

chauvinist—an extreme patriot, loyal beyond reason (from Nicholas Chauvin)

chimera—wild dream or fanciful imaginative creature (Gr. myth)

cupidity—greed, avarice (Rom. myth)

halcyon—peaceful, tranquil (Gr. myth)

hector—to bully or pick on; *harass* (Gr. myth)

jovial—jolly, good-natured, fond of laughter (Rom. myth)

lethargy—sluggishness, *torpor, languor, lassitude* (Gr. myth)

malapropism—a hilarious misuse of words (Sheridan, *The Rivals*)

mentor—respected guide or counselor; teacher (Gr. myth)

mercurial—*volatile;* changing easily (Rom. myth)

mnemonics—the art of improving memory through association (Gr. myth)

muse—source of inspiration; a poet; v., *muse = to ponder or mull over* (Gr. myth)

narcissism—self-love; extreme egotism (Gr. myth)

nemesis—relentless pursuer of evildoers; any jinx or *bane* (Gr. myth)

quixotic—idealistic but impractical (Cervantes, *Don Quixote*)

stentorian—obnoxiously loud (Gr. myth)

tantalize—to torment or tease, often with something unobtainable (Gr. myth)

thespian—actor or actress (from Thespis, a Greek)

- -

From the Animal World

asinine—stupid or ridiculous; lacking good judgment

bellwether—a leader whom others follow (from the belled sheep who leads his flock)

bovine—slow-moving, stolid, slow-witted, as cows and oxen

canine—referring to dogs or anything doglike

carnivorous—meat-eating

denizen—a normal inhabitant, either plant or animal

feline—like cats (big and small) in behavior, character, or appearance

herbivorous—plant-eating

prehensile—able to grasp quickly and naturally, as a monkey's prehensile tail grasps a branch (a *prehensile* mind grasps ideas easily)

ruminate—to ponder repeatedly, slowly, and thoughtfully, the way a cud-chewing animal deals with its food

simian—like apes or monkeys in character, behavior, and appearance

whelp—any youngster *(pup)*; v., to give birth (dogs)

Roots

HOM, HOMO (L); ANTHROP (Gr)   MAN, HUMANKIND

the *homage* virtue deserves (honor, respectful tribute)

abominable *homicide* (killing of a human being)

a course in *anthropology* (study of humankind's origins)

a victim of *misanthropy* (hatred of people in general)

MAN, MANU (L)   HAND

a recent royal *mandate* (formal command or order)

emancipated the poor bird (set free, especially from captivity or bondage)

our *manifest* destiny (obvious, easy to recognize)

NOMEN, NOMIN (L); ONYM (Gr)   NAME

ancient botanical *nomenclature* (any system of naming)

a *nominal* fee for the job (in name only; insignificant)

famous *pseudonym,* Mark Twain (lit., false name; pen name)

— —

Depressing Adjectives

This list is a little longer than the rest. Spend some extra time today, or save a few words for Day 9 if you need to.

acrid—deeply bitter (comments); sharply pungent (smoke)

ambiguous—vague and unclear; lacking definition

apocryphal—of doubtful origin (an *apocryphal remark*)

arduous—demanding, difficult

banal—stale, overused, *trite, hackneyed* (opp. of *novel*)

belligerent—looking for a fight, *bellicose, feisty, pugnacious, truculent*

caustic—biting, corrosive, *incisive, cutting, trenchant, mordant*

contrite—sorrowful for some wrong; *penitent, remorseful*

credulous—innocent, *gullible, naive, ingenuous*

didactic—designed to teach; now often means boring or *pedantic,* like the behavior of a know-it-all

dogmatic—stubborn, strongly opinionated, *dictatorial, doctrinaire*

dubious—doubtful, questionable (opp. of *indubitable*)

erratic—on no set course, wandering, nomadic; *devious*

flagrant—conspicuous in a very negative way; glaring, gross

futile—hopeless

garrulous—extremely talkative, gabby, *loquacious* (opp. of *taciturn* or *reticent*)

heretical—against accepted teaching or practice (n., *heresy*)

inane—foolish and silly, *asinine*

infamous—famously bad, *notorious* (n., *infamy*)

insipid—boringly dull and bland, dopey

irascible—easily annoyed or angered, testy, grumpy, *choleric, splenetic*

lax—loose and unstructured; slack; *negligent* (opp. of *stringent*)

oblivious—unaware, as *oblivious of my existence*

ostentatious—noticeably showy in display, *pretentious*

parochial—limited in outlook or scope, narrow, restricted (opp. of *catholic = universal*)

pedestrian—everyday, common, ordinary, dull

pompous—self-important, often arrogant in manner; high-flown or ornate, as *pompous speech or writing*

prodigal—wildly extravagant or lavish in spending

prosaic—dull, *banal,* lacking originality

recalcitrant—tough to manage or control, *refractory,* unruly

redundant—needlessly repetitive; *tautological*

reprehensible—earning disapproval or blame; blameworthy

servile—lit., like a servant; very submissive

stagnant—not moving, *static,* stationary

stolid—showing no emotion, *impassive, phlegmatic; bovine*

terse—brief and to the point, *curt* even to rudeness

verbose—wordy (opp. of *pithy, succinct, concise*)

Roots

ORA (L) SPEAK or PRAY

a lengthy, tiresome *oration* (formal speech or talk)

from the mouth of the *oracle* (giver of wise advice)

massive *orifice* of a whale (mouth; any opening through which things go)

PAS, PATH (Gr) FEELING, SUFFERING, DISEASE

known for her *compassion* (*sympathy* plus a desire to help)

eyed the beets with *apathy* (lack of interest or feeling)

view his plight with *empathy* (a feeling exactly like another's; vicarious sharing of emotion)

his course in *pathology* (study of the nature of disease)

— —

Words from Science

This list is short, so today would be a good time to review your flashcards from previous lists. (You *are* making flashcards, aren't you?)

anomaly—something different from the norm; irregularity or abnormality

antithesis—a direct opposite; *antipodes* = *exact opposites*

coalesce—to come together, join, mix, unite

doldrums—"the blues"; a state or place of inactivity, *listlessness,* or collapse

dormant—temporarily inactive, inert, or asleep; *latent*

hypothetical—for purposes of discussion, *theoretical* (n., *hypothesis* = *a supposition*)

ignition—the act of kindling or firing up (a motor or a person's mind or emotions)

incendiary—adj., highly exciting, *inflammatory,* as *an incendiary speech* (n., a bomb or explosive device)

inert—motionless, idle, static, dormant (n., *inertia*)

innocuous—harmless, *benign* (opp. of *noxious, malignant*)

metamorphosis—very noticeable change of form or character

mutable—changeable, not permanent (opp. of *immutable*)

skeptical—uncertain or doubtful; questioning

velocity—speed or rapidity of motion; rate of occurrence, especially when rapid, as *the velocity of change*

volatile—quick to show emotion; easily triggered or exploded

Roots

PED (L); POD (Gr)   FOOT

wanting to *expedite* shipment (speed up a process)

an *impediment* to progress (obstacle, anything in the way)

an *expedient,* but regrettable, idea (workable, often selfish way to achieve an end)

the speaker's *podium* (raised platform to stand on)

QUER, QUIR, QUIS (L)   ASK, SEEK

dissatisfied, *querulous* tone (whining, complaining)

an amused, *quizzical* look (questioning, teasing)

victim of an *inquisition* (official questioning, often excessively thorough)

REG, RIG, RECT (L)   RULE, RIGHT, STRAIGHT

a new, strict *regime* (method of government)

his *incorrigible* behavior (delinquent, unmanageable)

hoping to *rectify* the problem (to set right, correct)

— —

Pleasant Verbs

adhere—to stick to, abide by (n., *adherent = believer*)

advocate—to talk in favor of, support, recommend (n., *advocate = a lawyer, or one who supports you*)

alleviate—to lessen the severity or intensity of something bad; to *allay, soothe, relieve, mitigate*

ameliorate—to make better, improve

articulate—to speak distinctly and well (adj., *articulate = well-spoken, persuasive*)

ascertain—to make certain, to find out for sure

augment—to add to, increase in size or amount

comply—to agree to, go along with (rules, ideas, wishes) (adj., *compliant = docile, tractable*)

conciliate—to calm someone's anger by agreeable behavior; to *appease, pacify, reconcile, mollify, placate*

condone—to overlook (an offense); to pardon or excuse

converge—to come together, meet

deter—to forestall, to "head off" or stop

discern—to see, as to *discern the campfire in the night;* to reason, conclude, or detect by more than sight alone; to note differences by careful discrimination

disseminate—to disperse or spread (ideas, knowledge) as though sowing seeds

emulate—to strive to equal; imitate, copy

enhance—to make better or more desirable

enthrall—to charm, entrance, as though by a spell

extol—to praise highly, even extravagantly

facilitate—to "smooth the way"; to make easier

flaunt—to show off, display proudly

heed—to pay attention to

innovate—to do something new; to be original

pacify—to calm, *appease, mollify, conciliate, placate*

preclude—to forestall (a bad outcome); to hinder, avert, *prevent*

rejuvenate—to give new life; to make youthful again

revere—to honor, worship, respect highly (n., *reverence*)

sanction—to authorize, *endorse,* approve (**Note:** pl. n., *sanctions = forceful measures to ensure compliance with law*)

scrutinize—to examine minutely (n., *scrutiny*)

solicit—to seek something (support, donations, customers)

temper—to moderate or adjust *(to temper discipline with love);* to strengthen through hardship *(tempered in war);* to soften *or* toughen metals during manufacture

venerate—to admire, revere, honor, worship (adj., *venerable = worthy of admiration*)

Roots

SCI (L)   KNOW

with a clear *conscience* (mental seat of moral judgment)

not being *omniscient* (all-knowing)

ESP—one form of *prescience* (foresight, foreknowledge)

STRING, STRICT (L)   TIE, BIND TIGHTLY

a *stringent* rule (rigid, strict)

her throat was *constricted* by fear (rigid, unrelaxed)
narrow *stricture* of belief (tight restraint or limit)

TANG, TING, TACT, TIG (L)   TOUCH, BORDER ON

a *tangible* difference (noticeable, perceptible)
contingent on student vote (dependent on)
fur with *tactile* appeal (ref. to the sense of touch)
contiguous garden plots (touching, bordering on)

— —

Potluck

abstract—without substance, *theoretical* (opp. of *concrete*)
barren—not fertile; lacking progeny (children, crops, etc.)
cognizant—aware, conscious of
concede—to yield, give in, or give way (n., *concession*)
cryptic—hard to decipher, puzzling, *enigmatic*
dichotomy—division into two groups or ideas at odds with one
  another; lit., cut in two
diffident—shy, lacking self-confidence (opp. of *arrogant*)
diverse—different, unlike, dissimilar, as *diverse careers*
enigma—complex puzzle, mystery, *conundrum*
expurgate—to abridge, cut; to censor for questionable material
fortuitous—happening by chance, accidental, not on purpose
germane—fitting and appropriate; *pertinent, relevant*
incontrovertible—absolute, beyond doubt, *indisputable*
inevitable—bound to occur, unavoidable
inexorable—not movable by any means; *relentless,* inflexible
innate—inborn, natural, inherent (talents, personality traits, physical
  appearance, fears, instincts)
intrinsic—internal, inherent (opp. of *extrinsic* = *external*)
irony—the use of words to convey meaning other than the literal meaning; an expression or happening implying its opposite; *sarcasm*
mundane—of the material world, as opposed to the spiritual; everyday, ordinary, dull, commonplace
nuance—subtle undertone of meaning; *nicety*
obscure—unclear, vague, faint; mysterious or enigmatic; remote, as *an
  obscure hideout;* ambiguous

paradox—a contradiction in terms; as *the occurrence of icy hail in summer is a paradox*

pervade—to *permeate,* to become part of something else, as *smoke pervaded the air* (adj., *pervasive*)

relevant—important, significant (to what is being considered); *germane*

rhetoric—the skill of fine speaking and writing; also, pompous or hypocritical language, as *empty rhetoric*

superficial—on the surface; unimportant, insignificant

tortuous—winding, twisted, as *a tortuous mountain road* (Don't confuse with *torturous = cruelly painful*)

truncate—to cut short, curtail

vacillate—to waver among choices, to dither around

vicarious—felt or experienced through another person, as *I get a vicarious thrill watching Bob ski*

Roots

TERR (L)   LAND, EARTH
lovable Yorkshire *terrier* (lit., earth dog)
a *subterranean* animal (underground)
interment at Greengage (lit., into the earth; burial)
disinter the body (take out of the earth, dig up)

THE (Gr); DEI (L)   GOD
one prominent *theologian* (expert on religion)
most vocal *atheist* around (one denying God's existence)
as if she were a *deity* (a god; heavenly being)

VEN, VENT (L)   COME
convene the meeting (call to order; cause to come together
loves *The Ark of the Covenant* (pledge, promise, contract)
prior to their *advent* (arrival, coming)

— —

Word Groups Worth Knowing

Check out these word groups. Certain ideas and personality traits have given birth to many word sets.

To Soothe Injured Feelings or Fears

placate	allay (fears, worries)
mollify	alleviate (pain, suffering)
pacify	calm
conciliate	appease

Antonyms: aggravate, exacerbate, annoy, irritate

For Those Lacking Worldly Knowledge

naive	unsophisticated
ingenuous	unaffected
innocent	natural

Antonyms: sophisticated, urbane (men), street-smart, polished, affected

For the Unemotional

bovine	phlegmatic
impassive	stoic (mainly unemotional)
stolid	apathetic

Antonyms: volatile, emotional, sensitive, demonstrative

For Those Like Scrooge

stingy	penurious
tight	penny-pinching
parsimonious	

Antonyms: generous, lavish, prodigal, philanthropic

Rigidly Set in Feelings or Behavior

obdurate	inflexible
adamant	stubborn
unyielding	

Antonyms: flexible, accommodating, adaptable, pliable

For Clichés—Those Dull, Overused Expressions

trite   hackneyed
banal   stale

Antonyms: fresh, novel, inventive, original, new

For Thinkers

keen   perspicacious
perceptive   acute
discerning   sagacious
astute   judicious (wise)

Antonyms: obtuse, dense, dull, slow-witted

For Fighters

belligerent   aggressive
bellicose   feisty
truculent   pugnacious

Antonyms: pacific, peaceable, conciliatory

For Talkers

loquacious   chatty
gabby   prolix
garrulous   long-winded
verbose   effusive (gushy)

Antonyms: succinct, pithy, terse, concise, curt, reticent

Roots

VIA (L)   ROAD, WAY

deviate from tradition (swerve, take a different course)
a *devious* path (roundabout or remote)
having a *devious* mind (tricky, deceitful)
impervious to rain (lit., no way through, impenetrable)

VOC, VOKE (L)   CALL

music to *evoke* memories (call forth)
career that is *vocation* (job) and *avocation* (hobby)
revoke that order (lit., call back; rescind or take back)

QUICK TIP

Words often function as many different parts of speech.

For example: Think of the word *rank*.

As verb—I *rank* high in my class.

As noun—What *rank* has she attained in her class?

As adjective

> —The *rank* growth of weeds clogs our pond. (lush or excessive)

> —Jim is a *rank* amateur at tennis. (as an intensifier)

> —The *rank* odor of sewage hurts my nose. (offensive)

> —Their *rank* disobedience needs correcting. (flagrant)

If the answer choices don't seem to go with the other words in a sentence, you might be looking for the wrong meaning of a word. Ask yourself, what other meaning can this word have?

UNIT 3

CRITICAL READING

Are you on schedule?

Check the PLAN OF ATTACK on pages vi–viii.

Like Gaul, in Caesar's *Gallic Wars*, the new SAT is divided into three parts:

- $\frac{1}{3}$ Critical Reading; $\frac{1}{3}$ Writing; and $\frac{1}{3}$ Math.
- Each third is worth a total of 800 points . . . on a good day.

This unit will help you to do your best on the Critical Reading segment.

Success with Reading Passages

First, the layout:

Time:	70 minutes (Two 25-minute sections; one 20-minute section)
Question Types:	Reading Passages with multiple-choice answers
	—passages ranging from 400 to 850 words
	—short passages of 100 words, more or less
	Sentence Completion problems
Points:	800

Reading passages cover the humanities, the social and physical sciences, and fiction. They are chosen from college-level reading

33

matter, because you need to be able to interpret that type of material correctly in order to succeed in college.

To quote the College Board: the Critical Reading section:

"measures students' ability to identify genre, relationships among parts of a text, cause and effect, rhetorical devices, and comparative arguments."

The passages are usually interesting, so don't worry about slogging through "killer reading" laden with indecipherable jargon. Basically, this test segment will seem like any SAT from the last ten years. You will need a strong vocabulary—a college-level vocabulary—to fully comprehend these test materials.

Why So Much Emphasis on Language Skills?

While some folks seem magically able to repair cars, or paint memorable pictures, or bat balls deep into left field, most of us depend on our language skills to make a living. You can count on it: *your language will shape your life*.

Here's another truth: Roughly 90 percent of college work is based on reading comprehension, so you can see why questions testing language proficiency now take up $\frac{2}{3}$ of the SAT.

Basic HOW-TO for the Critical Reading Section

1. **Examine past SATs to gain familiarity** with question types and answers.

2. **Be very careful about recording answers.** Be sure the question number matches the number on your answer sheet. Some people record answers in the test booklet, then transfer them carefully in a batch to the answer sheet.

3. **Never grab the first appealing answer!** Eliminate answer choices one by one. Cross them out in your test booklet.

4. **Make an educated guess whenever you eliminate two wrong answers.** You have a 33 percent chance of getting the answer right even if you're guessing.

5. **Choose direct, simple answers.** Often the longer answers are designed to sound impressive so that you'll pick them.

6. **If the question and answer choices are from outer space, do not guess.** Leave that answer space blank on your answer sheet. Blanks are not good, but you lose $\frac{1}{4}$ of a right answer for every wrong answer.

7. **If you have a strong hunch about an answer choice, pick it,** especially if you've eliminated one or two other answer choices.

8. **The unknown is sometimes the answer.** If you've eliminated all but one answer, and that answer is unknown to you, pick it anyway. The others were wrong, remember?

9. **Don't dither around on any question.** Move on to the next question so that you collect as many right answers as possible. You can contemplate the weirdos later, if there's time.

10. **Answer your best kinds of questions first.** Your job is to record as many right answers as you can before time runs out. *Each right answer is worth the same number of points, no matter how easy or how hard*.

    You do not have to answer ALL of the questions, but you do need to make a serious try on all the ones for which you have some hope.

11. **"Killer questions" are any that you cannot answer.** Usually hard questions come near the end of a test section, but they can come anywhere in Critical Reading segments. Snarl at these questions and move on.

12. **Keep track of time.** Before test day, practice with old SATs so that you have a "feel" for the 30-minute testing segment. *Managing time is a major test-taking skill*.

Want to Eliminate Answers? Watch for These Patterns

You'll have five answer choices for each verbal question. After examining too many SATs to even think about, here's what I discovered for way over half of the questions:

- One answer covers too much ground. It is too broad, too "big" in some way.

- One or more answers are too narrow, too restricted in outlook—too "small" in some way.

- One answer is apt to parrot the passage, repeating exact phraseology. It may be tempting, but is often too narrow or limited in scope.

- One answer may be off the wall—wacko—illogical. Find it and laugh.

- One answer will be right. It will be specific and will stand up to any test you apply for accuracy.

Be meticulous about eliminating wrong answers one by one, keeping the above possibilities in mind, and you'll get good at finding correct answers.

KEY Word Alert!

Certain words send big messages. They signal shifts in attitude or tone; they set up a contrast or comparison; they foreshadow positive or negative outcomes—*something* to note. We call those Key Words.

Many words signal a change—a contrast. They include *but*, *although*, *however*, *uncharacteristically*, *atypically*, *illogically*, *abnormally*, *curiously*, *strangely*, *ironically*, *nevertheless*, *even so*, *on the other hand*, *nonetheless*, *unless*, *moreover*, *except*, *yet*, and other similar words. These words point to something different from what has gone before. They are *shift points* in the sentence or paragraph and you need to mark them.

Words that hint at similarities or like ideas being compared include *and*, *moreover*, *like*, *always*, *ever*, *faithfully*, *regularly*, *dependably*, *reflected*, *echoed*, *repeated*, and so on.

Words that suggest cause and effect concepts include *so*, *thus*, *because*, *since*, *as a result*, *unless*, *except*, *but*, *therefore*, and so on.

Remember that each word in a sentence has a JOB to perform. The key words may seem small or ordinary, but they are chock full of meaning that you need to note. Often *major shifts occur within the verbs in sentences*, such as *echoed*, *reflected*, *downgraded*, *vacillated*, and so on.

What Kinds of Questions Are Asked?

Questions on reading passages generally fall into these categories:

- Main point or central theme of the passage.
- Author attitude or tone. How does the writer *feel* about his material?
- Genre recognition.
- Author's rhetorical purpose? What does the writer hope to accomplish with this essay . . . this specific example . . . this analogy . . . this comparison?
- Basic facts contained in the material.
- Implications of the material, asking you to draw conclusions (to infer meaning) based on material in the passage.
- Use of various words in context, i.e., What does this word mean *here*?

How to Read for the Main Point or Central Theme

Everything written or said has a point to make. Why write or speak if you don't have a point?

Typical SAT Questions on the Main Point include:

- The author's primary purpose in the passage is . . .
- This passage is mainly concerned with . . .
- This passage/these paragraphs primarily suggest that . . .
- The passage as a whole most completely answers which question? (Answers are in the form of questions.)

In order to locate correct answers, try the following approach:

- First, skim all the questions quickly before reading the passage. Now you know what to read for. (If you hate this idea, okay, but try it a few times before deciding against it.)

- Read quickly on this "main idea hunt." Mark any meaty or summarization sentences with asterisks. Underline anything that seems to be a major conclusion or viewpoint. You'll need these sentences later.

- In the first paragraph, look for the main idea. How about at the end of that paragraph? No? Then perhaps it's summarized near the end of the passage.

- If you're unsure of the main idea after reading quickly one time, move on to your *in-depth reading* of the passage. As you work, the major focus of the piece will become clearer and you can answer any question on the main idea.

Reading to Decode Attitude or Tone (Mood)

You should be able to decide on the author's attitude toward his or her material, or the overall tone of the passage, after one quick read. How? By circling words the author chooses. If the writer says someone is "a pitifully poor excuse" as a manager, then he or she thinks the manager is a total dimwit. Any answer showing admiration for the manager would be wrong. *Authors always reveal attitude by their choice of words*. For the paragraphs that follow, circle words that will guide you to correct answers about author attitude or the tone (mood) of the piece.

Practice A

Another lamentable aspect about the current economy is the dwindling number of jobs in the clothing sector. Blouses, slacks, socks, and underwear—garments that we wear and replace regularly—now are manufactured by willing workers overseas who have no labor unions to protest unsavory working conditions, and no preconceived notions of how much their jobs are worth.

Question

The writer's outlook (attitude) on the current economy is best summarized as

(A) puzzled

(B) uninformed

(C) impatient

(D) disheartened

(E) ambivalent

Question

The writer would most likely characterize workers overseas as

(A) somewhat greedy

(B) rather naïve

(C) basically enslaved

(D) lacking in skills

(E) patient and perceptive

Answers

In the first paragraph, did you circle "Another lamentable aspect"? This opening phrase tells you that there are *other aspects* (previously discussed, no doubt) to be *lamented* (regretted, deplored) in the current economic picture. This writer feels he has much to *bemoan*. Therefore he is not *puzzled* (A) at all; he is definite. He is not *uninformed* (B) either, as he cites working conditions overseas and appears knowledgeable. He may be *impatient* (C) but we can't find support for that in this passage, and we must support answer choices with material in the passage. Last, he is not *ambivalent* (E), which means feeling two ways about a topic, or perhaps being unsure of what to feel. This writer is plainly depressed about the economy and therefore *disheartened* (D) is the most accurate answer choice.

The second question asks you to determine how the writer feels about overseas workers. Did you circle the phrase "willing workers"? Those overseas workers are eager for the jobs. Did you note that they apparently ignore "unsavory working conditions"? They have no workers' unions to protest bad working environments, and they also have "no preconceived notions of how much their jobs are worth"—no inherited any ideas of what they should be paid. Look at the answer choices.

(A) *somewhat greedy?* No support for that in the passage. (B) *rather naïve?* Meaning, are they *unaware of many things* garment workers could have, such as unions to represent them and better working conditions? Yes, they are *innocent* like that, so *naïve* is a keeper. (C) *basically enslaved?* No, because they are willing workers. (D) *lacking in skills?* No support in the passage. (E) *patient and perceptive?* We can guess *yes*, but we'd be guessing, because we can't find support for this anywhere in the passage.

Thus, (B) *rather naïve* is by far the most accurate answer, given this brief excerpt.

Practice B

"Colonel Reynolds, V.C., glared sternly across the table at Miss Sylvia Reynolds, and Miss Sylvia Reynolds looked in a deprecatory manner back at Colonel Reynolds, V.C.; while the dog in question—a foppish pug—happening to meet the colonel's eye in transit, crawled unostentatiously under the sideboard, and began to wrestle with a bad conscience."

—from *The Uncollected Wodehouse*,
writings by English satirist P. G. Wodehouse

Question
The tone of this brief excerpt is best described as

(A) familial

(B) wrathful

(C) humorous

(D) irritable

(E) intellectual

Answer
Any doubts? Reread the paragraph for overall "feeling," then eliminate answer choices one by one. The writer shows us "a foppish pug" who catches the colonel's eye and decides to hide under the sideboard (a

dining room buffet on legs) and confront his guilt. Eliminate answers one by one: (A) *familial*. We might infer that the colonel is Sylvia's father, but that connection does not dominate this paragraph. (B) *wrathful*. Even though the colonel is angry, the feeling of the entire paragraph is not one of great wrath. (C) *humorous*.
The idea of a dog wrestling with a bad conscience is in itself laughable, and the most obvious choice so far. This would be a keeper. (D) *irritable*. Again, the feeling of anger or irritation does not permeate the entire paragraph. Only the colonel is angry. (E) *intellectual*, the "doesn't make sense" answer. Thus, *humorous* is the only logical choice. We eliminated the others.

***Sharpen your skills in Mood/Tone decoding* by trying the following exercise.**

For nonfiction: The following words might describe the tone (mood) of an interesting, basically serious piece of factual literature—the only kind we'll find on SATs. After each word, write your definition, then double-check with your favorite dictionary.

Approving/admiring _____ Didactic _____

Uneasy/ambivalent _____ Respectful _____

Sympathetic _____ Disinterested _____

Reluctant agreement _____ Analytical _____

Indifferent _____ Reflective _____

Emphatic disapproval _____ Nostalgic _____

Colloquial/chatty/relaxed ____ Informative _____

Detached _____

For fiction. Fiction can exhibit a variety of moods that are typically inappropriate for nonfiction, or factual literature. The job of fiction is to tell a story, even when tons of facts are involved, and so it has great latitude in choice of tone. (If we're studying factual material, we can hope it is light and entertaining, but its main job is to inform, to communicate information.)

Jot down your definitions for each of the fictional moods here:

Satirical _____   Whimsical/fanciful _____

Sympathetic _____   Speculative _____

Nostalgic _____   Deeply thoughtful _____

Introspective _____   Tragic _____

Condescending _____   Farcical _____

Romantic _____   Stark _____

Detached/objective _____   Subjective _____

Ironic _____   Bitter _____

Bleak _____   Provocative _____

Well, that's just a sample. Again, check your dictionary to see that you're on the right track for word meanings.

Genre Recognition

In literature, genre refers to the *literary form* of the writing. The three main categories are *poetry*, *fiction*, and *drama*. Within those are finer distinctions, which you will recognize by scanning the examples below.

Genre	Examples
Epic Poetry	*Beowulf* (England); *The Poetic Edda* (Norway); *The Iliad* and *The Odyssey* (Greece)
Tragedy	Dramas, including *Hamlet*; *Death of a Salesman*; *Hedda Gabler*; novels such as *The Grapes of Wrath*
Comedy	*Les Miserables*; *Hatchet*; *Innocents Abroad* NOTE: *Comedy* means only that the story turned out satisfactorily for the protagonist, not that the material was *humorous*.

Genre	Examples
Satire	*Don Quixote*; *Gulliver's Travels*; *The Adventures of Huckleberry Finn*; *Holes* (by L. Sachar); *Catch-22*; *Player Piano*; Molière's plays
Farce	*The Taming of the Shrew*; *Charley's Aunt*; *Mrs. Doubtfire*; some *Saturday Night Live* skits
Folklore	Paul Bunyan (tall tales); *The Three Bears*; fairy tales; many of *The Canterbury Tales* by Chaucer
Fable	Short story with a moral, often with a satirical tone; *The City Mouse and The Country Mouse*; Aesop's Fables; *Animal Farm* (G. Orwell)
Romance	Stories with plots/scenes removed from common life, e.g., *Pride and Prejudice*; Wordsworth's poetry; *The Call of the Wild*; *The House of Seven Gables*; *Jane Eyre*; *Wuthering Heights*
Science Fiction	*The Time Machine*; *1984*; *The Giver*; *Jurassic Park*; The *Dune* series
Historical Fiction	*Northwest Passage*; *The Red Badge of Courage*; *Cold Mountain*; *Hawaii*; *Cane River* (L. Tademy)
Fantasy	*The Jungle Book*; *The Hobbit* and *The Lord of The Rings* trilogy; *Watership Down*; *Charlie and the Chocolate Factory*; *Charlotte's Web*
Horror-fiction	*Frankenstein* (also considered a romance); *Firestarter*, *Carrie*, *The Stand*, et al. (S. King)
Realistic Fiction	*Little Women*; *The Old Man and the Sea*; *Their Eyes Were Watching God*; *The Best Christmas Pageant Ever*

Genre	Examples
Mystery	*The Moonstone* (W. Collins); Agatha Christie titles; the Nancy Drew and Hardy Boys mysteries
Wit/Humor	*The Education of Hyman Kaplan* (L. Rosten); *The Egg and I* (B. MacDonald); *Skipping Christmas* (J. Grisham)

The idea of genre is fairly fluid. Some factual memoirs like *The Dog Who Wouldn't Be*, by Farley Mowat, are hilarious. Some mysteries are witty and crammed with facts. (Read Aaron Elkins.) Even so, books within a particular genre always have many things in common.

Reading for Author's Rhetorical Purpose

Rhetoric is the *art of using language (or speech) to convince others*. Skillful rhetoric accomplishes the writer's purpose. It gets the job done.

What jobs might an author want to do? Think about a humorous book, such as *All Creatures Great and Small*, by James Herriot. Herriot's rhetorical purpose is *to amuse*, *to entertain*, *and also to inform* his readers about life as a country vet in Yorkshire, England.

What do Stephen King, writer of horror, and Michael Crichton, writer of science fiction, have in common? Their rhetorical purpose is *to enthrall*—to keep you reading; their tales tear along at a furious pace.

Looking over several recent SATs, we found terms that you need to recognize when speaking of rhetorical purpose.

Writers may be trying to: *document* something; *present* or *offer* a persuasive argument; *analyze* reasons or causes or results; *explain* something; *appeal* to your sense of fairness, or appeal for advice; *pose* or *ask* questions; *consider* two sides of a vexing question . . . in short, writers may have an enormous variety of reasons for writing the way they do.

Read carefully in order to answer questions on rhetorical purpose. Note the author's vocabulary. Tone (mood) and rhetorical purpose are closely linked.

Practice C

Look back to *Practice A* on page 38, under *Reading to Decode Attitude or Tone (Mood)*. Reread that paragraph about garment workers.

Question

The writer's main rhetorical purpose in this paragraph is to

    (A) whine about the loss of jobs in the garment industry

    (B) explore many problems in the current garment industry

    (C) offer reasons to explain why jobs have moved overseas

    (D) protest the unsavory working conditions overseas

    (E) deplore the innocence of foreign workers

Answer

In case you are thinking that this paragraph is too short to serve as an example, please remember that every paragraph has a job to do in any piece of writing. Here, we hope you'll agree that *whining* (A), is too strong, although the writer is clearly not happy. Nor is he *exploring many problems* in the garment industry (B). The passage is too brief for (B) to be correct. The main job of this paragraph is (C), *offering reasons to explain why jobs have moved*, and the other choices are simply red herrings, parroting words/ideas in the passage.

Reading for Facts and Examples

Another type of SAT question tests whether or not you understood the use of key facts or examples in a passage. As you read any passage, *put a check mark in the margin next to lines with important facts*, *dates*, *proper names*—any fact that seems important. Or use a highlighter to illuminate facts.

    Examples and facts buttress an author's argument; that is their rhetorical purpose. They prove a point or make it more eloquently. For example, exact dates along with statistics may be used to show how a substance in the environment, such as CO^2 in the air, has increased over time.

    Therefore, you need to find the facts or illustrative examples fast. This checkmark technique works. Try it as you work with the Practice Passages in this unit. Answering questions based on facts should become both easier and faster for you.

Reading for What Is Suggested or Implied, Not Stated

Questions on what was implied in a passage are often the hardest. How do you tell what was implied? Again, the answer is *author's word choice*. And you may need to gather information from a couple of places in the passage to draw your conclusion. Again . . . you cannot do this with a quick, casual reading. You must read carefully and mark the passage as you go.

Don't *reach* for an answer. You must find support in the material given. Let's practice with this passage.

Practice D

Line   When I disengaged myself, as above mentioned, from private
     business, I flattered myself that, by the sufficient though moderate
     fortune I had acquired, I had secured leisure during the rest of my
     life for philosophical studies and amusements. I purchased all Dr.
5   Spence's apparatus, who had come from England to lecture in
     Philadelphia, and I proceeded in my electrical experiments with
     great alacrity; but the public, now considering me as a man of
     leisure, laid hold of me for their purposes, every part of our civil
     government, and almost at the same time, imposing some duty
10   upon me. The governor put me into the commission of the
     peace; the corporation of the city chose me one of the common
     council and soon after an alderman; and the citizens at large
     elected me a burgess to represent them in Assembly. This latter
     station was the more agreeable to me, as I was at length tired
15   with sitting there to hear debates, in which, as clerk I could take
     no part, and which were often so uninteresting that I was
     induced to amuse myself with making magic squares or circles or
     anything to avoid weariness; and I conceived my becoming a
     member would enlarge my power of doing good. I would not,
20   however, insinuate that my ambition was not flattered by all these
     promotions; it certainly was; for considering my low beginning,
     they were great things to me; and they were still more pleasing,
     as being so many spontaneous testimonies of the public's good
     opinion, and by me entirely unsolicited.

Question

We can infer that the author's primary rhetorical purpose in this passage is to

(A) review his retirement plan

(B) recall his feelings about certain events in his life

(C) counter accusations that he had not aided the public good

(D) amuse readers with his activities after leaving private business

(E) arouse admiration for his many talents

Answer

Eliminating one by one,

(A) Answer is too narrow. He begins with his retirement plan, but that's all. See lines 7–19, where he recounts new responsibilities.

(B) Yes. This is very autobiographical in tone; in fact, it's from Ben Franklin's autobiography. Reread to double-check.

(C) "Doesn't make sense" answer. Look at the list of his public jobs!

(D) Again, too narrow. He was just explaining in a lighthearted way. See lines 13–19.

(E) He isn't really bragging. This is an even-tempered, objective recounting of how Franklin was hastily re-employed—this time by the public—just when he thought he had retired. Reread lines 19–24 where he says he hadn't looked for these honors, but that they "flattered" him.

Question

Although the author was immensely "flattered" (lines 19–24) by his new responsibilities, this passage implies that he might also have felt

(A) rather annoyed by all that new work

(B) quite surprised that the public needed his help

(C) overjoyed to be embarking on a new phase in life

(D) a twinge of regret at losing time to study and experiment

(E) some apprehension about his busy, demanding future

Answer

Study the question AND the passage. You should look for something that is *different from feeling flattered*. Note the key word *although*.

(A) The passage cannot support this choice.

(B) Again, we can't find support in the passage, but we can assume this was true. Keep for now.

(C) *Overjoyed* is awfully strong, but there's an undercurrent of Franklin's excitement. Keep for now.

(D) Yes. Read lines 1-7, then "imposing some duty upon me" in lines 9-10. He had looked forward to his studies and had begun electrical experiments with new equipment. He proceeded "with great alacrity" (lines 6-7)—clearly excited—yet now he cannot do those things. The passage supports this answer choice.

(E) Apprehension regarding the future is possible, but no support for this choice is in the passage.

Answer (D) is the best choice, because we find support in the early lines of the selection, and we cannot find support anywhere for the other answer choices.

Conclusion: Even for questions that ask what is *implied* (hinted at) in a passage, you will be able to find support for one answer.

Reading Vocabulary in Context

When an SAT question asks for the meaning of a word used in a reading passage, it is not asking what you think the word means. It is asking what the word means *in this particular context*.

Words frequently have multiple meanings, so be sure to see how the word in question is being used this time around . . . *right here in this passage*.

Practice E

Reread the portion of Ben Franklin's autobiography on page 46 to answer these two questions:

Question

In line 9, the word "imposing" most nearly means

(A) placing

(B) taking advantage of

(C) establishing by authority

(D) forcing

(E) fobbing off

Answer

(A) Substitute *placing* in the sentence. It works. Keep for now.

(B) Try "taking advantage of *some duty on me*." Weird.

(C) *Establishing by authority* some duty on me. Maybe . . . Keep for now.

(D) *Forcing?* This answer is too strong. (The "too big" answer type.)

(E) *Fobbing off* duties on Franklin? Not logical. He's honored by these new posts of responsibility.

While answer (A) is the simplest one, it also works best. In this context, the jobs imposed on Franklin were *placed upon him* by an admiring public. You can use *impose* other ways. For example: He always *imposes on* our good will. The government *imposed* a new tax. But in this sentence, only *to put or place* works as a meaning of *to impose*.

Question

In line 21, the word "low" is used to mean

(A) not high

(B) disgraceful

(C) humble

(D) depressed

(E) unappealing

Answer

Substitute the answers in the passage, one by one. (A), My *not high* beginning? Probably not. (B), *disgraceful* beginning? Not that we're aware of. Keep going. (C), *humble* beginning? Makes the most sense. Best so far. (D), *depressed* beginning? Maybe, but not as good as (C). (E), *unappealing* beginning? Word usage is strange here. Thus we're left with *humble* as a meaning for *low*, and that sounds just right. Your English ear is a helpful asset, especially if you're a reader.

NOTE: Words tested on SATs and PSATs are often simple, everyday words. Your job is to pay close attention to the way the word is being used *this time*. By eliminating answers you should get most of these questions right, and they take less time than some others.

Reading Paired Passages

You may see short or medium-length paired passages on the new SAT that will be similar to any paired passages on tests to date. Try this approach to paired passages:

- Read Passage 1 carefully. Mark it, and answer only those questions that pertain to this passage. (May be only one or two for short passages.)
- Now, read Passage 2.
- Answer questions that pertain only to it. Mark this passage as you would any other passage.
- The last questions ask you to compare or contrast the two passages.

  1. *Consider differences* in tone, point of view, author style, attitude toward the same topic, anything that differentiates one passage from the other.

  2. *Consider similarities* in tone, style, attitudes—all the things that both passages have in common—places where they agree.

Practice F

Read the following two passages to get an idea of working with paired passages.

Passage 1

Line   *One Hundred Years of Solitude,* Gabriel Garcia Marquez's most
    famous novel, is often cited as the seminal work in the movement
    in Latin American fiction known as magic realism. Some critics have
    argued that magic realism was a departure from the tradition of so-
5   cial realism in Latin American fiction that so often concerned itself
    with the struggles and oppression of poor or indigenous people.
    However, the presence of magical events in the novels of the magic
    realists does not mean that those authors have abandoned social
    commentary. Rather, they have immersed themselves so fully in the
10 belief systems of their characters—usually poor people with strong
    ties to native or African roots—that the appearance of supernatural
    beings or the occurrence of strange events occasions no surprise or
    disbelief. Indeed, what is "real" in magic realism is the magic itself;
    it is fully accepted by both author-narrator and characters as simply

15   part of normal life. The presence of the supernatural distinguishes
     magic realism from other types of realism; the fact that the super-
     natural is mingled with the real world distinguishes it from science
     fiction or fantasy, and this acceptance of the supernatural as normal
     and real distinguishes magic realism from ghost stories and other
20   tales of the supernatural.

Passage 2

     While carefully chronicling the struggles of African American
     people at various points in U.S. history, Toni Morrison's novels
     often include elements of the magical or supernatural, so much so
     that many critics have mentioned Morrison's works in the same
25   breath with those of the magic realists of Latin America. *Song of
     Solomon,* for instance, ends with Milkman, the protagonist,
     apparently having learned to fly; the title character of *Beloved* is a
     ghost, killed in infancy and now come to life as a young woman
     the age the baby would have been had it lived. When asked about
30   the presence of the supernatural in her novels, Morrison says, "I
     want my work to capture the vast imagination of black people.
     That is, I want my books to reflect the imaginative combination of
     the real world, the very practical, shrewd, day to day functioning
     that black people must do, while at the same time they encom-
35   pass some great supernatural element. We know that it does not
     bother them one bit to do something practical and have visions at
     the same time."

Question

According to information provided by the passages, which of the
following is a similarity between *One Hundred Years of Solitude* and
Beloved?

   (A)   Both feature ghosts as main characters.
   (B)   Both emphasize the magical over the realistic.
   (C)   Both combine realistic events with supernatural events.
   (D)   Both are considered to be seminal works of magic realism in
         their respective countries.
   (E)   Both draw on African folk traditions for their depiction of
         magical events.

Answer

This question asks you to pull together information from both passages. Neither author actually says very much about the novels in question; you have to take what the author of Passage 1 says about magic realism in general and what the author of Passage 2 says about Morrison's novels in general and apply those comments to the novels mentioned in the question to come up with the right answer, which is (C).

Look at the wrong answer choices. In questions that compare two passages, at least some of the wrong answer choices are likely to apply to one passage but not the other.

Answers (A) and (E) apply only to *Beloved* in Passage 2. Passage 1 does mention "African roots" in line 11, but we don't know whether any African folklore appears in *One Hundred Years of Solitude.*

Answer (D), meanwhile, applies only to Passage 1. The author of Passage 2 does say that some critics have linked Morrison's works to magic realism, but that doesn't make them *seminal*, which means *seedlike, having the power to originate or create.*

Answer (B) is just plain wrong, using the language of both passages to say the *opposite* of what both passages say.

Question

Which of the following techniques is NOT used in EITHER passage?

(A) defining a term
(B) refuting an assertion
(C) providing an example
(D) quoting an authority
(E) analyzing a literary text

Answer

These "NOT questions" can be tricky. You have to be careful in eliminating answer choices. In this case, check each answer choice to see whether *either* author uses that technique. If the technique appears in Passage 1 *or* Passage 2, you can eliminate it.

Does either author *define a term*? Yes, in fact, Passage 1 "is primarily concerned with" (to use SAT language) defining magic realism.

Does either author *refute an assertion*? Yes, Passage 1 refutes the assertion that magic realism is a departure from social realism.

Does either author *provide an example*? Both do—Passage 1 opens with an example and Passage 2 cites two novels by Morrison.

Does either author *quote an authority*? Well, what is Toni Morrison if not an authority on her own novels?

Luckily, choice (E) is right; neither passage *analyzes* a literary text. Although both passages are about literature, they do not analyze the work itself. Neither author breaks a literary text down into its parts in order to understand it better.

Question

Would the author of Passage 1 be likely to agree with the characterization of Toni Morrison's novels as examples of magic realism?

- (A) Yes, because Morrison immerses herself in the struggles of African American people.
- (B) Yes, because Morrison's characters accept magical events as real within a realistic setting.
- (C) Yes, because the examples cited in Passage 2 show that Morrison includes supernatural events in her fiction.
- (D) No, because magic realism is indigenous to Latin America.
- (E) No, because Morrison's emphasis on practicality and shrewdness is incompatible with magic realism.

Answer

The *because* clauses are more important here than whether you think the answer is *yes* or *no.* In order for the author of Passage 1 to agree that Morrison's novels are magic realist, the novels would have to meet author 1's criteria for magic realism. Passage 1 says that magic realist novels combine the supernatural and the realistic and, perhaps most importantly, *the supernatural is accepted by narrator and characters as normal and real* (lines 13–15). Morrison makes a similar point about her own novels at the end of Passage 2: "[I]t does not bother them one bit to do something practical and have visions at the same time." (As you were reading Passage 2, this would have been a good place to mark a circled 1 or somehow indicate that this comment corresponds closely to something said in the first passage.) The answer, then, is (B).

Answers (A) and (C) would have Morrison meeting only part of author 1's criteria. Answers (D) and (E) give as reasons things that the author of Passage 1 does not cite as criteria for magic realism.

Short Paragraphs . . . the "New" Reading Passages

This is just more of the same, folks, only in snippets. Focus carefully on the paragraph(s) in question, treating every word with the respect it deserves. Watch for those key words and for significant meaning in the verbs of these paragraphs.

You may find questions on rhetorical purpose, author's style, tone or mood, language usage, purpose of examples, and vocabulary in these shorter passages.

Practice G

Line Shortly after [H.L.] Mencken's death, colleagues at the *Baltimore*
Sun-papers opened a locked box containing a note about the
handling of his obituary. Mencken had requested only a brief
notice, with no accompanying editorial or biographical sketch. He
5   might well have suspected that this request could not be honored. His passing generated numerous retrospectives in Baltimore,
throughout America, and abroad.

Since that time, as was the case during his career, Mencken
has been the subject of numerous attacks—some justified, others
10   patently unfair. For the most part, though, acclaim has super-
seded censure.

Question

We can assume that Mencken spent his career as a(n)

(A) political figure in Baltimore

(B) journalist

(C) extremely popular editor

(D) writer known mainly in Baltimore

(E) vain and controversial figure

Answer

Answer (A) has no support in the passage; politics are not mentioned.

Answer (B) says he had "colleagues" at the *Baltimore Sun-papers*, so this is a keeper for now.

Answer (C) is contradicted in line 9, where the author says Mencken has been "the subject of numerous attacks."

Answer (D) is possible at first glance, yet this idea is strongly contradicted in lines 6-7, where the passage mentions "numerous retrospectives in Baltimore, throughout American, and abroad."

Answer (E) is trickier. Consider that Mencken himself asked for no editorial or biographical sketch to accompany his obituary. If he had been a *vain* man, he'd have desired both, most likely. He was *controversial*, however. Remember that an answer has to be totally correct, not partially. Therefore, answer (B) remains as the only choice after eliminating the others.

Question

In line 10, the word *patently* is used to

(A) express strong emotion

(B) help the cadence of the sentence

(C) undercut the importance of the "attacks"

(D) emphasize the injustice of some of the "attacks"

(E) alter the meaning of the adjective "unfair"

Answer

Answer (A) may get some support just because of the sentence where it appears. But *patently* itself does not express strong emotion; it means *obviously, readily or openly visible; clearly*.

Answer (B) is the "ha-ha" choice.

Answer (C) is just off the mark—too narrow in its scope.

Answer (D) says that *patently* is used as a word of emphasis, which is often true of adverbs—think about *very, terribly, quickly*. While some attacks on Mencken were "justified," others were "*patently unfair*." They were *clearly unjust* (unfair) attacks. Keep this answer!

Answer (E) contends that the noun *unfair* has been changed (altered) in meaning. An adverb cannot change a word's meaning.

Instead, *patently* stresses just *how unfair* some of those attacks on Mencken were.

Thus, we go with answer (D), the logical choice.

Practice H

(1) Green spaces, trees, and places to walk around, drive by, and enjoy add pleasure to urban life. (2) The highest level of commitment must be expended to maintain our natural areas because they are among our most valuable resources. (3) Through parks we are able to learn about and respect the animals and plants that have every right to live alongside us. (4) The learning that goes on in the parks is wonderful. (5) We need to encourage all age groups to come and enjoy. (6) Bird watching, plant identification, fishing (where permitted), learning about wild edibles (look but don't bite)—are all vital to the urban dweller. (7) It is easy to lose sight of the larger picture when we become involved in our everyday activities. (8) Cities have culture and excitement, but they also need nature. (9) Our souls, too, need nourishment.

Question

The writer's main rhetorical purpose in this piece is to

(A) educate readers about urban life

(B) describe the benefits of living in an urban environment

(C) encourage involvement with nature in an urban setting

(D) discourage a narrow focus on everyday activities

(E) enumerate the valuable resources available in urban areas

Answer

Answer (A) is off focus, and too broad. This piece centers on nature within the urban environment.

Answer (B) is too broad. This brief piece does not list/enumerate the benefits of (urban) city life.

Answer (C) can be tested by checking all sentences. All appear to encourage the city-dweller to interact with nature in parks and elsewhere. This one is a keeper.

Answer (D) is too narrow. Only one sentence addresses this topic.

Answer (E) is a rephrasing of Answer (B), and therefore incorrect.

Thus, only answer (C) can be supported by the sentences in this paragraph.

Question

A crucial guideline for all writers is "Show, Don't Tell." In this brief essay, the sentence that comes closest to embodying that rule is

(A) sentence 9

(B) sentence 1

(C) sentence 4

(D) sentence 8

(E) sentence 6

Answer

Answer (A), the last sentence in the piece, acts as a summation sentence, but draws no picture for the readers.

Answer (B), the first sentence in the piece, is an introductory or topic sentence. It is very general in nature, not specific or colorful enough to draw any pictures for the readers.

Answer (C), sentence 4, is general, dull, and amazingly redundant.

Answer (D), sentence 8, is also too general.

Answer (E), sentence 6, is the best of the answer choices given. It gives the reader *bird watching, fishing, and identification of wild edibles* as specific things that nature provides. Here is at least a *hint* of a picture to keep our interest.

NOTE: If the writer had said "*watch* wild birds, *fish for trout and small perch, and identify* edible bulbs and grasses," the verbs (and specific nouns) would have given the sentence more life. Don't disguise good verbs as nouns or gerunds When writing your essay, *avoid generalities*. Be specific. No one can resist intriguing, concrete, colorful, sensory details.

Summary: Know-How for Critical Reading Questions

1. Try to skim questions before reading each passage. Do NOT read the answer choices.

2. Read the passage quickly once to determine the main idea. Mark it if you can.

3. Reread. Carefully. You can use these marks for critical places:

   ** for Main Points or meaty, summation sentences.

   • for facts and examples.

   Q for quotes you may refer to.

   Underline words revealing shifts in tone/viewpoint/outcome.

   Circle words that indicate mood (tone). Informative pieces won't have a mood as such, since they are written to inform, not to invoke a mood.

4. Answer questions as quickly as possible, eliminating one at a time. Be sure to record answers for all the ones that you know. Save the stinkers for last, only if you have time to go back and ponder. On a really tough question, your chance of getting the right answer is slimmer anyway.

Timing for Critical Reading Segments

As we go to press, the College Board is planning on nine separate test segments: *two are 20 minutes long, one is 35 minutes, and six of them are 25-minute segments*. One of those 25-minute segments will test new questions for validity before they are used in an actual SAT. That segment will not count toward your test score, but it may be hard to figure out which one it is, so give each test segment your best effort.

Each time you begin a new test segment, scan it first. Decide which questions or reading passages you like best and do them first.

Any Sentence Completion questions here? Do them first. They take less time than reading passages.

Keep an eye on your watch.

By practicing with the questions in this book, you will learn how long it takes you for each kind of question. Note your time requirements here:

(Your name goes here) Time Chart for CRITICAL READING segments

I NEED _____ minutes for short reading passages (about 100 wds.).

I NEED _____ minutes for paired, shorter passages (maybe 200 words total).

I NEED _____ minutes for medium-length passages (400–600 wds.).

I NEED _____ minutes for longer passages (600–850 wds.).

I NEED _____ minutes for a unit of 8 to 10 Sentence Completion questions.

What if you discover you're a slow worker? Well, many brilliant people work *very* slowly. But on an SAT, time is in short supply, so you must make a choice. Either plan ahead and practice until you can work faster OR decide to eliminate one passage (plus its questions) in each Critical Reading section. Do not race through every question just to prove you can finish them all.

Slow workers will score more points if they do a careful job on a selected number of questions.

Short passages take only a few minutes. But longer passages (500–850 words) can take 15 minutes or more. *Consider omitting the longest passage (or the most demanding one) or saving it for last*. Be sure to scan its questions for ones you can answer quickly—such as words in context—and be sure to record your answers in the correct place on the answer sheet.

For longer, paired passages, save more time for Passage 2 questions, because at the end of those are a few questions pertaining to *both* passages.

Practice Reading Passages

For the following reading passages, practice reading and answering questions as rapidly as you can. Learn the directions now, so that you won't waste time with them on test day.

> Answer the questions based on what is stated or implied in the passage as well as any introductory material that might be supplied.

The passages are as close to actual test passages as possible. As on standardized tests, they come from a variety of reading materials.

All answers to the following seven passages begin on page 324.

PRACTICE CRITICAL READING 1

The following passage is from a nineteenth-century American novel about the whaling industry. The setting is on board the ship Pequod. *Here, the chief mate of the ship, Starbuck, is presented and his character described. The historical time is about 1850.*

Line   The chief mate of the *Pequod* was Starbuck, a native of Nan-
        tucket. He was a long, earnest man, and though born on an icy
        coast, seemed well adapted to endure hot latitudes, his flesh
        being hard as twice-baked biscuit. Transported to the Indies, his
5   live blood would not spoil like bottled ale. He must have been
        born in some time of general drought and famine. Only some
        thirty arid summers had he seen; those summers had dried up all
        his physical superfluousness. But this, his thinness, so to speak,
        seemed no more the token of wasted anxieties and cares, than it
10   seemed the indication of any bodily blight. It was merely the
        condensation of the man. He was by no means ill-looking; quite
        the contrary. His pure tight skin was an excellent fit; and closely
        wrapped up in it, and embalmed with inner health and strength,
        like a revivified Egyptian, this Starbuck seemed prepared to
15   endure for long ages to come. For be it Polar snow or torrid sun,
        like a patent chronometer, his interior vitality was warranted to
        do well in all climates. Looking into his eyes, you seemed to see

there the lingering images of those thousand-fold perils he had calmly confronted through life.

20   Yet, for all his hardy sobriety and fortitude, there were certain qualities in him which at times seemed well nigh to over-balance all the rest. Uncommonly conscientious for a seaman, and endued with a deep natural reverence, the wild watery loneliness of his life did therefore strongly incline him to

25 superstition, which in some organization seems rather to spring, somehow, from intelligence than from ignorance. Outward portents and inward presentiments were his. And if at times these things bent the iron of his soul, much more did his far-away domestic memories of his young Cape wife and child, tend to

30 bend him still more from the original ruggedness of his nature, and open him still further to those latent influences which, in some honest-hearted men, restrain the gush of dare-devil daring, so often evinced by others in the more perilous vicissitudes of the fishery. "I will have no man in my boat," said Starbuck, "who is

35 not afraid of a whale." By this, he seemed to mean, not only that the most reliable and useful courage was that which arises from the fair estimation of the encountered peril, but that an utterly fearless man is a far more dangerous comrade than a coward.

        Starbuck was no crusader after perils; in him courage was

40 not a sentiment; but a thing simply useful to him, and always at hand upon all mortally practical occasions. Besides, he thought, perhaps, that in this business of whaling, courage was one of the staple outfits of the ship, like her beef and her bread, and not to be wasted. Wherefore he had no fancy for lowering for whales

45 after sun-down; nor for persisting in fighting a fish that too much persisted in fighting him. That hundreds of men had been so killed Starbuck well knew. What doom was his own father's? Where, in the bottomless deeps, could he find the torn limbs of his brother?

50   With memories like these in him, and, moreover, given to a certain superstitiousness, as has been said; the courage of this Starbuck, which could, nevertheless, still flourish, must indeed have been extreme. But it was not in reasonable nature that a man so organized, and with such terrible experiences and

55 remembrances as he had; it was not in nature that these things

should fail in latently engendering an element in him, which,
under suitable circumstances, would break from its confinement,
and burn all his courage up. And brave as he might be, it was that
sort of bravery chiefly visible in some intrepid men, which, while
60　abiding firm in the conflict with seas, or winds, or whales, or any
of the ordinary irrational horrors of the world, yet cannot
withstand those more terrific, because more spiritual terrors,
which sometimes menace you from the concentrating brow of an
enraged and mighty man.

65　　　Men may seem detestable as joint stock-companies and
nations; knaves, fools, and murderers there may be; men may
have mean and meager faces; but, man, in the ideal, is so noble
and so sparkling, that over an ignominious blemish in him all his
fellows should run to throw their costliest robes. That immaculate
70　manliness we feel within ourselves, so far within us, that it
remains intact though all the outer character seem gone; bleeds
with keenest anguish at the undraped spectacle of a valor-ruined
man. But this august dignity I treat of, is not the dignity of kings
and robes, but that abounding dignity which has no robed
75　investiture. Thou shalt see it shining in the arm that wields a pick
or drives a spike; that democratic dignity which, on all hands,
radiates without end from God; Himself! The great God absolute!
The center and circumference of all democracy! His omnipres-
ence, our divine equality!

1. The word "transported"
   (line 4) describes which of
   the following?

   (A) "flesh" (line 3)
   (B) "biscuit" (line 4)
   (C) "blood" (line 5)
   (D) "ale" (line 5)
   (E) "He" (line 5)

2. Starbuck was thin chiefly
   because he

   (A) was burdened with
       worry and anxiety
   (B) had an inherited
       digestive illness
   (C) was still a very young
       man
   (D) had a compact, efficient
       constitution
   (E) had a rare sort of blood
       disorder

3. In line 7, the word "arid" most nearly means

(A) long and fretful
(B) dull and uneventful
(C) dry and parched
(D) unhappy and painful
(E) disturbing and frightening

4. Starbuck is compared to an Egyptian mummy (lines 12–15) in order to emphasize his

(A) strong belief in a preordained fate
(B) extraordinary durability
(C) intellectual strength and interests
(D) antecedents in historical time
(E) rigid moral convictions

5. In line 23, "endued with" most nearly means

(A) possessed of
(B) in need of
(C) weakened by
(D) wishing for
(E) sanctified by

6. Which of the following best describes the author's attitude toward Starbuck?

(A) He understands and respects Starbuck.
(B) He feels Starbuck is weak and fearful.
(C) He envies and fears Starbuck.
(D) He feels Starbuck is cruel and mean.
(E) He thinks Starbuck is good and faultless.

7. By describing Starbuck as "uncommonly conscientious" (line 22), the author implies that most seamen are

(A) unskilled and lazy
(B) violent and aggressive
(C) self-indulgent and weak
(D) reserved and individualistic
(E) careless and indifferent

8. Starbuck's natural predisposition toward bold, courageous action was tempered chiefly by

(A) the authority of the ship's captain
(B) the unpredictability of his crew mates
(C) his innate fear of dying
(D) thoughts of his family back home
(E) a humble spirit and fear of God

9. The "thousand-fold perils" that Starbuck "calmly confronted" in his life (lines 18–19) accounted for which of the following traits as primary in his character?

   (A) A profound, sometimes disabling superstition
   (B) Prudence and a capacity for judicious caution
   (C) An occasional failure of nerve caused by memories of his father and brother
   (D) A heroic yet reckless disdain for danger and imminent calamity
   (E) A matchless self-confidence in his own talents and experience

10. The deaths of Starbuck's father and brother (lines 46–49) were most likely the result of

    (A) a vengeful fate
    (B) a violent storm
    (C) hapless accidents
    (D) reckless judgment
    (E) faulty equipment

11. The author implies that Starbuck's nobility of character can be compromised only by

    (A) the dangers and fury of a stormy sea
    (B) a cowardly and weak boat crew
    (C) the sinister power of whales
    (D) an angry and vengeful God
    (E) anyone possessed of a cosmic anger

12. The author would most strongly agree with which of the following ideas?

    (A) Life at sea for long periods provides people with unusual chances to purify the spirit.
    (B) A life of action is most often preferable to a life of contemplation.
    (C) Life on land nurtures domestic values; life at sea is destructive of human values.
    (D) Violence and egotism in human nature are common elements that will ultimately prevail.
    (E) Anger and hatred are always present in the human heart and when yielded to may destroy a person's soul.

13. The author's style or voice is best described as

   (A) informal and conversational

   (B) witty and sophisticated

   (C) formal and orotund

   (D) elegant and decorative

   (E) fearful and prophetic

14. In the final paragraph, the author's purpose is to

   (A) celebrate the glories of God

   (B) shift the focus from Starbuck to kings, God, and social leaders

   (C) end the narrative on a level of logical inquiry

   (D) transmute the particular person to the universal ideal human being

   (E) contrast Starbuck's virtues with his potential for failure

PRACTICE CRITICAL READING 2

The passages below are adapted from two different essays. The first was written in the seventeenth century, and the second was written about 1870. Both authors are English.

Passage 1

Line   It is a capital misery for a man to be at once both old and
ignorant. If he were only old, and had some knowledge, he might
lessen the tediousness of decrepit age by divine raptures of
contemplation. If he were young, though he knew nothing, his
5   later years would serve him to labor and learn; whereby in the
winter of his time he might beguile the weariness of his pillow
and chair. But now his body being withered by the stealing length
of his days, and his limbs wholly disabled for either motion or
exercise, these, together with a mind unfurnished of those
10   contenting speculations of admired science, cannot but delineate
the portraiture of a man wretched.

   A gray head with a wise mind is a treasury of grave precepts,
experience, and judgment. But foolish old age is a barren vine in
autumn, or a university to study folly in: every action is a pattern

15   of infirmity: while his body sits still he knows not how to find his mind's action: and tell me if there be any life more irksome than idleness. I have numbered yet but a few days,[1] and those, I know, I have neglected; I am not sure they shall be more, nor can I promise my head it shall have a snowy hair.

20   What then? Knowledge is not hurtful, but helps a good mind; anything that is laudable I desire to learn. If I die tomorrow, my life today shall be somewhat the sweeter for knowledge: and if my day prove a summer one, it shall not be amiss to have my mind my companion. Notable was the answer that Antis-

25   thenes[2] gave when he was asked what fruit he had reaped of all his studies. "By them," saith he, "I have learned both to live and to talk with myself."

Passage 2

    Suppose it were perfectly certain that the life and fortune of every one of us would depend upon our winning or losing a

30   game of chess. Don't you think that we should all consider it a primary duty to learn at least the names and the moves of the pieces? Do you not think that we should look with a disapprobation amounting to scorn, upon the father who allowed his son, or the state which allowed its members, to grow up without

35   knowing a pawn from a knight?

    Yet it is a very plain and elementary truth, that the life, the fortune, and the happiness of every one of us do depend upon our knowing something of the rules of a game infinitely more difficult and complicated than chess. It is a game which has been

40   played for untold ages, every man and woman of us being one of the two players in a game of his or her own. The chessboard is the world, the pieces are the phenomena of the universe, the rules of the game are what we call the laws of Nature. The player on the other side is hidden from us. We know that his play is

45   always fair, just, and patient. But also we know, to our cost, that he never overlooks a mistake, or makes the smallest allowance for

---

[1] The author wrote this short essay before he was 20 years old.
[2] An Athenian philosopher who lived about 444–365 B.C.

ignorance. To the man who plays well, the highest stakes are paid, with that sort of overflowing generosity with which the strong shows delight in strength. And one who plays ill is
50   checkmated—without haste, but without remorse.

Well, what I mean by Education is learning the rules of this mighty game. In other words, education is the instruction of the intellect in the laws of Nature, under which name I include not merely things and their forces, but men and their ways; and the
55   fashioning of the affections and the will into an earnest and loving desire to move in harmony with those laws. For me, education means neither more nor less than this. Anything which professes to call itself education must be tried by this standard, and if it fails to stand the test, I will not call it education, whatever may be the
60   force of authority, or of the numbers, upon the other side.

That man has had a liberal education who has been so trained in youth that his body is the ready servant of his will, and does with ease and pleasure all the work that, as a mechanism, it is capable of; whose intellect is a clear, cold, logic engine, with
65   all its parts of equal strength, and in smooth working order; ready like a steam engine, to be turned to any kind of work, and spin the gossamers as well as forge the anchors of the mind; whose mind is stored with a knowledge of the great and fundamental truths of Nature and of the laws of her operations; one who, no
70   stunted ascetic, is full of life and fire, but whose passions are trained to come to heel by a vigorous will, the servant of a tender conscience; who has learned to love all beauty, whether of Nature or of art, to hate all vileness, and to respect others as himself.

1. In line 1, the word "capital" most nearly means

   (A) centrally fixed
   (B) critically important
   (C) lesser quality
   (D) little understood
   (E) much discussed

2. According to the author in Passage 1, the pains of old age can be made more bearable if one

   (A) is sufficiently wealthy
   (B) has inherited good genes
   (C) is well educated
   (D) is naturally courageous
   (E) has sympathetic friends

3. According to the author in Passage 1, the chief advantage in being young is that one has

   (A) strength and good health
   (B) opportunities to travel and meet new people
   (C) prospects of good employment
   (D) future years in which to study and acquire knowledge
   (E) time to enjoy life without spending it all on tiresome work

4. In line 6, the "winter" of one's time most nearly means

   (A) years of illness and bad health
   (B) youth and its normal ignorance
   (C) years of unrewarding hard labor
   (D) times of misfortune and bad luck
   (E) old age and its infirmities

5. Which of the following is the most striking characteristic of the language in Passage 1?

   (A) Rich use of figures of speech
   (B) Simple and direct sentences
   (C) Rhetorical questions and logical answers
   (D) Unusually complex verbal structures
   (E) Abstract diction and argument

6. In line 27, the phrase "to talk with myself" is a metaphorical way of saying

(A) loneliness is unavoidable

(B) old age is a second childhood

(C) being selfish loses friends

(D) thinking is excellent conversation

(E) a love of ideas will invite many admirers

7. The author of Passage 1 most disdains which of the following?

(A) Old age and infirmity

(B) Scandal and bad repute

(C) Poverty and homelessness

(D) Pain and death

(E) Indolence and sloth

8. The fundamental assumption the author of Passage 2 makes about life is that

(A) it is dominated by a cruel and malign force

(B) behind the material world is a more or less benign power that challenges mankind

(C) what happens to human beings is largely determined by chance

(D) there is no force or power in the universe superior to mankind's intelligence

(E) human beings can lay claim to having a part of the divine being within themselves

9. Which of the following best states the definition of the educated person as described by the author of Passage 2?

(A) A person is educated who through self-discipline has learned the ways of self, nature, and society and lives in harmony with those ways.

(B) An educated person is a gamester and a good sport, taking victory humbly and defeat with grace.

(C) An educated person has trained himself diligently in a profession or business and succeeds through a combination of struggle and good luck.

(D) An educated person is one who knows that fate is neutral and even careless in dealing with people but who still believes in victory.

(E) A person who has acquired an education is versed in the sciences and arts and is able to outwit fate and Nature in the game of life.

10. "The player on the other side" (lines 43–44) in its challenge to human players is best described as

(A) sinister and unknowable
(B) absolute and dictatorial
(C) generous and loving
(D) exacting and unforgiving
(E) dishonest and secretive

11. The phrase "to . . . spin the gossamers" (lines 66–67) is a metaphor for

(A) developing architectural plans
(B) dreaming and imagining
(C) learning the mind's psychology
(D) getting rid of lazy thinking
(E) solving problems mathematically

12. According to the passage, a "stunted ascetic" is one who

(A) is born with a physical disability
(B) values natural law over artistic beauty
(C) has a kind and saintly manner
(D) needs much respect and affection
(E) is too strict and pinched in spirit

13. The authors of both passages value which of the following most highly?

    (A) Sociability and good spirits
    (B) Honesty and frankness
    (C) Knowledge and learning
    (D) Wealth and influence
    (E) Good health and longevity

14. The authors of both passages believe that acquiring an education is possible only

    (A) for those who are born to privilege and opportunity and take advantage of them
    (B) when society provides appropriate educational institutions and opportunities for its citizens to use them
    (C) when one strives to learn and makes being a diligent student a lifelong habit

    (D) for those born with above-average intelligence and a strong drive to succeed
    (E) for those who can play the game of life like a gambler and beat Nature and fate at their own game

15. The authors of the two passages are alike in that they both

    (A) are young men in their early twenties
    (B) speak with conviction
    (C) reveal their own weaknesses
    (D) are whimsical and only half serious
    (E) have served as professional educators

PRACTICE CRITICAL READING 3

Line   Although a complex nervous system is not essential for behaviour—protozoans get by quite nicely with only rudimentary sense cells—the scope and sophistication of behaviour within the animal kingdom is quite clearly linked with the evolution of
5   neural complexity. The behavioural capacities of protozoans and

earthworms are extremely limited compared with those of birds and mammals. What, then, are the properties of a nervous system which make complex behaviour possible?

10 . . . True nervous systems are only found in multicellular animals. Here they form a tissue of discrete, self-contained nerve cells or *neurons*. Like any other type of animal cell, neurons comprise an intricate system of cell organelles surrounded by a cell membrane. . . . Unlike other animal cells, however, they are specialised for transmitting electrical messages from one part of

15 the body to another. This specialisation is reflected both in their structure and their physiology.

A neuron has three obvious structural components. The main body of the cell, the *soma,* is a broad, expanded structure housing the nucleus. Extending from the soma are two types of

20 cytoplasm-filled processes called *axons* and *dendrites.* Axons carry electrical impulses away from the soma and pass them on to other neurons or to muscle fibers. Dendrites receive impulses from other neurons and transport them to the soma. All three components are usually surrounded by *glial cells.* Although glial

25 cells are not derived from nerve tissue, they come to form a more or less complex sheath around the axon. In invertebrates, the glial cell membranes may form a loose, multilayered sheath in which there is still room for cytoplasm between the layers. In this case the arrangement is known as a *tunicated axon.* In vertebrates the

30 sheath is bound more tightly so that no gaps are left. The glial cells are known as Schwann cells and are arranged along the axon in a characteristic way. Each Schwann cell covers about 2 mm of axon. Between neighbouring cells there is a small gap where the membrane of the axon is exposed to the extracellular medium.

35 These gaps are known as the nodes of Ranvier. Axons with this interrupted Schwann cell sheath are called *myelinated* or *medullated* axons. The formation of the myelin sheath enhances enormously the speed and quality of impulse conduction.

1. The question in lines 7–8 serves primarily to

   (A) introduce the description of neural specialization that follows
   (B) signal a shift in topic from animal behavior to the capacities of nervous systems
   (C) cast doubt on the previous discussion of simple animal behavior
   (D) highlight one of the enduring mysteries of biology
   (E) emphasize the differences between simple and complex neural systems

2. According to the passage, the components of nerve cells that perform jobs opposite to one another are

   (A) the cell organelles and the cell membrane
   (B) the soma and the muscle fibers
   (C) the glial cells and the cytoplasm
   (D) the axons and dendrites
   (E) a tunicated axon and glial cells

3. It can be inferred from the passage that the neural systems of vertebrates receive

   (A) fewer messages than do the neural systems of invertebrates
   (B) interrupted messages due to the gaps known as the nodes of Ranvier
   (C) electrical messages at too great a speed for assimilation
   (D) electrical messages more quickly and accurately than do the neural systems of invertebrates
   (E) specialized electrical messages only

4. The word "medium" in line 34 most nearly means a(n)

   (A) average or mean
   (B) surrounding environment
   (C) position between two extremes
   (D) material used for a specific function
   (E) agent through which something is transmitted

5. One major difference between invertebrate and vertebrate neurons is

   (A) their structural components
   (B) the tightness of the glial cell sheath
   (C) their neural complexity
   (D) the number of cytoplasm-filled processes known as axons and dendrites
   (E) the presence of a glial cell sheath

PRACTICE CRITICAL READING 4

The everyday life of the average man—his whole political, economic, and social life—was transformed during Late Antiquity. The free and natural forms of the early [Roman] Empire, the multiplicity and the variation of life under a decentralized administration, were replaced by homogeneity and uniformity under an ever-present and increasingly more centralized hierarchy of civil officials.

1. The author is most probably going to elaborate on which of the following themes?

   (A) The natural forms of the early Roman Empire
   (B) The burgeoning centralized nature of government
   (C) Variations for Roman citizens under a decentralized government
   (D) The growing standardization of lifestyles for Romans
   (E) Facets of early Roman modes of existence

PRACTICE CRITICAL READING 5

Line   Two centuries ago, a pair of intrepid men conducted a two-year
exploration and science experiment that has inspired hundreds of
articles and books, all drawing on the information Lewis and
Clark amassed in their westward trek to the Pacific. In a 1995

5   book, Daniel Botkin termed it "the greatest wilderness trip ever
recorded." Ever since that trip, when Meriwether Lewis and
William Clark left Mississippi behind them in 1804, adults and
children have wondered about the idyllic wilderness those two
men encountered.

10   Ah, but think a moment. Just how pristine could that
wilderness have been? We tend to view the early nineteenth
century as a time when nature in America was unspoiled by
man—a pure land, inviolate, and eternal. Yet given the amazingly
detailed information in the journals of Lewis and Clark, today's

15   scientists hold dissenting opinions. Lands rich in game were
inhabited by Native Americans who hunted that game for suste-
nance, but, more importantly, engaged in warfare among the
tribes. These behaviors no doubt played a significant ecological
role in controlling the distribution of game, as well as the

20   numbers of bison, elk, and other Western megafauna long before
Europeans settled there.

     According to ecologists and biologists, Indian hunters were
proficient enough to decimate or even obliterate populations of
large game such as bison within their tribal homelands. Between

25   warring tribes, however, big game sought safety in sizable buffer
zones. Hunters felt disinclined to linger in what could easily
become enemy territory, and thus, in a province threatening to
humans, big game thrived. These areas acted as preserves, and
may actually have kept the plains bison, elk, and other large

30   animals from extinction. Lewis and Clark reported that in these
preserves, large animals showed no fear of humans.

     This "war zone" theory appears in an article for *Conserva-
tion Biology* by Dr. Paul S. Martin, a paleoecologist at the
University of Arizona, and Christine R. Szuter, editor in chief of

35 the University of Arizona press. Martin feels that his theory at
    least partly accounts for the survival of bison, deer, elk, and bears,
    whereas other, larger species such as mammoths, camels,
    mastodons, giant sloths, and giant short-faced bears went extinct
    13,000 years ago. According to Martin and Szuter, "the land had
40 been stripped of most of its native megafauna through human
    influence" before Lewis and Clark arrived.
        Not everyone agrees with this theory, yet it raises questions
    for modern ecologists and scientists that beg consideration. If we
    wish to restore lands to their "natural" ecosystems, how do we
45 contrive an accurate picture of that system? How many millennia
    back are we prepared to think? Do we mean the state of the land
    before Native Americans discovered it? Before any humans arrived
    in North America? When the Europeans arrived? Also, different
    scientists have varied explanations for the disappearance of North
50 American megafauna, chief among them climatic change or dis-
    ease.
        Still, whatever the explanation, some conclusions seem
    inevitable. Paleo-Indians, who pre-dated the Native American
    tribes that we know, plus the Native Americans themselves had
55 multiple influences upon the early West, prior to the advent of
    Lewis and Clark. Indians constructed various earthworks, houses,
    towns, and trails; they cultivated fields. They hunted many species
    and set fires, with the result that pre-Columbian forests were
    more parklike than forests we know today. All such behaviors
60 ripple throughout an ecosystem. It is humans who generally
    decide whether the ripples escalate into waves or tsunamis.

1. According to Martin, Indian tribal wars were responsible for all of the following EXCEPT
    (A) location of various kinds of large game animals
    (B) alterations to the actual landscape
    (C) Native Americans' avoidance of certain locations
    (D) isolating tribes one from the other
    (E) inadvertent creation of game preserves

2. In line 1, the word "intrepid" is used to mean

(A) brilliant
(B) hardy
(C) dauntless
(D) highly qualified
(E) self-appointed

3. The author of this passage most probably wants readers to contemplate which of the following questions?

(A) How did Native Americans affect the landscape of the American West?
(B) Why did European colonists settle in the American West?
(C) What else is contained in the extensive journals of the Lewis and Clark expedition?
(D) When did the period of paleo-Indian influence end and that of more recent Native Americans begin?
(E) How will actions by today's humans affect our ecological system?

4. Lines 24–31 imply that

(A) these animals had adjusted to human contact
(B) these animals had had little or no human contact
(C) these animals were used to the appearance of different creatures
(D) these animals were trained by Native Americans to be more docile
(E) these animals expected to be fed by the humans who appeared

5. The rhetorical purpose of the first two sentences in the second paragraph (lines 10–11) is to

(A) slow the pace of the essay
(B) act as an introduction to the remainder of the essay
(C) establish a conversational, relaxed tone
(D) prepare the reader for the many rhetorical questions that will follow
(E) pose a disturbing question

6. The essay's author would most likely agree with which of the following?

(A) It is probably impossible to fully describe the flora and fauna in western North American prior to the time of the Lewis and Clark expedition.

(B) It is highly probable that paleo-Indians hunted the mastodon, the mammoth, and the giant sloth, plus others, to extinction.

(C) Climatic changes and disease most likely caused the extinctions of the mastodon, the mammoth, the giant sloth, and other megafauna.

(D) Early Native Americans lived so carefully upon the land that their influence was negligible in regards to the landscape.

(E) Human influence played a relatively minor role, all things considered, in the distribution and numbers of wild game.

7. Paragraph 4 (beginning with line 32) primarily serves to

(A) debunk a previously-held theory

(B) take readers back to an earlier time, paleontologically

(C) explain how easy it was for a species to become extinct

(D) add authority and scientific weight to the essay

(E) eradicate any doubt about Dr. Martin's theory

8. Based on information in the essay, which of the following probably had the LEAST effect on the megafauna of western North America?

(A) The presence of human beings

(B) The tendency of Native Americans to war with neighboring tribes

(C) Climatic change or disease

(D) The Native Americans' tendency to set fires

(E) The gradual disappearance of suitable forests and vegetation

9. By "pre-Columbian forests" (line 58), the author means

(A) North American forests when the Europeans settled there

(B) North American forests prior to the Native Americans' arrival

(C) North American forests before the western lands were inhabited by any humans

(D) North American forests prior to the arrival of Christopher Columbus

(E) any forests before humans altered them

PRACTICE CRITICAL READING 6

Line   "The tears were in my eyes, and I knew that Madame Renard was boiling with rage, for she kept on nagging at me: 'Oh, how horrid! Don't you see that he is robbing you of your fish? Do you think that you will catch anything? Not even a frog, nothing
5   whatever. Why, my hands are burning just to think of it.'

  "But I said to myself: 'Let us wait until twelve o'clock. Then this poaching fellow will go to lunch, and I shall get my place again.' As for me, Monsieur le Judge, I lunch on the spot every Sunday; we bring our provisions in the boat. But there! At twelve
10   o'clock the wretch produced a fowl out of a newspaper, and while he was eating, actually he caught another chub!

  "Melie and I had a morsel also, just a mouthful, a mere nothing, for our heart was not in it.

  "Then I took up my newspaper, to aid my digestion. Every
15   Sunday I read in the shade like that, by the side of the water.

  "Well, then I began to tease my wife, but she got angry immediately and very angry, so I held my tongue. At that moment our two witnesses, who are present here, Monsieur Ladureau and Monsieur Durdent, appeared on the other side of the river. We
20   knew each other by sight. The little man began to fish again, and he caught so many that I trembled with vexation, and his wife said: 'It is an uncommonly good spot, and we will come here always.'

  "As for me, a cold shiver ran down my back, and Melie kept repeating: 'You are not a man; you have the blood of a chicken in

25   your veins'; and suddenly I said to her: 'Look here, I would rather
     go away, or I shall only do something foolish.'

         "And she whispered to me as if she had put a red-hot iron
     under my nose: 'You are not a man. Now you are going to run
     away and surrender your place!'

30   "Well, I felt that, but yet I did not move while the little man
     pulled out a bream. Oh! I never saw such a large fish before, never!
     And then my wife began to talk aloud, as if she were thinking, and
     you can see her trickery. She said: 'That is what one might call
     stolen fish, seeing that we baited the place ourselves. At any rate

35   they ought to give us back the money we have spent on bait.' "

1. Monsieur Renard is most
    probably relating his story
    in a

    (A) town square
    (B) town council meeting
    (C) friend's sitting room
    (D) courtroom
    (E) local restaurant

2. The passage suggests that
    Monsieur Renard

    (A) is intimidated by his
         wife
    (B) respects his wife's
         feelings
    (C) rarely pays attention to
         his wife
    (D) abhors his wife
    (E) enjoys his wife's
         company on fishing
         trips

3. Monsieur and Madame
    Renard's attitude toward the
    "little man" is best described
    as one of

    (A) wounded indignation
    (B) seething hatred
    (C) abject depression
    (D) magnanimity in defeat
    (E) respectful admiration

4. Madame Renard's speeches
    are intended to

    (A) taunt her spouse about
         his lack of masculinity
    (B) goad her husband into
         action against the
         usurper
    (C) drive Monsieur Renard
         to commit a crime
    (D) tease her spouse to
         relieve the tedium of
         fishing
    (E) inflict misery on her
         inactive husband

5. Monsieur Renard's narrative style can best be described as

(A) light-hearted, but somewhat dull and wordy

(B) terse and angry, but interesting

(C) rambling and disoriented, but entertaining

(D) amusingly loquacious, but eloquent

(E) intense and wordy, but penetrating

PRACTICE CRITICAL READING 7

Line The Knight-Parsons dialogue [between the economist Knight and Parsons, a sociologist] ended in 1940 with an angry public exchange. Perhaps by this time Knight had also had enough of Parsons's penchant for abstract theorizing. In any event, Knight

5 was the originator of one of the better jokes about sociology, and he may very well have had Parsons in mind when he formulated it: "Sociology is the science of talk, and there is only one law in sociology. Bad talk drives out good talk."

1. This passage implies that the economist Knight apparently had "had enough of Parsons's penchant for abstract theorizing" because Knight himself

(A) had little patience with other scientists

(B) was interested in what was concrete or could be proved

(C) had a penchant for making suppositions

(D) enjoyed being the person who gave lectures

(E) took his profession far less seriously than Parsons did

2. Based on this brief excerpt, we may assume that Knight regarded sociology in what light?

(A) As a new and valuable science

(B) As the work of predictable professionals

(C) As the creation of undisciplined academics

(D) As sundry observations by wordy theorists

(E) As a science apt to undermine the work done in economics

More Practice on Critical Reading Passages

Working with some old, published SATs (see your guidance counselor), read and answer questions on all of the reading passages in *at least two old tests*. Practice reading as swiftly as you can, reading for the main point of each selection and the main point of each *paragraph*.

Pay attention to time. How long is it taking you to answer questions on a paragraph? On a short or medium passage? Are you able to answer questions on the longer passages in 13–15 minutes? Learn how you work and enter your results in the Timing Chart on page 59.

Are you beginning to think like the test-makers? Can you anticipate what kinds of questions might be asked on the reading material? When that day comes, and it will come with practice, you'll know that *you're in charge of this test*.

Success with Sentence Completion Questions

These questions ask you to complete the meanings of sentences by choosing the word or words that will make the most sense. So . . . *every word in each sentence is important*. Students who enjoy reading will do well. TV addicts will have more trouble, but practice makes a real difference, so let's get cracking.

First, the directions. They'll read something like the box shown here. Learn the directions now, as every minute counts on test day.

Blanks appear in one or two places in each of the following sentences to indicate a missing word or phrase. Choose the word(s) or phrase(s) that best complete the meaning of each sentence.

"Test Smarts" You Can Use

Key words point to the answer you want in every sentence.

Note the italicized words in the following examples. They are your clues to the needed words and sentence type.

Example A

Although Janie was *normally* _____, *she became* extremely _____ when it was time to get out of the pool, *insisting* that she needed more practice with the kickboard.

1. Is Janie behaving normally?

2. How is she behaving? Is she being insistent?

3. Is she normally the insistent type?

4. Is Janie's normal behavior the opposite of how she's acting now? Yes.

5. *This is a sentence of contrast:* one behavior contrasted with (opposed to) another.

6. The answer will be opposing words, such as *docile..stubborn.* Try reading the sentence with those words inserted. It makes complete sense, doesn't it?

Example B

The critic labeled the film _____, saying that *it was poorly cast and lacked substance.*

1. Why so many key words in a row?

2. Do the italicized words after the blank act as a definition of the unknown word? Yes.

3. *This is a definition sentence:* the key words explain, amplify, or define the missing word.

4. Try plugging in a word that fits the definition, such as *shallow* or *tasteless.* Now the sentence makes complete sense.

Example C

The *aggressive* _____ *and commitment* required to open the American West are *reflected* today in the _____ of modern business entrepreneurs.

1. Is that little word *and* really significant? You bet it is.

2. *And* links *similar* words, certainly not opposites.

3. The missing word and *commitment* must be closely linked and well described by *aggressive* to make logical sense.

4. These two nouns, _____ and *commitment,* are *reflected* (they show up again) in modern business entrepreneurs—today's pioneers in the business field.

5. *This is a sentence of comparison or coordination of similar ideas:* the key words told you so.

6. Try reading the sentence again, with words inserted: The aggressive *drive* and commitment required to open the American West are reflected today in the *actions* (or *thrust*) of modern business entrepreneurs.

Example D

Due to the _____ of qualified instructors, the obvious *concern* of modern education *is not the curriculum but* the _____ required to give it life.

1. *Due to* means *because of,* right?

2. *Because of* some problem with qualified instructors, the *concern* (worry) in education is *not* curriculum (what is being taught) *but* that problem with teachers.

3. *This is a cause-and-effect sentence* or *cause and result:* the key words tell you that one thing/situation is resulting in another.

4. Go ahead now and plug in your own words. Write your complete sentence here:

_____

_____

_____

_____

5. Did you come up with something like this? Due to the *lack* of qualified instructors, the obvious concern of modern education is not the curriculum but the *personnel* required to give it life.

Key Word Reminder

Remember the collection of key words from the earlier segment on Critical Reading, on page 36? Like *but* or *and*, many of them seem small; *however,* they play a major role in sentence completion questions. Every word in a well-constructed sentence has a job to do.

Certain Sentence Types Repeat

Learn these sentence types.

1. Contrast of one thing/situation with another. (Read Example A on page 83.)

2. Definition or explanation. (Read Example B on page 83.)

3. Comparison/coordination of similar ideas. (Read Example C on page 84.)

4. Cause and effect/result. (Read Example D on page 84.)

Knowing what sentence type you are working with will tell you what sort of words must be used to complete the meaning. Although not all sentences on standardized tests fit into these categories, you'll be surprised at how many do.

Negative vs. Positive Concepts Abound

Remember this example? *The critic labeled the film _____, saying that it was poorly cast and lacked substance.* Did the critic like the film? No. The word for this blank must be a *negative* word.

Any positive or even neutral word offered as an answer choice will be wrong and can be crossed out immediately.

How about this example? *The aggressive _____ and commitment required to open the American West are reflected today in the _____ of modern business entrepreneurs.* Is this a negative sentence as a whole? No, it appears to be fairly positive. Any negative answer choices can be eliminated immediately. *Commitment* is a fairly positive word, and the word linked to it by *and* must also be positive. For the second blank, a positive word or one with no negative connotations is a must. Why? Because the two nouns (_____ and *commitment*) are *reflected* today. They show up again in modern business pioneers, and they are still positive qualities.

Be alert for negative and positive word requirements. Ask yourself whether you want good words or bad ones. Is the general idea nice or nasty?

The Last Sentence Completion Questions Are Often Harder

In any set of sentence completion questions, the first few are apt to be relatively simple. One-word completions are the easiest and will take you only a few seconds. As you work through the problem set, however, the going may get rougher, and the answer choices may be words you've rarely seen. Eliminate all the answers you *know* to be wrong. Then choose the best one of those remaining.

QUICK TIPS

Read and reread the given sentence.

Examine it like a bug under a microscope. Circle key words if it helps you.

Note the key words as clues.

Pay special attention to the "little words": *so, because, and, yet, since, most, least, although, enough, moreover, typically, normally, curiously, however, uncharacteristically, unless, even though, nevertheless,* and so on. Note all *adverbs.*

Decide on sentence type—is it one of these?

(1) *Contrast* of one thing with another?
(2) *Definition,* with the word you're looking for defined or explained in the sentence?
(3) *Comparison* or *coordination* of similar ideas?
(4) *Cause and effect* or *result?*

Whomp up your own answer for the blank(s) before looking at the answer choices.

Do you want a positive or negative word? Positive word in the first blank and negative word in the second blank? What does the sentence need to make absolute logical sense?

Eliminate answer choices systematically.

Cross out the wrong ones in your test booklet, and circle the answers to keep for final decision time.

Timing for Sentence Completion Questions

Look ahead to see how many sentence completion sentences are on a given portion of your timed test.

Allow yourself 30 seconds to 1 minute per question. Practice with sentence completion questions should help make you a speedy, accurate worker.

As you practice, note how long it takes you to do a ten-question series of sentence completion problems.

PRACTICE SENTENCE COMPLETIONS 1

Directions for all practice exercises: Circle the word or words that best complete the meaning of the entire sentence. Answers begin at the end of the book on page 327.

1. Americans seem committed to the exploration of space, aware that the variety of information gained in the attempt is of _____ value—beyond precise calculation.
   - (A) dubious
   - (B) medical
   - (C) inconclusive
   - (D) inestimable
   - (E) calculable

2. James was _____ about joining a fraternity; yes, he wanted the society of compatible, like-minded friends, but he also craved _____.
   - (A) confused..education
   - (B) ambivalent..diversity
   - (C) delighted..companion-ship
   - (D) determined..solitude
   - (E) uninformed..knowledge

3. The principle behind mediation is _____, wherein people with _____ goals or philosophies reach agreement on common ground, with each side conceding a point now and then.

   (A) arbitration..identical
   (B) historic..similar
   (C) compromise..disparate
   (D) modern..current
   (E) dissension..divergent

4. Despite warnings from financial experts, some _____ investors still _____ dubious get-rich-quick schemes.

   (A) innocent..adhere to
   (B) credulous..succumb to
   (C) timorous..retreat from
   (D) skeptical..wait for
   (E) arbitrary..care for

5. Patience, who possessed a(n) _____ temperament at odds with her name, learned that office work was too repetitive and predictable for one of her nature.

   (A) placid
   (B) volatile
   (C) remote
   (D) benevolent
   (E) amicable

6. A dedicated sculptor, Wharton found himself _____ with his new acquaintances because they valued him more for his ability to regale them with _____ at endless parties than for his hard-won artistic achievement.

   (A) conversant..grisly details
   (B) incompatible..witty repartee
   (C) blessed..professional skills
   (D) disgusted..information
   (E) malcontent..frivolity

7. It is an unfortunate _____ that the countries most in need of restructuring their economic systems are the ones whose history, customs, or rulers have _____ the acquisition of modern education and technology.

   (A) situation..encouraged
   (B) error..frustrated
   (C) paradox..inhibited
   (D) concern..realized
   (E) contretemps..promoted

8. More scientific progress was made during the twelve _____ years of war than during the preceding fifty years of _____ and peaceful commerce.

    (A) disordered..frugality
    (B) subversive..intrigue
    (C) chaotic..tranquillity
    (D) glorious..depression
    (E) uneventful..sterility

9. Miracles are not _____ to scientific proof; their _____ rests entirely on faith.

    (A) immune..power
    (B) opposed..evidence
    (C) amenable..inevitability
    (D) convertible..vitality
    (E) susceptible..efficacy

10. Literary styles change, and Dickens or Hawthorne would be as astonished by the deliberate _____ of Hemingway, as Hemingway was appalled by their _____ of words.

    (A) terseness..profusion
    (B) prose..paucity
    (C) approach..variety
    (D) morass..style
    (E) passages..mastery

PRACTICE SENTENCE COMPLETIONS 2

1. Clara Peeters, a distinguished Flemish painter, is among the best of many talented women who have _____ the history of still life and flower painting.

    (A) created
    (B) enriched
    (C) rescued
    (D) validated
    (E) extended

2. Frontier settlements had only makeshift jails in empty storerooms and livery stables; in addition, security was _____ and guards were easily _____, so that escapes were not uncommon.

   (A) formal..angered
   (B) established..induced
   (C) feeble..converted
   (D) intermittent.. investigated
   (E) lax..bribed

3. Rhonda's belief that people's lives are predestined, determined by God or perhaps fate, makes her championship of free will and independence especially _____.

   (A) understandable
   (B) incongruous
   (C) specious
   (D) suspect
   (E) reprehensible

4. Ralph's young, ingenuous appearance belied his _____ bargaining skill in awkward negotiations, so that opponents were often surprised by his _____.

   (A) honest..approach
   (B) clever..failures

   (C) canny..acumen
   (D) innovative..retreat
   (E) plausible..illogic

5. As anyone who watches TV can _____, the determination of advertisers to feed us their messages along with our entertainment continues _____.

   (A) attest..unabated
   (B) reveal..to diminish
   (C) state..to be mystifying
   (D) deny..as before
   (E) verify..to wane

6. Emily found that her pet monkey had not only a _____ tail but a mind to match it; his inventive exploits displayed a _____ intelligence far beyond what she had expected in so young an animal.

   (A) talented..kind of
   (B) simian..destructive
   (C) sedulous..brief
   (D) prehensile..precocious
   (E) clever..malicious

7. In times past, society suffered from a _____ of information about diet and exercise, but recently we have been _____ reams of information on both topics.

   (A) deluge..deprived of
   (B) dearth..inundated with
   (C) paucity..denied the
   (D) plethora..showered with
   (E) misdirection..given

8. Known for her _____ and generosity, Mavis astonished her community by withdrawing her customary support from a charity and establishing a rival one in her own name, a gesture labeled as pure _____ by disgruntled former associates.

   (A) keenness..philanthropy
   (B) aggressiveness..conceit
   (C) geniality..insensibility
   (D) idealism..rudeness
   (E) altruism..narcissism

9. Because of our cherished conception of the friar as an honest _____ who has no need of worldly goods, Chaucer's portrayal of the _____ and mendacious cleric comes as a shock.

   (A) priest..perspicacious
   (B) cleric..efficacious
   (C) ascetic..avaricious
   (D) fanatic..grasping
   (E) lunatic..craven

10. When informed that their ideas are _____, many people both old and wise have refrained from sharing their patiently garnered knowledge with the young and smug whom they deem too _____ to appreciate it.

    (A) perceptive..conceited
    (B) ludicrous..grateful
    (C) revolutionary..hide-bound
    (D) vicarious..insular
    (E) obsolescent..myopic

Stop!

Are there, by any remote chance, some words given as answer choices in these exercises that you *didn't know*?? If so, you'd better check on their meanings. These words were taken from PSATs and SATs of recent years, and many are repeat offenders.

PRACTICE SENTENCE COMPLETIONS 3

1. Can we restructure education so that it teaches logic and _____, rather than the collection and recitation of facts divorced from useful application?

   (A) cohesiveness
   (B) reasoning
   (C) problem-solving skills
   (D) proven data
   (E) historical precedent

2. Popular in the 1970s, the young adult problem novel, as it was known in the publishing trade, was essentially _____ in nature, bent on conveying a moral lesson in modern slang.

   (A) frivolous
   (B) boring
   (C) modern
   (D) equivocal
   (E) didactic

3. Her school performance was consistently _____; in conferences, her parents debated with the instructors whether she was _____ or just plain bored.

   (A) lackluster..incapable
   (B) insipid..gifted
   (C) meteoric..attentive
   (D) slow..bright
   (E) erratic..deficient

4. Apparently greatly _____, the secretary of the corporation accepted the generous apology of her board chairperson.

   (A) perplexed
   (B) mollified
   (C) exaggerated
   (D) maligned
   (E) stimulated

5. An optimist by nature, Harold faced a difficult adjustment when his investments turned sour, and he was slow to regain his customary _____ after the _____.

(A) cheer..process
(B) hardiness..event
(C) wariness..disaster
(D) sanguinity..debacle
(E) outlook..result

6. Because the front-runner in a state election focused on _____ interests rather than the parochial ones of his constituency, he lost to a _____ who told the citizens what they wanted to hear about their own narrow concerns.

(A) private..campaigner
(B) catholic..demagogue
(C) wide-ranging..pioneer
(D) specific..candidate
(E) centralized..politician

7. For authors, composers, and painters who must work alone, an occasional, stimulating meeting with others in the solitary arts serves to _____ their self-imposed _____.

(A) combat..isolation
(B) expand..endeavors
(C) mitigate..agony
(D) destroy..talent
(E) allay..fears

8. Although E. B. White enjoyed the success of his children's novel *Charlotte's Web,* he was _____ to have it translated into a movie, which he feared might _____ the book.

(A) resigned..reproduce
(B) delighted..magnify
(C) reluctant..inaccurately reflect
(D) hesitant..skillfully depict
(E) ecstatic..lampoon

9. Many of the antique "finds" she holds most dear have been strictly _____, the result of happenstance or what is often termed serendipity.

(A) characteristic
(B) preposterous
(C) brilliant
(D) immaculate
(E) fortuitous

10. For too many faculty members and researchers, computers are still _____ challenge; for growing numbers of students, however, these remarkable machines are _____ the way they learn.

(A) an interesting..inhibiting
(B) a formidable..revolutionizing
(C) an absorbing..subverting
(D) a disabling..codifying
(E) a euphoric..solidifying

PRACTICE SENTENCE COMPLETIONS 4

Stop!
Remember to put the trickier sentences into your own words. Know what sort of word you need for each blank before you eliminate answers.

1. While critics praised the play highly, viewers did not flock to the theater, and the playwright reaped only a(n) _____ reward from its brief run.

(A) just
(B) modest

(C) embarrassed
(D) monetary
(E) precise

2. My economics textbook is _____ to read, yet when I read attentively, I understand the theories presented.

(A) exciting
(B) annoying
(C) objectionable
(D) demanding
(E) idealistic

3. The scientist decided to risk failure rather than _____ the data just so that he could be published in the leading scientific journal.

(A) augment
(B) implement
(C) rationalize
(D) distort
(E) gauge

4. Although children need shelter and protection, their need for _____ is just as great if they are to evaluate themselves and their world honestly.

(A) homes
(B) affection
(C) truth
(D) adjustment
(E) instruction

5. The considerate personality of Dr. Jekyll underwent a total _____ as he became Mr. Hyde, _____ character bent on evil.

(A) alteration..a dubious
(B) refurbishing..a masterful
(C) indoctrination..an original
(D) advancement..a different
(E) metamorphosis..a ruthless

6. If, as Shelley wrote, "The great instrument of moral good is the imagination," then we must not allow _____ to exclude totally our _____.

(A) harsh reality..idealistic goals
(B) creativity..fantasies
(C) unpleasant facts..daily lives
(D) religion..perception of life
(E) practicality..constructive ideas

7. In the nineteenth century, women on the American frontier were people of _____ determination whose _____ helped them conquer loneliness and privation.

   (A) questionable..character
   (B) fortunate..morality
   (C) average..modesty
   (D) relentless..tenacity
   (E) aristocratic..attitude

8. Even though certain forms of cancer now respond well to treatment, others have remained a(n) _____ continuing to puzzle physicians.

   (A) pestilence
   (B) allusion
   (C) eccentricity
   (D) enigma
   (E) provocation

9. A number of psychologists appear to believe that human intelligence is largely _____ and that to provide large sums of money to _____ intelligence in a structured environment is wasteful.

   (A) proven..portray
   (B) spiritual..define
   (C) theoretical..calculate
   (D) innate..cultivate
   (E) accessible..test

10. Believing himself supported by more than a _____ of evidence, the professor endeavored to prove that Beowulf was not the _____ his colleagues claimed, but an actual man whose existence was the basis for the Old English epic.

    (A) shred..persona
    (B) modicum..chimera
    (C) fabrication..demon
    (D) particle..heresy
    (E) aggregation..protagonist

More Practice with Sentence Completion Questions

After you have recovered from the foregoing exercises, if you feel the need for further practice and you have a copy of *Real SATs,* do as many of its sentence completion questions as you can stand. You will find that you are *much* better than you were. In fact, you will rarely miss any but the very nastiest—and maybe not even those.

UNIT 4

WRITING

Are you on schedule?

 Check the PLAN OF ATTACK on pages vi–viii.

"You learn best by reading a lot and writing a lot and the most valuable lessons of all are the ones you teach yourself. These lessons almost always occur with the study door closed."

Stephen King, *On Writing*, 2000

The new writing section on the SAT may not be welcome, but it is necessary. Your writing mirrors your thinking. If your writing is muddy, so is your thinking, and you know that muddy thinking won't work in college.

On the other hand, if you can write a clear essay—one that is well organized, logical, and convincing—then you are ready for college, where writing skills are critically important.

In the Writing section you'll find *multiple-choice questions* that take 35 minutes and are like questions on the SAT II: Writing Test. You can see a sample of this test online and study its questions—at the College Board Web site or at www.petersons.com. If you've taken a PSAT recently, you'll recognize these questions on grammar, diction, usage, and word choice.

If you get stuck as you work the practice questions in this book, get help from your English teacher or a friend who loves the topic.

Write an essay or two just to warm up. You CAN learn to write! It's a craft you can learn, not a gift reserved for a precious few. But writing gets better only through practice.

The Writing Section

Time:	60 minutes (One part = 25 minutes; one part = 10 minutes; the essay = 25 minutes)
Question Types:	Multiple choice on grammar, usage, diction (choice of words), correctness and effectiveness of written expression, and idiom.
	Essay; subscore ranges from 2 to 12
Points:	800

A Review of Grammatical Terms

Subject
The subject is the *who* or *what* that the sentence talks about.

My pet bat Loony has always been a little odd.

Predicate
The predicate must have a verb, and may have other material about the subject. It tells what the subject did (the action verb) or what the subject *is/feels/seems/appears* (a state-of-being verb).

Loony seemed friendly to my family right away.

Modifier
Modifiers tell something specific about the word they modify. They behave like adjectives or adverbs.

That large, groggy bat is Loony. (adjective modifiers)

Loony squeaks only to get attention. (adverb plus infinitive phrase as adverbial modifier)

Phrase
A phrase is a group of closely related words. Some phrases act as adjective or adverb modifiers.

The sleek bat under the window is named Ricardo. (adjectival modifier)

Most bats are quiet <u>during the day</u>. (adverbial modifier)

Noun phrases, which are *not modifiers*, do noun jobs, acting as single nouns. They can be subjects, objects, or predicate nouns.

<u>To fly freely</u> seems to be a bat's delight. (subject of verb *seems*)

My family enjoys <u>their acrobatic flying</u>. (gerund phrase as object of verb *enjoys*)

A bat specialty is <u>beeping high-frequency sounds</u>. (gerund phrase as a predicate noun)

Infinitive phrases may occasionally act as modifiers. For clear sentences—a must in writing—keep all modifiers close to the words they modify.

One elderly bat lacks the energy <u>to fly</u>. (infinitive phrase as adjective modifying the noun *energy*)

We think that a baby bat squeaked <u>to call her mother</u>. (infinitive phrase as adverb modifying the verb *squeaked*)

Sentence

A sentence must have a subject and a predicate and make sense all by itself. It is also called an *independent clause*.

<u>Loony and his bat family make me smile</u>.

Clause

A clause is a group of closely related words with a subject and a predicate. *Independent clauses* (sentences) express complete thoughts. *Dependent clauses* depend for sense on a word or words in the main (independent) clause.

A dependent clause pretending to be a sentence is called a *fragment*.

Bats fly. (Independent clause. Makes sense all by itself.)

Why bats fly (dependent clause/fragment)

As I watch Loony and his family (dependent clause/fragment)

Since Loony's family moved into our garage (dependent clause/fragment)

Clauses as Modifiers

A bat <u>that is as personable as Loony</u> is probably rare. (clause as adjective modifier)

I pet Loony <u>when he lands on my outstretched hand</u>. (clause as adverb modifier

Clauses as Nouns

<u>Why Loony decided to be my friend</u> is a mystery. (clause as subject)

I don't know <u>how old Loony is</u>. (clause as direct object)

Loony can fly to <u>any rafter he chooses</u>. (clause as object of preposition)

Run-on Sentence

Sometimes run-on sentences are called **comma splices,** because the writer has linked many ideas with commas and created a mess. Watch for this common error on the SAT! Always avoid using a comma to join two independent clauses *when there is no conjunction between them*.

NO: Loony circled and circled one evening, he was apparently flying just for sheer enjoyment.

YES: Loony circled and circled one evening, <u>as if he were flying just for sheer enjoyment</u>. (conjunction links the clauses, turning the second one into a dependent clause)

YES: Loony circled and circled one evening; he was apparently flying just for sheer enjoyment. (two closely-linked thoughts—nice place for a semicolon)

YES: Loony circled and circled one evening, apparently flying just for sheer enjoyment. (restructuring also fixes the problem)

YES: Loony circled and circled one evening. He was apparently flying just for sheer enjoyment. (two separate sentences)

Identifying Sentence Errors

The following practice questions reflect the most common writing errors. Watch for mistakes in grammar, usage, idiom, and diction (word choice). The explanatory answers start on page 330.

Step-by-Step Approach:

- Read the entire sentence carefully.
- Lightly cross out the underlined sections that you know are *correct*.
- Examine the remaining underlined section(s).
- Know *what* is wrong and *why* it is wrong when you select it as the error in the sentence. (Acting on a hunch works, too, but it's riskier.)
- If you decide nothing is wrong, select "No error" as your answer choice. "No error" will be your answer 10–20% of the time.

PRACTICE IDENTIFYING SENTENCE ERRORS 1

> *Directions:* Identify the grammatical error by selecting its corresponding letter. Write it in the margin. Wait to check answers until you've completed this set of practice questions. Answer choice (E) is always "No error."

1. My folks insisted that my little sister behave respectively in
   <u>(A)</u>
   church, <u>although</u> they were tense sitting through a long service
   <u>(B)</u>
   <u>while</u> she squirmed <u>between</u> them. <u>No error</u>
   (C)   (D)   (E)

2. If you <u>would have notified</u> me, I would have <u>made sure that</u> I
   (A)   (B)
   appeared at the dress rehearsal <u>in costume</u> and <u>on time</u>. <u>No error</u>
   (C)   (D)   (E)

3. On a big game photographic <u>safari</u>, each member of the tour
   (A)
   <u>was warned</u> to keep <u>their camera</u> ready, as a photo opportunity
   (B)   (C)
   <u>might appear</u> at any time. <u>No error</u>
   (D)   (E)

4. Worried about <u>raising</u> grocery costs, my dad planted a vast home
   (A)   (B)
   garden; he also <u>set out</u> six fruit trees. <u>No error</u>
   (C)   (D)   (E)

5. <u>Clearly</u> in a hurry, Sherry pushed the envelopes <u>toward</u> me,
   (A)   (B)
   saying, "Here's the films <u>you ordered</u>." <u>No error</u>
   (C)   (D)   (E)

6. One and a half inches <u>means</u> <u>a lot</u> to someone <u>whose</u> wishing to
   (A)   (B)   (C)
   <u>grow taller</u>. <u>No error</u>
   (D)   (E)

7. Many <u>have smiled</u> at the irony in the title United Nations, <u>as</u> that
   (A)   (B)
   august body <u>appears</u> united on so <u>few</u> occasions. <u>No error</u>
   (C)   (D)   (E)

8. The education curator <u>at the museum</u> noticed <u>less</u> people for the
(A)   (B)

lecture on dolphins <u>than</u> she <u>had expected.</u> <u>No error</u>
(C)   (D)   (E)

9. A puppy with bad habits or a kitten that <u>scratches the upholstery</u>
(A)

<u>seem</u> like trouble on foot <u>to some</u> , but not to those <u>who love</u>
(B)   (C)   (D)

pets. <u>No error</u>
(E)

10. "A new pair of trousers <u>is not</u> what I expected <u>to be</u> in this gift
(A)   (B)

bag," said Grampa, <u>clearly</u> surprised and pleased. <u>No error</u>
(C)   (D)   (E)

PRACTICE IDENTIFYING
SENTENCE ERRORS 2

Directions: Identify the grammatical error by selecting its corresponding letter. Write it in the margin. Wait to check answers until you've completed this set of practice questions. Answer choice (E) is always "No error."

1. <u>It's</u> annoying and also highly possible <u>that</u> the completion
(A)   (B)

of our house <u>would be</u> delayed, due to <u>inclement weather.</u>
(C)   (D)

<u>No error</u>
(E)

2. My pet Loony the bat is <u>kind of</u> <u>a worrisome</u> pet, <u>because</u> he's not
(A)   (B)   (C)

a totally normal bat, <u>and so</u> I never know what to expect.
(D)

<u>No error</u>
(E)

3. We <u>assured</u> our class advisor that she could depend on the prom
(A)

committee and <u>myself</u> <u>not to set</u> any new <u>precedents</u> for
(B)   (C)   (D)

ridiculous expenses. <u>No error</u>
(E)

4. Either the girls or the coach <u>calls</u> time out during basketball
(A)

games <u>I've attended</u>, <u>which</u> haven't been as many as I
(B)   (C)

<u>would have liked</u> . <u>No error</u>
(D)   (E)

5. Based on the <u>spate of errors</u> that <u>flood</u> every publication and
(A)   (B)

student paper, <u>its</u> somewhat tricky to put the apostrophe in
(C)

<u>its</u> place. <u>No error</u>
(D)   (E)

6. <u>Many a troop</u> of Boy Scouts <u>have spent</u> weekends at Camp
(A)   (B)

Wannalinga, <u>striving</u> to qualify <u>for</u> Canoeing, Camping, and
(C)   (D)

Wilderness Survival badges. <u>No error</u>
(E)

7. I'm sure <u>your</u> bound to take <u>offense</u> at some of my
(A)   (B)

<u>grampa's</u> opinions, such as his recent dictum that <u>we girls</u> should
(C)   (D)

never wear bikinis. <u>No error</u>
(E)

8. The <u>principal</u> told us he <u>would award</u> first prize to <u>whomever</u>
(A)   (B)   (C)

wrote the funniest essay in the <u>school's</u> writing contest.
(D)

<u>No error</u>
(E)

9. I see <u>where</u> your football team is <u>mired in</u> last place, and I'll
(A)   (B)

wager your <u>team's</u> <u>morale</u> is equally muddy. <u>No error</u>
(C)   (D)   (E)

10. <u>School's</u> hardly begun, and <u>already</u> my mom has sent Brad and
(A)   (B)

<u>me</u> some <u>healthy</u> snacks to keep in our room at the dorm.
(C)   (D)

<u>No error</u>
(E)

Improving Sentences

Knowing how to improve sentences is a critical writer's skill. It is editing to repair structural flaws. As you learn to enjoy editing, you'll begin to enjoy writing. Making something sparkle and shine is fun.

Here are some of the problems you'll be fixing in order to improve sentence clarity:

- Vague or incorrect pronoun reference
- Misplaced or dangling modifier
- Lack of parallel structure
- Coordination and subordination of sentence elements
- Awkward/inaccurate shifts in verb tense, person and number, voice, or mood
- Wordiness
- Awkward phraseology
- Run-on sentence/comma splice

PRACTICE IMPROVING SENTENCES 1

Directions: Select the answer choice that makes each sentence absolutely clear, avoiding redundancy, clichés, and structural flaws. Choice (A) is always the same as the given sentence. When the sentence has no errors, select (A). Write your answer choice in the margin beside the sentence number.

Be sure to read the answers, beginning on page 332. The answers *teach* the material for this part of your book.

1. I love the fact that Howard is always on time.

    (A) the fact that Howard is always

    (B) Howard's habit of arriving

    (C) the tendency Howard has to arrive

    (D) that Howard is always

    (E) it, because Howard always comes

2. Since my favorite brother is a pharmacist, it's no wonder I chose that for a career.

    (A) I chose that for a career.

    (B) I will choose it for a career.

    (C) I am choosing that for a career.

    (D) I chose pharmacy for a career.

    (E) that I chose that for a career.

3. The absence of professional theatre might prompt citizens to begin their own theatre, write their own plays, being creative all the time.

    (A) being creative all the time.

    (B) as well as creating all the time.

    (C) and thereby discover their own creativity.

    (D) and be creating like never before.

    (E) to create all the time.

4. To his dismay, Seth found that he couldn't do the problem, moreover, he couldn't even decide what the first step should be.

    (A) problem, moreover, he couldn't even decide

    (B) problem; moreover, he couldn't even decide

(C) problem, and what was worse moreover, he couldn't even decide

(D) problem; couldn't even begin to decide

(E) problem; couldn't even decide

5. The fire ants in my garden build mounds wherever <u>they choose, but they can resist the pesticides we use to eradicate them.</u>

(A) they choose, but they can resist the pesticides we use to eradicate them

(B) they choose, but they're resistant to pesticides

(C) they choose, since they're resisting the pesticides

(D) they choose, being able to resist the pesticides

(E) they choose, because they're resistant to our pesticides

6. In Africa, the Boer War was a time of great upheaval, of local misery, <u>and of larger portent than was realized at the time.</u>

(A) and of larger portent than was realized at the time.

(B) more portent than was realized then.

(C) because it was more portentous than anyone realized.

(D) since it was a portent of things to come, which was unrealized then.

(E) and at the time, something most portentous.

7. <u>The dean gives us a talk about manners in school about every two weeks.</u>

(A) The dean gives us a talk about manners in school about every two weeks.

(B) The dean gives us a talk about manners in school when it's been only two weeks.

(C) About every two weeks, the dean gives us a talk about manners in school.

(D) In school, the dean gives us a talk about manners, about every two weeks.

(E) A talk about manners is what the dean gives us in school, about every two weeks.

8. If <u>anyone wants to keep a job, they</u> must be conscientious about work.

   (A) If anyone wants to keep a job, they

   (B) Anyone who wants to keep a job, they

   (C) People who keep jobs, they

   (D) Those who want to keep jobs

   (E) If anyone wants a job, they

9. Our cat Fred is quite adventuresome, <u>and it causes him</u> to wander away often.

   (A) and it causes him

   (B) so that it makes him

   (C) and it is why he wanders away often.

   (D) because he is often known to wander away.

   (E) and that trait causes him

10. As I biked along the quiet street, <u>the houses were seen to be trim and fresh</u>.

   (A) the houses were seen to be trim and fresh.

   (B) the trim, fresh houses could be seen.

   (C) the houses, trim and fresh, could be seen by me.

   (D) I saw the houses, looking trim and fresh.

   (E) I looked at the trim, fresh houses.

PRACTICE IMPROVING SENTENCES 2

Directions: Select the answer choice that makes each sentence absolutely clear, avoiding redundancy, clichés, and structural flaws. Answer (A) is always the same as the given sentence. When the sentence has no errors, select (A). Write your answer choice in the margin beside the sentence number.

This time, try to decide what the error is *before* looking at any of the answer choices.

1. We had heard where the movie was already being shown, that it was well portrayed, and long, too.

   (A) where the movie was already being shown, that it was well portrayed, and long, too.

   (B) where the movie was shown already, how it was well portrayed, and it was long, too.

   (C) where the movie being shown was well portrayed, and why it was long.

   (D) that the movie was already being shown, that it was well portrayed, and that it was long.

   (E) that the movie was already being shown, being well portrayed and long.

2. Rain poured for over a week, consequently, we had to bail out our fishpond.

   (A) week, consequently, we had to bail out

   (B) week. Consequently, we had to bail out

   (C) week and so consequently, we had to bail out

   (D) week so that's why, consequently, we had to bail out

   (E) week, we had to bail out

3. The trouble <u>with this present situation was that</u> we owe more thanks than can ever be expressed.

   (A) with this present situation was that

   (B) with that situation was that

   (C) with this present situation was because

   (D) with this present situation came about because

   (E) with this present situation is that

4. At the end of the movie classic *Casablanca*, <u>it shows clearly the depth of the man's love</u> for the woman he sends away to safety.

   (A) it shows clearly the depth of the man's love

   (B) it is clear the depth of the man's love

   (C) viewers see clearly the depth of the man's love

   (D) it's clear how deep the man's love is

   (E) it clearly is a man's deep love

5. Rachel Carson wrote eloquent essays <u>and they communicate</u> the need for respecting our fragile world.

   (A) and they communicate

   (B) and that is why they communicate

   (C) essays, they communicate

   (D) that communicate

   (E) about communicating

6. <u>Blowing across the sands, the boy smelled the unmistakable odor of dead fish.</u>

   (A) Blowing across the sands, the boy smelled the unmistakeable odor of dead fish.

   (B) Having been blown across the sands, the boy smelled the unmistakeable odor of dead fish.

   (C) The boy smelled the unmistakable odor of dead fish blowing across the sands.

   (D) The boy smelled, blowing across the sands, the unmistakable odor of dead fish.

   (E) The unmistakable odor of dead fish, blown across the sands, was smelled by the boy.

7. During her senior year, Gretchen scored a first at the national music contest; which was a dream come true.

   (A) national music contest; which was a dream come true.

   (B) national music contest, which, for her, was a dream come true.

   (C) national music contest. Which was a dream come true.

   (D) national music contest, a dream come true, that it was.

   (E) contest, which was a dream come true.

8. Señor Carlo is one of our school's most popular teachers and he is the head of the language department, as well as being head of our drama productions.

   (A) Señor Carlo is one of our school's most popular teachers and he is the head of the language department, as well as being head of our drama productions.

   (B) Señor Carlo, head of language and drama at our school, is one of our most popular teachers.

   (C) One of our school's most popular teachers is Señor Carlo, who is head of both our language and drama departments.

   (D) Head of our language department and also of drama productions at our school is Señor Carlo, one of our most popular teachers.

   (E) Being head of both the language and drama departments at our school is Señor Carlo, one of our most popular teachers.

9. Seen from the deck of our sailboat, the house back on shore appeared tiny.

   (A) Seen from the deck of our sailboat, the house back on shore appeared tiny.

   (B) The house back on shore appeared tiny, seen from the deck of our sailboat.

   (C) Back on shore the house appeared tiny, seen from the deck of our sailboat.

   (D) In our sailboat, from the deck, the house back on shore appeared tiny.

   (E) Back on shore, the house seen from the deck of our sailboat appeared tiny.

10. To attend all the campus basketball games, seats must be reserved one year ahead of the season.

   (A) To attend all the campus basketball games, seats must be reserved one year ahead of the season.

   (B) To attend all the campus basketball games, one year ahead of season the seats must be reserved.

   (C) To attend all of the campus basketball games, you must reserve seats one year ahead of the season.

   (D) Attending all the campus basketball games means that seats must be reserved one year ahead of the season.

   (E) Seats must be reserved one year ahead of the season, in order to attend all the campus basketball games.

Improving Paragraphs

The main reason for improving any sentence or paragraph is clarity. You must make sure that you said exactly what you meant to say. In addition, a paragraph needs to have:

1. A clear focus, with no extraneous material

2. Coherence = logical structure, organization

3. Standard English (good grammar)

If your writing also has a consistent tone, uses active verbs, contains a variety of sentence types, and is concise, well, yeah! Go to the head of the class.

But for now . . . consider the lowly paragraph. Like all other aspects of writing (sentences, essays, books, plays—even grocery lists), paragraphs have a *beginning, middle, and end*.

The beginning of a paragraph—the first sentence or two— usually gives the topic or theme of the paragraph. If part of a longer work, the opening sentence(s) in a paragraph will link back to what has gone before. In works with many paragraphs (most writing), a topic sentence may be either unneeded or found anywhere in the first paragraph.

Occasionally, the main idea of a paragraph, or even an entire essay, is implied, as in satiric writing. For example, the newspaper comics "Cathy," "Zits," and "Opus" regularly suggest their main points rather than saying them literally.

The middle of a paragraph enlarges on the topic with additional information in examples, quotes, anecdotes, and so on.

The end of a paragraph usually leads the reader to the next paragraph in a work filled with paragraphs. (The world has few paragraphs that have escaped and are running around on their own.) If the last sentences end the entire essay, they should echo the theme established in the beginning, making a conclusion that drives the point home. If it's the last paragraph in a chapter of a book, then its job is to lure the reader on. (Charles Dickens is famous for his chapter endings, known as cliff hangers, which leave the protagonist in such a perilous state that the reader is compelled to continue.)

Improving paragraphs is the daily job of full-time writers. They regularly repair the same errors that you fix in your own writing, and that will appear on the SAT.

Grammar faults such as
—subject-verb disagreement
—incorrect verb tense
—errors in tense sequence
—shift in verb voice from active to passive
—incorrect pronoun case
—lack of antecedent for a pronoun

—incorrect punctuation
—incorrect idiom
—wrong choice of word (diction)
—incorrect usage of words/ phrases
—cloudy pronoun reference
—pronoun shifts (for example, from I to you)

Structural faults such as
—lack of parallelism
—lack of clarity in any element
—sentence fragments (incomplete sentences)
—misplaced or dangling modifiers
—incorrect coordination of sentence elements
—incorrect subordination of sentence elements

—lack of sentence variety (for example, too many short, punchy sentences in a row)
—wordiness/redundancy
—run-ons/comma splices
—awkward phrasing
—rambling discourse/lack of focus

What Makes a Good Paragraph?

An award-winning paragraph has a focused point, made clearly, although not always in the first sentence. Supporting sentences include examples, quotes, narrative, authoritative sources, and so on. The paragraph may be one of persuasion, argument and proof, definition or explanation, cause and effect, classification and analysis (to explain processes or systems step by step)—all common ways to develop paragraphs.

This jewel of writing contains no unnecessary words or extraneous facts, avoids clichés, and links sentences one to another with absolute clarity.

How Can Anyone Do All This?

By not trying too hard. Don't use a great many big words to impress. Save the stunner word for special occasions. Outline what you want to say and organize the outline until it flows logically. Write slowly and think hard. Block out the world and focus only on the writing.

PRACTICE IMPROVING PARAGRAPHS 1

Directions: Some portions of this early draft need revision. It is the opening paragraph of a student's essay for history class. Questions on it will cover grammar, usage, and diction, plus organization and development (structure). Select answers based on the conventions of standard written English.

(1) One of the most intriguing figures of the eighteenth century, a person who was both adventurer and wrecker, whose biography reveals the conflicts of ego mixed with a love of history and concern for the common good, is Napoleon Bonaparte. (2) He was born in 1769. (3) His birthplace was the island of Corsica, a restless, half-barbaric place at the time. (4) His mother matched the place and she was in the habit of "birching" her sons with a stout switch, and Napoleon remembers being beaten when he was sixteen. (5) While his father was a somewhat boring lawyer. (6) Although Napoleon had many siblings, he was the only one in his family to become famous, perhaps because he was extremely bright with a humongous memory. (7) He was also considered ill-tempered and overbearing, because he

was profoundly patriotic like his hot-headed mother. (8) It is fortunate that the French governor of Corsica became his patron and Napoleon received an excellent military education. (9) His numerous, detailed notebooks from this education still exist.

1. Of the following choices, which one makes the best revision of sentence 1, the topic sentence of this paragraph?

   (A) Both adventurer and wrecker, Napoleon Bonaparte stands out as an intriguing eighteenth-century figure whose biography reveals the subtle conflicts of ego mixed with love of country and concern for the common good.

   (B) Napoleon Bonaparte, who was both wrecker and adventurer, stands out in the eighteenth century because his biography reveals the subtle conflicts of ego mixed up with a love of country and concern for the common good.

   (C) In the eighteenth century, the most intriguing figure is Napoleon Bonaparte, whose biography reveals the subtle conflicts of ego warring with a love of country and concern for the common good—a person who was both wrecker and adventurer.

   (D) A person who was both adventurer and wrecker in the eighteenth century is Napoleon Bonaparte, whose biography reveals the subtle conflicts of ego mixed with love of country and concern for the common good.

   (E) The subtle conflicts of ego mixed with concern for the common good and love of country characterize Napoleon Bonaparte—adventurer and wrecker—one of the most intriguing figures of the eighteenth century.

2. Keeping in mind the best possible topic sentence, which of the following revisions would be most effective for sentences 2 and 3?

(A) His birthplace was the island Corsica, in 1769, a restless and half-barbaric place at the time.

(B) He was born on the restless, half-barbaric island of Corsica in mid-century, 1769.

(C) A restless, half-barbaric place, Corsica was Napoleon's birthplace in 1769, the middle of the eighteenth century.

(D) His birthplace was the island of Corsica, in 1769, when it was a restless and half-barbaric place back then.

(E) On the island of Corsica, in 1769, Napoleon was born when the place was both restless and half-barbaric.

3. Consider the following choices and select the revised sentence that most succinctly expresses the ideas in sentence 4 of the original draft.

(A) His mother, who seemed to be as wild as Corsica itself, regularly "birched" her many sons with a stout switch; Napoleon remembers being beaten when he was sixteen.

(B) He grew up on Corsica with his brothers, who were all "birched" by their mother, who was as wild as Corsica itself. Napoleon remembers being beaten when he was sixteen.

(C) Napoleon remembers being beaten by his mother with a stout switch when he was sixteen, because she was in the habit of "birching" him and his brothers, since she was wild herself like the island of Corsica.

(D) He grew up with a mother as wild as Corsica, who regularly "birched" her sons with a stout switch; Napoleon recalled being beaten at age sixteen.

(E) Napoleon's mother was much like Corsica, and in the habit of "birching" her many sons with a stout switch, according to Napoleon who recalled being beaten at age sixteen.

4. Of the following editorial choices, which is the best way of working with the material in sentence 5? *While his father was a somewhat boring lawyer.*

(A) Put information about Napoleon's parents in one sentence at the very beginning of the essay.

(B) Leave it in this place, but rewrite to create a complete sentence. For example, <u>In contrast to his mother, Napoleon's father was a somewhat boring lawyer.</u>

(C) For the sake of unity, cut it from this paragraph. Maybe it will fit in the essay later.

(D) Because they're more important, put the information about both parents ahead of the information about Corsica.

(E) Research Napoleon's father so that several sentences could be written about him here, giving a fuller picture of Napoleon's background.

5. Which of the following is the best revision of the underlined segment in sentence 6, below?

Although Napoleon had many siblings, he was the only one to become famous, <u>perhaps because he was extremely bright with a humongous memory</u>.

(A) maybe because he was hugely smart, with a great memory.

(B) perhaps because he had an outstanding mind linked to a prodigious memory.

(C) perhaps because he had an awesome memory and was extremely bright as well.

(D) no doubt due to his fine mind and his memory, which was prodigious.

(E) probably because he was extremely bright and had an amazing memory.

6. When considering logic, and therefore clarity, which of the following changes in sentence 7 (shown below) would improve it the most?

He was also considered ill-tempered and overbearing, because he was profoundly patriotic like his hot-headed mother.

(A) Though he was profoundly patriotic like his hot-headed mother, he was also ill-tempered and overbearing.

(B) While he was profoundly patriotic like his mother, he also was considered to be ill-tempered and overbearing by others.

(C) In addition, he was considered ill-tempered and overbearing, while he was also profoundly patriotic like his hot-headed mother.

(D) Like his hot-headed mother, however, he was patriotic, although he was also ill-tempered and overbearing.

(E) While he was profoundly patriotic like his mother, he was also ill-tempered, just like she was, and overbearing.

7. Which of the following revisions would end the paragraph more gracefully than the first draft version?

(A) Despite his shortcomings, Napoleon benefited from the patronage of the French governor of Corsica, who saw that the intelligent boy received an excellent military education. Fortunately for historians, Napoleon recorded his education in numerous, detailed notebooks.

(B) It is fortunate that Napoleon received an excellent military education, thanks to the French governor of Corsica, and we have his numerous, detailed notebooks that describe this period in his life.

(C) Thanks to Napoleon's numerous, detailed notebooks from his military education, we know that the French governor of Corsica acted as his patron.

(D) Napoleon received an excellent military education because the French governor of Corsica acted as his patron; we know this because Napoleon's numerous, detailed notebooks from this education still exist.

(E) Numerous, detailed notebooks illuminate the period of Napoleon's life when he received an excellent military education, thanks to the French governor of Corsica, who became his patron.

PRACTICE IMPROVING PARAGRAPHS 2

Directions: Some portions of the following essay need revising. It is the first draft of a student's essay, written in response to this assignment in ecology class: *Write about a plant (or plants) with economic value in today's world.*

(1) If you haven't heard of the plant named chufa (pronounced choo-fa), relax. (2) You're not alone. (3) Of course, if you live on the Mediterranean coast of Spain you know all about chufa, one of the most beloved and economically important plants in that region. (4) From chufa's peanut-sized tubers come many treats, chief among them the classic milky beverage called *horchata*, whose history goes back thousands of years to the Nile river valley in Egypt.

(5) This popular drink—a mixture of mashed chufa tubers plus water, sugar, and cinnamon—boasts a sweet, nutty flavor hinting at almonds or coconut. (6) Today it is served chilled, in cafes known as *horchaterias*. (7) Long ago, Spaniards took chufa to Mexico, where it was an instant success among wealthier people. (8) The traditional Spanish *horchata de chufa* remains much the same, but a modern version made with rice and known as *horchata de arroz*, has a different, less distinctive flavor.

(9) Another reason for this plant's popularity, and a major economic opportunity for farming and ecotourism, is chufa's appeal as

food for both wild and tame animals. (10) Turkeys, deer, feral hogs, and waterfowl quickly learn to dig beneath its grassy tops for the tubers below. (11) Turkeys in particular go crazy for these tubers packed with sugar, carbohydrates, protein, oil, and fiber. (12) In fact, one savvy land manager in the southeastern U.S. calls chufa a "turkey magnet."

(13) Thanks to the turkeys' eager foraging, sizable craters form in the chufa plot that attract other wildlife. (14) Large and small fowl visit the chufa craters and proceed to dig. (15) Deer drop by and hogs. (16) Before long, the chufa plot becomes a veritable restaurant in the wild, providing feed along with an incomparable viewing opportunity for humans. (17) Here, turkey gobblers strut their stuff before the hens. (18) Cardinals meet other cardinals. (19) Critters large and small set aside their differences in order to enjoy a delicious meal together.

(20) I don't know about you, but this picture reminds me strongly of the holiday Americans call Thanksgiving.

1. Select the answer choice that describes the purpose(s) achieved by the first paragraph in this essay.

   (A) It gives the historical background of the topic under discussion—the chufa plant that originated in the Nile valley.

   (B) It promises readers a relaxed, chatty discussion of an otherwise boring topic, a plant.

   (C) It establishes the informal tone of the essay and makes a thesis statement: chufa is an economically significant plant.

   (D) It introduces an economically important plant, which was the assignment for the essay.

   (E) It entices us to read on by being written in a casual, offhand tone.

2. Which answer choice best expresses the writer's overall purpose in the second paragraph?

   (A) To make readers want to taste horchata, especially horchata de chufa.

   (B) To prove that chufa is currently an economic necessity in Spain by describing the popularity of horchaterias.

   (C) To add interesting information to that given in the first paragraph.

   (D) To offer a specific example of how one historical use of chufa is also a modern economic success.

   (E) To act as a transition between paragraphs one and three.

3. Of the following, which is the writer's main purpose for the underlined portion in sentence 9, shown below?

   Another reason for the popularity of this plant, and a major economic opportunity for farming and ecotourism, is chufa's appeal as food for both tame and wild animals.

   (A) Further support for main thesis.

   (B) Emphasis on the importance of the topic—economically valuable plants.

   (C) Emphasis on the popularity of chufa.

   (D) To avoid having the separate aspects of the topic read like a list.

   (E) Transition from the first half of the essay to the second.

4. For both writer and reader, paragraphs three and four function in what way(s)?

(A) As enlargement of the topic: chufa's economic value in today's world.

(B) As support for the main thesis using specific, visual examples, facts, and a quote.

(C) To appeal to a different economic audience altogether.

(D) To make the conclusion in paragraph five more logical or meaningful.

(E) As the clincher for the main thesis that chufa is an economically important plant.

5. The writer should reorganize the sentences in paragraph two for the sake of logical, orderly flow, known as coherence. Select the answer choice that lists the sentences in the best order to achieve coherence.

(A) Sentence 5, then sentences 7, 6, and 8.

(B) None. All sentences are in logical order.

(C) Sentence 7, then 5, 6, and 8.

(D) Sentence 6, then 5, 7, and 8.

(E) Sentence 5, then 8, 6, and 7.

6. Sentence 20, seen below, needs revising. What should a careful writer do to correct one of its flaws?

I don't know about you, but this picture reminds me strongly of the holiday Americans call Thanksgiving.

(A) Begin the sentence with "This picture . . ."

(B) Insert the pronoun "we" before Americans.

(C) Substitute "we" for the word "Americans," which is unnecessary.

(D) Turn this declarative sentence into an interrogative one, which would provide a more intriguing concluding sentence.

(E) Eliminate the first person pronouns, I and me, which have not appeared elsewhere, and revise accordingly.

7. Reread sentence 20, seen in question 6. In light of the entire essay, which of the following revisions offers a more satisfying conclusion than this first draft?

(A) This picture reminds us all of Thanksgiving, doesn't it?

(B) That sounds like our American Thanksgiving feast, with the addition of an ancient and attractive plant called chufa.

(C) The chufa plant seems to be something that should have appeared at the first Thanksgiving in the New World.

(D) I don't know about you, but right now I'm thinking of our holiday called Thanksgiving, built around good food, family, and friends.

(E) Thus, you can see many reasons why chufa grass with its edible tubers would make a sterling addition to the crops currently grown around the world for animal feed, as well as being a popular woodland feed for animals to be viewed by ecotourists.

Writing the Essay

The best thing you can do to get ready for the 25-minute essay on the SAT is to write a few essays in preparation. This unit offers guidelines for presenting your thoughts on paper in an interesting, competent manner, followed by some topics for practice essays.

Try to remain calm about this essay. No one is expected to produce a brilliant essay in a mere 25 minutes! This will be a first draft and everybody knows that.

Your essay will be graded by two trained readers looking for clarity and coherence (logical organization). They'll also be happy if they find a clear thesis statement (your main point) and solid support for it with examples from books, plays, your life, history, quotations—anything that supports the point you're making. If you finish with a conclusion that reiterates your thesis—perhaps a clincher comment—AND you avoid major grammatical errors, your score will be a 4, 5, or 6 and everyone will be delighted.

Now That We've Mentioned Scoring . . .

Take time to examine the requirements for scores on the essay segment of the writing test. This rubric is similar to the one used now for the SAT II: Writing Test.

Score of 6

A paper in this category demonstrates clear and consistent competence, though it may have occasional errors. Such a paper:

- effectively and insightfully addresses the writing task
- is well organized and fully developed, using clearly appropriate examples to support ideas
- displays consistent facility in the use of language, demonstrating variety in sentence structure and range of vocabulary

Score of 5

A paper in this category demonstrates reasonably consistent competence, though it will have occasional errors or lapses in quality. Such a paper:

- effectively addresses the writing task
- is generally well organized and well developed, using appropriate examples to support ideas
- displays facility in the use of language, demonstrating some syntactic variety and range of vocabulary

Score of 4

A paper in this category demonstrates adequate competence with occasional errors and lapses in quality. Such a paper:

- addresses the writing task
- is organized and adequately developed, using examples to support ideas
- displays adequate but inconsistent facility in the use of language, presenting some errors in grammar or diction (choice of words)
- presents minimal sentence variety

(Continued on p. 129)

Score of 3
A paper in this category demonstrates developing competence. Such a paper may contain one or more of the following weaknesses:

- inadequate organization or development
- inappropriate or insufficient details to support ideas
- an accumulation of errors in grammar, diction, or sentence structure

Score of 2
A paper in this category demonstrates some incompetence. Such a paper is flawed by one or more of the following weaknesses:

- poor organization
- thin development
- little or inappropriate detail to support ideas
- frequent errors in grammar, diction, and sentence structure

Score of 1
A paper in this category demonstrates incompetence. Such a paper is seriously flawed by one or more of the following weaknesses:

- very poor organization
- very thin development
- usage and syntactical errors so severe that meaning is somewhat obscured

NOTE: Remember to *use your best handwriting*. The scorers (trained professionals) must be able to read your paper. If they have to *decode it*, you're in trouble.

The College Board's advice on the essay should help you to feel calmer: " . . . even with some errors in spelling, punctuation, and grammar, a student can get a top score on the essay."

What Will You Write ABOUT?

According to current College Board advice, the writing prompt will most likely "be persuasive in nature and will ask the student to take a position on an issue and support it with reasons and evidence from his or her reading, experience, and observation."

Fair enough. Everyone has opinions. *Supporting one* with appropriate reasons and examples, however, means justifying it— making it believable to others. Think for a minute now on some of your opinions. How do you feel about:

1. Ethics?
   Do you have ethics? Are they important? WHAT are they? Where did they come from?

2. Conserving Species?

   • Do we need all these species? Why?

   • Are any animal or plant species unnecessary?

3. Repeating History?

   • According to Sir Arthur Quiller-Couch, "Those who cannot remember the past are condemned to repeat it." Do you agree or disagree? Support your position.

Is your brain humming? Of course, because all of us form opinions early in life. Intelligent people decide WHY they have those opinions. Are they logical or emotional? In order to write a thoughtful, well-reasoned essay, start thinking in depth about some of your opinions.

HOW Will You Write?
The Three-Step Essay System

Step One

Outline. Allow three to five minutes for this step on the SAT. At this time you do two of the most important jobs.

First, decide on your thesis (main point), which is termed "addressing the task," being sure that you are answering the question. Begin by jotting down a rough idea of your main point. Keep this idea in mind throughout. If you wander off course, you'll get no points at all. Be sure that your idea *addresses the writing task*.

Tailor the essay to suit your audience, in this case two professional readers (teachers).

List what you want to say about your main idea—in any order. This is your supporting material, which must be relevant to your audience; otherwise it's worthless. Three to five ideas are plenty.

Second, organize those ideas. Consider (1) chronological order, (2) order of importance, (3) spatial order, (4) comparison and contrast, or (5) developmental order. Don't dither, just pick one that seems logical for the subject matter. Number the supporting ideas in the order you have chosen.

During these few minutes, your mind is hard at work. Once you have the map of your essay—its outline—you will find it much easier to begin writing.

Step Two

Begin writing. Somewhere in the first paragraph, state your main point clearly. *If you normally work fast*, you may be able to write many paragraphs, and you can use this first paragraph to hook the reader, be witty, show off a quote you love that is right on target, or relate an intriguing incident that leads to . . .

Paragraph TWO, in which you really should tell the reader where this thing is going. That is, *what is the point of* all this writing?!

If you write slowly, and know you'll manage to eke out only a few paragraphs, state your thesis somewhere in that first paragraph.

Treat your supporting ideas respectfully. Showcase them with active verbs and adjectives that let readers feel, smell, taste, hear, and see what you are writing about. You are a painter without paints, remember? You have words instead.

Form your sentences in your head before writing them down. Write each one with care. See a weak noun or verb? Erase it and replace it with a specific word that creates a picture in the reader's mind.

Link one sentence to another clearly. At the beginning of each new paragraph, use transitional words or phrases to join it to the paragraph that went before.

Vary the length and style of your sentences. If most of them begin with an opening clause or phrase, like this sentence, readers will soon fall asleep. Brief, punchy sentences move the prose along, but a series of them reads like a list. Variety in sentence length and structure is critical.

The LAST paragraph is a summation or concluding paragraph. It is expected to restate the thesis, taking the piece full circle, something that readers find highly satisfying. This paragraph may have several sentences that bring all the information together in a general overview, or it may consist of only one "clincher" sentence as in the essay on chufa (page 124).

Step Three

Proofread for the last few minutes. If you correct a few grammatical errors (missing or misplaced commas, subject-verb disagreement, wrong pronoun case), this editing time will be well spent. You may also substitute vivid words for colorless ones. After all, *what you have written is a first draft.* Like professional writers who routinely correct errors and alter vocabulary in their early drafts, you need to be serious about this writing step.

Golden Rules of Writing

Even though playwright Lillian Hellman wrote ". . . don't listen to writers talking about writing or themselves," those who write just keep on yapping. Here are some favorite rules:

• SHOW, DON'T TELL

All of your writing will improve if you can remember this one rule. If I describe Herbert as heaving a ball at the garage, grumbling to himself, and kicking the gravel, you know that Herb is angry. I have *shown* you how angry he is. If I merely tell you, "Herbert was really, really angry," you get no picture whatsoever. As you can see, the difference between showing and telling is huge.

Showing readers involves using precise words—words that are specific, definite, and concrete. Those words paint pictures. Broad, sweeping statements and vague generalities put readers to sleep and paint zero pictures. Everyone loves specific details.

Showing readers demands that you use action verbs and the active voice.

> **YES:** *Active voice*: Ralph brandished his sword over his head.

> **NO:** *Passive voice*: The sword was brandished by Ralph over his head.

All forms of to be (*am*, *is*, *are*, *was*, *were*, *be*, *been*, and *being*) merely describe state of being, but do not convey any sense of action to the reader. You can almost always choose better verbs than forms of to be or state of being verbs like seem, feel, appear, become, rest, remain, stay, and so on.

Showing the reader often involves dialogue between two people. Even heated discussions among several people. Because we are so used to talking, we are delighted to find it in prose. This truth explains why quotations are so effective. They're apt to be more lively than the other prose, and they lend authority to an argument.

Showing the reader always involves appealing to our senses of sight, touch, hearing, smell, and taste. I will feel cheated as a reader if you write about a young seal *without* describing the color and velvety feel of his baby-soft fur, plus the sound of his joyous bark. I want to be there—to see and feel and hear that beautiful mammal.

• LESS IS MORE
This rule says, "Please be concise." Don't keep saying the same thing over and over, in different ways. All writers need to examine each sentence and each paragraph to see how many words can be edited OUT.

For example, you can nearly always eliminate both; at this point in time; and first and foremost. It is, it was, there is, there are are the deadwood sentence starters. Get rid of the fact that; in the case of; and hundreds more.

• NO CONFLICT, NO STORY
This rule may seem odd in this context, but I believe it will be helpful. Think about your favorite books and movies: *To Kill a Mockingbird*, *Star Wars*, perhaps the Harry Potter series. Those stories are full of suspense, conflict, tension, all of which readers love. Humans have an innate love of an exciting story.

To create tension (conflict) in writing, show both sides to a question—the pro and the con—the possible versus the impossible—and you'll be turning your topic into a story. For instance, *good vs. evil* is the basic conflict in the Harry Potter books, in biblical stories, in *Star Wars*, in *To Kill a Mockingbird*, even in *The Tale of Peter Rabbit*.

The best nonfiction will illuminate important conflicts as well. Consider Jeff Shaara's books on the Civil War, David McCullough's biography, *Truman*, and Bill Bryson's hilarious adventure on the Appalachian Trail, *A Walk in the Woods*. Readers (and viewers) basically insist on some amount of tension or conflict—just ask the people in TV, movies, and publishing.

• CONSIDER THE READER
If you can, read E. B. White's *Elements of Style* and William Zinsser's *On Writing Well*. These writers know what they're talking about, and they're funny, too. Above all, they beg us to keep our readers in mind as we work. What follows is a distillation of their outstanding advice.

1. Stay on track. Don't wander off into another topic.

2. Avoid jargon and acronyms.

3. Choose a tone for your essay and be consistent.

4. Be direct. Don't waffle. Don't say what *isn't*. Say what *is*.

   NO: Today doesn't seem to be very sunny.

   YES: Today is cloudy.

5. Vary sentence length and structure.

6. Avoid overly-impressive words, but a stunner here or there can work.

7. Remember the stress positions in sentences and paragraphs. Readers expect to find the subject somewhere near the beginning of the sentence, and the topic sentence near the beginning of the paragraph, in the *minor stress position*. They look for the new or most vital piece of information at the end of the sentence or paragraph, in the *major stress position*.

8. Keep related words together. Check each sentence to see that modifiers are next to the words they modify, or darned close! A participial phrase at the beginning of the sentence MUST modify the subject of the main clause.

9. Write parallel thoughts in parallel grammatical form. This structure aids the flow of sentences and ideas, and has greater impact on the reader.

   NO: I love writing more than to garden. (1 gerund object, 1 infinitive)

   YES: I love <u>writing</u> and <u>gardening</u>. (two gerund objects)

10. Remember that punctuation is vital for the reader. Learn its rules if you want your prose to shine.

Warming Up with Practice Essays

Now it's time to write. Go somewhere quiet, and tell the world not to interrupt. Learn the directions for writing the essay. Ours may not be exact, as no one has seen the new test yet, but they'll be very close. Read again the College Board's scoring rubric on pp. 128-129. You'll need No. 2 pencils, blank paper, and a timer. Set the timer for 25 minutes.

PRACTICE ESSAY 1

Directions: Read carefully the following quote.

"Enlighten the people generally, and tyranny and oppression of body and mind will vanish like evil spirits at the dawn of day."
—Thomas Jefferson, in a letter of April 1816

Assignment: What is your view of Jefferson's idea that enlightenment, which is education, will free people so that they no longer suffer from tyranny of any kind? In your essay, support your position with an example (or examples) from literature, the arts, science and technology, current events, or from your own observation. Stop writing after 25 minutes.

Evaluating Essay 1

Take your essay to your favorite English teacher, along with the College Board's scoring rubric. Together, read and evaluate your essay, partly by answering the following questions:

1. Your thesis statement was

_____

_____

_____

_____

_____

2. Your supporting examples included the following specific, concrete information, quotes, examples, and anecdotes:

_____

_____

_____

_____

_____

3. Your concluding sentences summarized the material you presented or restated your thesis (main point) in what way? Did you think of a clincher sentence or example?

_____

_____

_____

_____

_____

4. Problems to work on before writing the next essay include:

_____

_____

_____

_____

5. Strengths in this essay include:

_____

_____

_____

_____

6. Estimated score for this essay is _____.

PRACTICE ESSAY 2

Again, reread the College Board's scoring rubric. You can see that answering the question that was asked (addressing the task) and coherence (logical organization) are vital. As before, you'll need No. 2 pencils and blank paper. Set the timer for 25 minutes.

Directions: Consider the following information and quote.

The man we call "the father of conservation," Aldo Leopold, published *A Sand County Almanac,* in 1929. In it, he defined conservation as follows:

"Conservation is a state of harmony between men and land. Despite nearly a century of propaganda, conservation still proceeds at a snail's pace; progress still consists largely of letterhead pieties and convention oratory. On the back forty we still slip two steps backward for each forward stride."

(NOTE: When this book was written, "men" meant all humankind, and most people were related to someone on a farm, laughingly referred to as "the back forty.")

Assignment: Explain whether or not you believe that Leopold's observations have relevance today. Are we still going back two steps for every one we take forward? Is conservation still a thing of political promises at election time? Support your position in the essay with pertinent, specific examples from science and technology, literature and the arts, current events, or your own experience.

Evaluating Essay 2

Take your essay to your favorite English teacher, along with the College Board's scoring rubric. Together, read and evaluate your essay, partly by answering the following questions:

1. Your thesis statement was

   _____

   _____

   _____

   _____

   _____

2. Your supporting examples included the following specific, concrete information, quotes, examples, and anecdotes:

   _____

   _____

   _____

   _____

   _____

3. Your concluding sentences summarized the material you presented or restated your thesis (main point) in what way? Did you think of a clincher sentence or example?

   _____

   _____

   _____

   _____

   _____

4. Problems to work on before writing the next essay include:

   _____

   _____

   _____

   _____

5. Strengths in this essay include:

_____

_____

_____

_____

_____

_____

6. Estimated score for this essay is _____.

PRACTICE ESSAY 3

Last time! Again, set your timer for 25 minutes.

Directions. Read and consider the following information and quote.

> In an interview in *Black Women Writers at Work*, Toni Morrison responded to a question about the cost (in personal terms) of her success. The interviewer seemed to think that Ms. Morrison might be gaining many fine things but losing privacy and several valuable personal freedoms because she had become so well known. In response, Ms. Morrison said, in part: "I don't subscribe to the definition of success I think you're talking about . . . a life surrounded by material things . . . I continue to live my life pretty much as I always have, except I may live a little better now because I can make some choices I wasn't able to before. . . . But in terms of meaningful things, relationships with other people, none of that has changed. What changes is not always the successful person; other people change."

Assignment: Compare your idea of success with Toni Morrison's view of her own success as a poet. In what way(s) do you agree with her, or disagree? Support your viewpoint in the essay with specific examples from all walks of life, from literature or the arts or sciences, or from your own observation.

Evaluating Essay 3

Take your essay to your favorite English teacher, along with the College Board's scoring rubric. Together, read and evaluate your essay, partly by answering the following questions:

1. Your thesis statement was

_____

_____

_____

_____

2. Your supporting examples included the following specific, concrete information, quotes, examples, and anecdotes:

_____

_____

_____

_____

3. Your concluding sentences summarized the material you presented or restated your thesis (main point) in what way? Did you think of a clincher sentence or example?

_____

_____

_____

_____

4. Problems to work on before writing the next essay include:

_____

_____

_____

_____

5. Strengths in this essay include:

_____

_____

_____

_____

_____

6. Estimated score for this essay is _____.

Glossary: Diction and Idiom

A short text cannot hope to cover all the stumbling blocks in diction and idiom, but here are some frequently troublesome items for your review.

Problem Words	*Standard Usage*
affect	The hot sun *affects* my skin, burning it quickly. (makes a difference to, changes in some way) Her *affected* accent is laughable. (phony, put on)
effect	What *effect* does the sun have? (noun meaning result or consequence) The prisoner *effected* his escape. (to bring about)
aggravate	Hiking *aggravates* her swollen ankle. (to make worse)
all ready	Our choir is *all ready* to sing. (pronoun + adverb)
already	We have *already* taken our places. (adverb)
all right	My answers were *all right*. (pronoun + adjective) Would it be *all right* for me to borrow these books? (unit adverb)
alright	"Iffy" usage. *All right* is preferred.
a lot	I owe *a lot* to my swimming coach.

Problem Words	Standard Usage
all together	Let's sing *all together*, when the music starts. (pronoun + adverb)
altogether	He's a new cat *altogether* after his bath. (adverb)
among	We shared the pizza *among* the six of us. (more than two)
between	Let's share that pizza *between* the two of us.
anxious	I'll be *anxious* until I hear the doctor's report. (nervous, worried and upset)
bad	Sam feels *bad* about his brother's accident. (predicate adjective)
badly	Is his brother *badly* hurt? (adverb)
capitol	The U.S. *capitol* in Washington is handsome. (government building)
capital	What a *capital* idea! How much *capital* can you give to the fund? Is that a *capital* letter?
censor	A film *censor* has interesting stories. (noun, a person)
to censor	Was it wise to *censor* their conversation? (to edit or delete questionable material)
censure	I cringed under my parents' hasty *censure*. (harsh or hostile criticism)
to censure	Dad said he'd *censure* me any time I rammed the car into the garage. (to criticize harshly)
complement	The second algebra course *complements* the first. (something that completes or goes well with)
compliment	Your *compliments* are too generous, but who does not enjoy being complimented?
concerned with	That office is *concerned with* school matters only.

Problem Words	Standard Usage
could have	We *could have* studied Latin this year. (<u>Of</u> is never a helping verb.)
different from	His study plan is *different from* mine.
discrete	We study the *discrete* systems of the frog, beginning with the digestive system. (separate, distinct)
discreet	Amy met Tracy *discreetly*, in the library, so that they could plan their party in private. (showing good judgment)
disinterested	A judge must render a *disinterested* verdict. (unbiased)
done	Cakes are *done*; people are *finished*.
uninterested	My cat Sophia is *uninterested* in your cat Bob. (not interested)
divers	*Divers* reasons convince people to remain in school. (several in number)
diverse	After graduation, we'll all go our *diverse* ways. (different, dissimilar, unlike)
elude	My sneaky cat *eluded* my grasp. (to escape notice or to escape being caught)
allude	If you *allude* to his graying hair, he frowns. (to refer to indirectly, obliquely)
good	He looks *good* on the balance beam. (predicate adjective after linking verb)
hanged	People are *hanged*; jackets are *hung*.
healthy	I walk every day to keep *healthy*.
healthful	*Healthful* fruits aid in promoting good health.
human	*Human* beings may be called *homo sapiens*.
humane	Saving the drowning cat was a *humane* act.

Problem Words	*Standard Usage*
immigrate	The U.S. now has many who have *immigrated* in the hope of finding a stable existence. (to move into another place)
emigrate	The potato famine forced many Irish people to *emigrate* to America. (leave home, go elsewhere)
imply	Are you *implying* that I'm late? (to suggest, hint)
infer	From your remarks, I *infer* that I am expected to arrive early. (to deduce, conclude)
its	The cat was wet; *its* fur was soggy. (possessive pronoun)
it's	*It's* a pity you don't like cats. (pronoun + verb; <u>it is</u>)
kind of a—sort of a	*Kind of a* and *sort of a* do not exist.
lend	I'll *lend* you some money. (<u>Loan</u> is a noun.)
less	The pool has *less* water today. (Use less for <u>things that cannot be counted</u>, such as liquids, meat, uproar, liberty.)
few	*Few* cookies are left. (Use <u>few</u> for things that <u>can be counted</u>.)
lie	*Lie* down on the bed to rest. (recline, as on a bed)
lay	*Lay* down your weapons instantly! (put or place)
	Hens *lay* eggs . . . sometimes. (put or place— here in a nest)
lose	I'm afraid I'll *lose* my keys. (misplace)
loose	Is that a *loose* tooth? (not securely attached; detached, free)
	Puritans railed against *loose* morals.

Problem Words	Standard Usage
metal	The symbol for the *metal* lead is *Pb*.
mettle	That horse showed his *mettle* today! (spirit, courage)
might have	He *might have* left already. (Remember that <u>of</u> can never be a helping verb.
nauseous	Hog lagoons have *nauseous* odors. (revolting, disgusting)
nauseated	He's always *nauseated* at sea. (sick to one's stomach)
past	In *past* times we kept a few goats. (adjective)
passed	As time *passed*, the goats grew older. (verb)
precedence	Your claim takes *precedence* over mine. (comes before, supersedes)
precedents	Earlier court decisions have set *precedents*. (examples or rules for anything similar that follows)
prophecy	Your *prophecy* of bad weather is coming true. (noun—meaning prediction)
prophesy	Cassandra *prophesied* that the Greeks would destroy Troy. (verb—meaning to foretell)
prosecute	You'd better *prosecute* that case in small claims court. (to bring legal action)
persecute	Sylvester *persecutes* Tweety Bird. (to harass, annoy)
raise	*Raise* your head off the pillow. (to lift up)
rise	Please set the bread out to *rise*. (to move up, like dough)
	Certain costs keep on *rising*.
reason . . . is because	Wrong, wrong, wrong.

Problem Words	Standard Usage
reason . . . is that	The *reason we agreed is that* I gave up the fight. (noun clause as predicate noun after a linking verb)
respectably	Please dress *respectably* for this dinner.
respectfully	Address an older person *respectfully*. (in a respectful way)
respectively	Ellen and Stuart won first and second place, *respectively*. (in the order named)
see that	We *see that* your team won. (see where is slang)
than	Richard is taller *than* Sue. (comparison)
then	We will leave *then*, after the movie. (adverb of time)
their	*Their* boat is a floating disaster. (possession)
they're	I guess *they're* going to replace it. (pronoun + verb; they are)
there	I wouldn't go *there* if I were you. (adverb of place)
tortuous	The *tortuous* mountain road wound slowly upward. (winding, twisted)
torturous	Recovering from the accident was a *torturous* experience he'd like to forget. (cruelly painful as torture is)
unique	*Unique* means the only one of its kind. (Things cannot be very unique or sort of unique. They either are or they aren't.)
used to	We *used to* go to the beach every summer. (repeated past action)
vocation/avocation	Brad's interest in finance has been both a *vocation* (job career) and an *avocation*. (hobby)

Problem Words	Standard Usage
who's	*Who's* going to go clamming with me? (pronoun + verb <u>who is</u>)
whose	I'd like to know *whose* dog this is. (possession)
your	*Your* dog is in the house. (possession)
you're	Do you know if *you're* going to the party? (pronoun + verb; <u>you are</u>)

"The discipline of the writer is to learn to be still and listen to what his subject has to tell him."

—Rachel Carson

UNIT 5

MATH FAMILIARITY FOR AN SAT OR PSAT

Are you on schedule?

✓ **Check the PLAN OF ATTACK on pages vi–viii.**

Successful tennis players are people whose muscles are so familiar with correct stroke motion that they would feel awkward moving in any other way. Good drivers subconsciously know "Brake, turn, accelerate, straighten out" every time they go around a bend in the road. Success on the SAT math section is based on the same sort of familiarity. If, upon seeing a problem, you subconsciously know a path to its solution and the instructions for filling out the answer, you will do well. The only way to develop this sort of familiarity is to practice: hit a ball against a backboard 100 times, spend an afternoon parallel parking between two garbage pails, or do math problems, lots of them, of every type you might encounter on test day.

Panic Plan for the SAT includes a collection of the types of math problems you need to practice to succeed with the SAT. As you work through them, if you come across a type of math problem you don't recognize, go to a teacher or savvy friend and learn what you need to know. For the problems that you recognize, use *Panic Plan* to strengthen your subconscious recognition of the problems, the topics they test, and the steps to their solutions.

For the rest of this introduction we'll preview the new SAT, the math topics it now covers, and the two types of problems you'll see. Then we'll review some generally helpful hints for doing math problems. In the subsequent sections we'll cover one or more of the topics tested by the SAT. Each section starts with a set of key **terms and definitions**—the vocabulary for doing this type of problem. Then it lists key **formulas and guidelines.** After that are **problems to**

watch for, typical ways the topic may be tested on the SAT. Finally there are a set of **practice problems.**

In case you missed it, there is a three-week lesson plan at the beginning of the book. As you go through it, or your own schedule, keep a small notebook or 3 × 5 cards of new problems or tricks that you will want to refer back to as you study. Good luck!

The New Test

In 2005 the College Board and ETS are releasing a completely re-vamped SAT—don't you feel lucky? What can you expect on the new math portion of the test?

Time:	70 minutes of math in three sections: Two 25-minute sections and one 20-minute section. This is down 5 minutes from previous versions.
Question Formats:	Multiple choice and "grid-ins." No quantitative comparisons.
Topics:	Arithmetic, Algebra I, Geometry, and new to this test, Algebra II

The College Board's stated intent in developing the new test is to align itself with classroom practice and predict success in college. According to the College Board, 97 percent of college-bound high school students take Algebra II by their junior year; so, the SAT is testing three years of math. Success, in or out of college, involves applying knowledge through data analysis and interpretation. It requires synthesizing multiple concepts. Arithmetic is an assumed step in larger problems.

• **New Test Topics**
The following table summarizes the topics and lists the pages in *Panic Plan* where they are covered.

Topic	Page
• Numbers and Operations	
Sequences Involving Exponential Growth	237
Sets (Union, Intersection, Elements)	160
• Algebra and Functions	
Absolute Value	157
Rational Equations and Inequalities	210
Radical Equations	180
Integer and Radical Exponents	180
Direct and Inverse Variation	251
Function Notation	232
Concepts of Domain and Range	232
Functions as Models	233
Linear Functions—Equations and Graphs	251
Quadratic Functions	251
• Geometry and Measurement	
Geometric Notation	186
Special Trigonometric Properties	199
Properties of Tangent Lines	189
Coordinate Geometry	203
Qualitative Behavior of Graphs and Functions	256
Transformations and Their Effect on Graphs and Functions	253
• Data Analysis, Statistics, and Probability	
Data Interpretation, Scatter-plots and Matrices	254
Geometric Probability	242

This *is* a long list. And these are just the "new" topics. There's no mention of the old staples like arithmetic, factoring, fractions, percentage, decimals, rates, and word problems.

The Two Question Formats

There are two formats of questions on the math section of the SAT: multiple choice and grid-ins. By the time you take the SAT you should know the instructions for each.

• Multiple Choice

Multiple-choice problems are shown with five options marked (A) through (E). For example:

1. The average of four consecutive even numbers is equal to:

   (A) the first number

   (B) the second number

   (C) the third number

   (D) the fourth number

   (E) None of the above

In your answer booklet you will see:

1. (A) (B) (C) (D) (E)

The answer is E, none of the above, so you will fill in the oval in the E column in row 1. Make sure you fill in the oval completely; otherwise, the automatic scoring system will miss your answer.

1. (A) (B) (C) (D) ●

Remember, using the **process of elimination,** once you have *disproved* some answers, you can guess at the solution with a better chance of getting it right.

• Grid-In

Student-produced response questions, commonly called "grid-ins," don't offer you a set of possible answers. Instead, using a grid like the ones shown on the next page, you are to construct the solution from scratch. Because a grid can represent roughly 13,000 distinct solutions, guessing is not an option. The instructions for grid-in problems are on the next page. Throughout this unit, several questions in each practice set are set up as grid-ins, so you'll get plenty of practice with them.

Directions for Student-Produced Response Questions

Each of the remaining 10 questions requires you to solve the problem and enter your answer by marking the ovals in the special grid, as shown in the examples below.

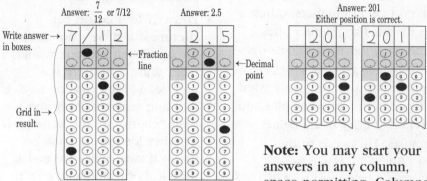

Note: You may start your answers in any column, space permitting. Columns not needed should be left blank.

- Mark no more than one oval in any column.
- Because the answer sheet will be machine-scored, **you will receive credit only if the ovals are filled in correctly.**
- Although not required, it is suggested that you write your answer in the boxes at the top of the columns to help you fill in the ovals accurately.
- Some problems may have more than one correct answer. In such cases, grid only one answer.
- No question has a negative answer.
- **Mixed numbers** such as $2\frac{1}{2}$ must be gridded as 2.5 or 5/2.

  (If $\boxed{2\,1\,/\,2}$ is gridded, it will be interpreted as $21/2$, not $2\frac{1}{2}$.)

- **Decimal Accuracy:** If you obtain a decimal answer, **enter the most accurate value the grid will accommodate.** For example, if you obtain an answer such as 0.6666..., you should record the result as .666 or .667. **Less accurate values such as .66 and .67 are not acceptable.**

Acceptable ways to grid $\frac{2}{3} = .6666\ldots$

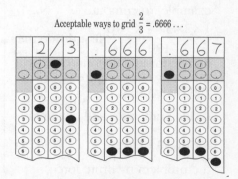

Helpful Hints

Let's review some basic approaches to SAT math problem solving right here. Some people like crunching numbers, others like to visualize number lines. Some are good with calculators and others need to see an equation written out; some want to work from first principles and others do better memorizing formulas. This leads to the first hint.

- **Know thyself.** If you have strengths, use techniques and work at problems that play to your strong suit. If you have weaknesses, be prepared to skip problems that test them. Remember, all problems count equally towards your score. This is a timed test; so, *three minutes spent on one difficult problem could be better spent on three that you know how to do.*

- **Simplify.** If the arithmetic looks complex, try to simplify first. For example, to compute $\dfrac{1\times2\times3\times4\times5\times6}{180}$ first divide the numerator and denominator by 2 and then 3 to get $\dfrac{4\times5\times6}{30}$. Then divide numerator and denominator by 30 to get $\dfrac{4}{1} = 4$. Working the problem by brute force,

$$\frac{1\times2\times3\times4\times5\times6}{180} = \frac{720}{180} = 4,$$

will end up with the correct answer, unless you make a mistake along the way.

- **Draw information on pictures.** If there's no picture for a problem and one would help, draw it. If there is a picture, add information to it. If two line segments have the same length, put the same hash or other identifying mark on them. If two angles are equal, note it. For example, a quadrilateral might be marked as:

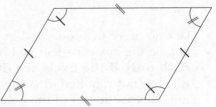

- **Visualize abstract concepts.** For SAT-level math, such as absolute value, some people visualize number lines, and others think of distances: $|a - b|$ is the distance between a and b, which can never be negative. I think of absolute value as a black box into which you stick one expression, and get another one out according to a pair of rules: If the input, $a > 0$, then output a; otherwise, output $-a$.

- **Use consistent units.** If a problem is presented in

different units, such as inches and feet, remember to convert and work the problem in the same unit. Usually the smaller unit is the simpler one.

- **Step back and look for patterns or approximate.** If a problem involves a lot of arithmetic, try to approximate the answer and look for patterns. The answer may be clear without doing any arithmetic. For example, which sum is greater?

$$\left[\frac{1}{1} + \frac{1}{2} + \ldots + \frac{1}{10}\right] \text{ or}$$

$$\left[\left(\frac{1}{1}\right)^2 + \left(\frac{1}{2}\right)^2 + \ldots + \left(\frac{1}{10}\right)^2\right]?$$

The first is greater because

$$\frac{1}{1} \geq \left(\frac{1}{1}\right)^2, \frac{1}{2} > \left(\frac{1}{2}\right)^2,$$

$$\left(\frac{1}{3}\right) > \left(\frac{1}{3}\right)^2, \text{ and so on. You}$$

don't need to square the fractions or do the addition.

- **Trial and Error.** With multiple-choice questions, you have the answer right in front of you. Some questions, especially word problems, readily lend themselves to picking possible solutions one by one, and trying them until you find the right one. This often takes longer than solving the problem directly, but helps a lot when you're not sure how to attack a question.

- **Use common sense.** For many problems you can quickly look at them and determine a reasonable approximation to the answer. For example, you know that .06 × 54 is

$$\frac{6}{100} \times 54 \approx 6 \times \frac{50}{100} = 3;$$

so, the answer you calculate better be a little more than 3.

Arithmetic

This section reviews arithmetic including working with negative numbers and factoring, sequences, and set notation.

Addition, Subtraction, Multiplication, and Division

Arithmetic, the manipulation of numbers as opposed to, say, geometric figures or variables, manifests itself everywhere in the SAT. You must be able to perform the four basic arithmetic operations—addition, subtraction, multiplication, and division—both accurately and quickly. To mirror the SAT I, we're not going to harp on arithmetic. If you're having trouble, pick up a grocery receipt, total the items, and confirm that you come to the same total as the cash register. If you're having trouble with subtraction, do it backward: start with the total, subtract off each item, and expect to get to zero when you're done. Practice multiplication by figuring out what the sales tax should be and confirming that you're correct. Next time you get in the car, check the time and the odometer reading. Practice division by computing your average speed when you get out of the car. If you're feeling up to it, note the cost of gasoline and compute the cost of the trip.

Formulas and Guidelines

• **Quick tests for divisibility:**

A number is divisible by	If
2	The last digit in the units place is 2, 4, 6, 8, or 0.
3	The sum of its digits is divisible by 3. For example, 87 is divisible by 3, because 8 + 7=15, which is divisible by 3, because 1 + 5 = 6, which is divisible by 3.
5	The last digit in the units place is 0 or 5.
10	The last digit in the units place is 0.

• **Fractions are shorthand for division:** $\frac{3}{5}$ is shorthand for $3 \div 5$.

• **a(b + c) = ab + ac: Multiplication and Division distribute over Addition and Subtraction.**

Example: Simplify $\dfrac{111+33-66}{3}$

$= \dfrac{3(37 + 11 - 22)}{3}$ Factor the 3 out of each term of the numerator.

$= 37 + 11 - 22$ Divide 3 out of the numerator and denominator.

$= 26$

Problems to Watch For

- **Tens and 0's are easy and fast to manipulate with a relatively low chance for error.** When operating on long lists of numbers, look for pairs that combine to 10 or cancel one another out.

   Example: Simplify $3 - 7 + 2 + 3 + 4 + 8$.

   1. Notice that $3 + 4 - 7 = 0$, so you can cross out these three numbers leaving $2 + 3 + 8$.

   2. Pair off the 2 and 8 to leave $10 + 3 = 13$.

   Example: Simplify $5 \times 7 \times 4$.

   1. First multiply the 4 and 5 to get 20.

   2. Easily finish off the multiplication: $20 \times 7 = 2 \times 7 \times 10 = 14 \times 10 = 140$.

- **When dividing two numbers do it in steps.**

   Example: Simplify $720 \div 180$.

   1. Divide both 720 and 180 by 10 to get $72 \div 18$.

   2. Divide both 72 and 18 by 3 to get $24 \div 6$—we know that 72 is divisible by 3 because $7 + 2 = 9$, which is divisible by 3.

   3. Divide both 24 and 6 by 2 to get $12 \div 3 = 4$.

   4. It doesn't matter in what order you do the simplification.

- **When you add something t times, it is the same as multiplying it by t.**

   Example: Solve $\dfrac{n^2 + n^2 + n^2}{3}$ for $n = 7$.

   You could do this by saying $n^2 = 49$; so $n^2 + n^2 + n^2 = 49 + 49 + 49 = 147$ and $\dfrac{147}{3} = 49$.

   Alternatively, a more efficient way to work the problem is to first combine the n^2's:

   1. $\dfrac{n^2 + n^2 + n^2}{3} = \dfrac{3n^2}{3} = n^2$

   2. When $n = 7$, $n^2 = 49$.

Negative Numbers and Absolute Value

Terms and Definitions

- **Negative number:** A number less than 0. Note that $-p$ is not necessarily negative because p could be -5, in which case $-p = -(-5) = 5$.

- **Absolute value** ($|x|$): The distance a number is from zero. Alternatively, a function that takes a value x, and, if $x < 0$, returns $-x$; otherwise, returns x.

Formulas and Guidelines

- **Adding with negatives:** To add two negatives, add them as though they were positives and negate the answer. To add a negative and a positive number, compute the difference of their absolute values. The sign of the result is the sign of the number with the greater absolute value. For example, given the problem $-4 + 3$, think: the difference between 4 and 3 is 1, and 4, the negated number, has the greater absolute value, so $-4 + 3 = -1$.

- **Subtracting with negatives:** If a negative number follows a subtraction sign, change the subtraction to addition and change the negative to a positive.

  Example: $-4 - (-3) = -4 + 3 = -1$.

- **Multiplying with negatives:** Multiplication is really just repeated addition. Put another way, if two numbers have the same sign, their product is positive; otherwise, their product is negative. Notice that this implies that x^2 is positive for all x other than 0.

- **Dividing with negatives:** This follows the same rules as multiplying with negatives.

- $a > |x|$ **can be rewritten as** $-x < a < x$.

- $a > |x|$ **can be rewritten as** $a < -x$ **or** $x < a$.

Rule	Explanation	Mnemonic Example
pos × pos = pos	Once positive, always positive.	$1 \times 1 = 1$
neg × pos = neg pos × neg = neg	You're adding a negative number to itself several times. Several negatives should make a "bigger" negative.	$-1 \times 1 = -1$ $1 \times -1 = -1$
neg × neg = pos	Visualize a negative number as a debt and a positive number as a cash balance. If you have negative debts, then you have a positive balance.	$-1 \times -1 = 1$

Problems to Watch For

- **If you multiply a negative number by itself an even number of times, the result is positive.** For example, $(-2)^{102} > 0$.

- **If you multiply a negative number by itself an odd number of times, the result is negative.** For example, $(-2)^{101} < 0$.

Factoring

Factoring is usually tested in one question on an SAT. However, being able to factor a number into its prime factors is necessary for simplifying fractions and doing division.

Terms and Definitions

- **Factor:** An integer that evenly divides another number is a factor of the other number. If $y = ab$, then a and b are factors of y.

- **Prime number:** A number greater than 1 whose only factors are 1 and itself. An example is 7 because the only integers that evenly divide it are 1 and 7. Other prime numbers include 2, 5, 11, and 13.

- **Prime factors:** The prime factors of a number are the unique set of prime numbers that when multiplied together yield the number. The prime factors of 12 are 2, 2, and 3 because $12 = 2 \times 2 \times 3$. The number 4 is not a prime factor because it is not a prime.

Formulas and Guidelines

- **Uniqueness of prime factors:** Two numbers are equal if and only if their prime factors are the same.

Problems to Watch For

- **Some problems on the SAT give you the product of a set of variables and ask you to determine what the variables might be.** First factor the product into its prime factors.

  Example: The product of three integers greater than 1 is 30.

  What is the maximum difference between any two of the numbers?

  1. Factor 30 into its prime factors:
     $30 = 2 \times 3 \times 5$.

  2. The maximum difference between any two of 2, 3, and 5 is the greatest minus the least: $5 - 2 = 3$.

Sets

Terms and Definitions

- **Set ({}):** A collection of objects (not necessarily numbers) with no duplicates. For example, {1, 2, 3} is a three-member set.

- **The empty set ({} or ∅):** The set with no elements.

- **Element or Member (∈):** An object that is in a set. For example,
  $1 \in \{1, 2, 3\}$.

- **Order of a Set (‖):** The number of objects in a set. For example, $|\{ \clubsuit, \blacklozenge, \heartsuit, \spadesuit \}| = 4$.

- **Union (∪):** The union of two sets is a new set that includes all of the members of the first two. For example, {1, 2, 3} ∪ {1, 2, 4} = {1, 2, 3, 4}. Notice that the 1 and 2 are not repeated.

- **Intersection (∩):** The intersection of two sets is a new set that includes elements that are members of **both** of the original sets. For example, {1, 2, 3} ∩ {1, 2, 4} = {1, 2}.

- **Set Difference (−):** The set difference of two sets is the set of elements that are members of the first set but **not** members of the second set. For example, {1, 2, 3}—{1, 2, 4} = {3}. Notice that there is no negative element.

- **Integers:** Counting numbers (1, 2, 3,...), their opposites (−1, −2, −3,...), and 0.

- **Positive:** Greater than zero.

- **Negative:** Less than zero.

- **Non-negative:** Greater than **or equal to** zero.

- **Venn Diagram:** A graphical representation of the union and intersection of two or three sets. For example: In the Venn diagram representation of {1, 2, 3, 5}, {1, 2, 4}, and {1}. The elements "3" and "5" are only in Set A. "4" is only in Set B. "2" is in Sets A and B, but not C. And, "1" is in all three sets.

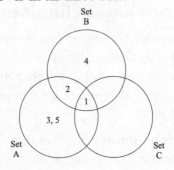

Problems to Watch For

Know the relationships among integers, zero, negatives, non-negatives, positives, primes, rational numbers, etc. **One representation is a tree.**

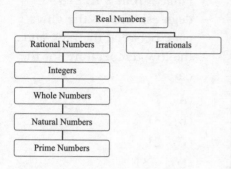

Another is used in the following example problem.

Example:

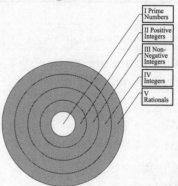

1. The figure above shows a subset relationship between five sets of numbers. Which ring has exactly one element in it?

   (A) I

   (B) II

   (C) III

   (D) IV

   (E) V

The inner circle includes all of the primes. Listing the first two, "2", and "3" proves that it has more than one element. The second ring includes all positive numbers that are not primes. Every even number except "2" is in this ring, among others. The non-negative integers include every positive integer plus "0"; so, "0" is the only element in the third ring. The answer is C.

PRACTICE PROBLEMS IN ARITHMETIC

Answers begin on page 336.

1. What is the sum of the integers between $-x$ and x inclusive when x is 3?

    (A) -3
    (B) -1
    (C) 0
    (D) 1
    (E) 3

2. How many unique pairs of positive integers can be multiplied together to yield 24?

    (A) 2
    (B) 3
    (C) 4
    (D) 5
    (E) 6

3. On a given day in February, the temperature in a town ranged from -12 to 19 degrees. What is the difference between the high and the low temperature for the day?

    (A) 7
    (B) 31
    (C) 21
    (D) -31
    (E) -21

4. The union of the sets of integers divisible by 2 and integers divisible by 4 is

    (A) $\varnothing$
    (B) $\{0\}$
    (C) the set of integers divisible by 2
    (D) the set of integers divisible by 4
    (E) the set of integers divisible by 8

5. The intersection of the sets of prime numbers and even numbers is

(A) $\varnothing$

(B) {1}

(C) {2}

(D) {1, 2}

(E) {0, 1, 2}

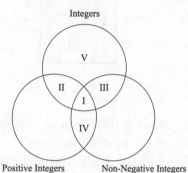

Integers

V

II   III

I

IV

Positive Integers   Non-Negative Integers

6. Which of the regions in the diagram has exactly one element?

(A) I

(B) II

(C) III

(D) IV

(E) V

7. $|y - x| - |x - y| =$

(A) 0

(B) $-2x$

(C) $2x$

(D) $2y - 2x$

(E) $2x - 2y$

8. A and B are sets. If $|A| = 6$, $|A \cup B| = 12$, and $|A \cap B| = 2$, what is $|B|$?

(A) 2

(B) 4

(C) 5

(D) 6

(E) 8

9. If $|-x| > |-y|$, then

(A) $x > y$

(B) $y > x$

(C) $x^2 > y^2$

(D) $y^2 > x^2$

(E) None of the above are necessarily true

10. If $p \times 9 \times 10 \times 11$ is divisible by 24, which of the following could be p?

(A) 2

(B) 3

(C) 4

(D) 5

(E) 6

The directions for grid-ins are on page 153.

11. Rounded to the nearest integer, what is $620 \div 60$?

12. If $2 \times 3 \times 4 \times 5 \times 6 \times 7 = 6 \times a \times 42$, then $a =$

13. If $1 + 2 + 3 + \ldots + 19 + 20 = 21x$, what is x?

14. What is the result of adding all of the even integers between 1 and 100 inclusive, and subtracting all of the odd integers between 1 and 100 inclusive?

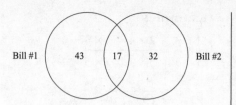

Bill #1   43   (17)   32   Bill #2

15. The number of Senators voting "yes" on each of two bills is shown in the above Venn diagram. What is the average number of "yes" votes on the two bills?

Fractions

One usually thinks of a fraction in the form $\dfrac{a}{b}$; however, we'll consider other types of part-whole relationships such as percentages, ratios, and decimal arithmetic. For many percentage, ratio, and decimal problems, rewrite the problem using fractions. This simplifies problem solving because everything that follows

uses a single set of rules—fewer things to keep in mind.

Basic Fractions

Terms and Definitions

• **Fraction:** A fraction is shorthand for a division problem. The fraction $\dfrac{a}{b}$ is equivalent to $a \div b$. You can also think of a fraction as a part-whole relationship: $\dfrac{a}{b}$ means a parts of something that has a total of b parts. Some people like to think of a pie cut into b pieces from which a person takes a of those pieces.

• **Rational Number:** Any number that can be written as a fraction. For example, $-\dfrac{3}{2}$, but not $\sqrt{2}$ or π.

• **Numerator:** The "top" of a fraction. In $\dfrac{a+b}{c}$, $a + b$ is the numerator.

• **Denominator:** The "bottom" of a fraction. In $\dfrac{a+b}{c}$, c is the denominator.

• **Reciprocal:** The reciprocal of b is $\dfrac{1}{b}$. When b is a fraction, the reciprocal of b is the fraction inverted. For example, the reciprocal of $\dfrac{3}{5}$ is $\dfrac{1}{\frac{3}{5}} = \dfrac{5}{3}$.

Formulas and Guidelines

If you're unsure of one of the following rules while taking the SAT, test it on two simple fractions.

- **Equivalence rule for fractions:** $\dfrac{a}{b} = \dfrac{ac}{bc} = \dfrac{a \div c}{b \div c}$

  Examples:

  $\dfrac{20}{25} = \dfrac{20 \div 5}{25 \div 5} = \dfrac{4}{5}$, and

  $\dfrac{20}{25} = \dfrac{20 \times 4}{25 \times 4} = \dfrac{80}{100}$

- **Adding fractions:**

  $\dfrac{a}{c} + \dfrac{b}{c} = \dfrac{a+b}{c}$

  Before you can add two fractions, the denominators must be the same. Also, note that the denominator does not change. To alter an expression so that the denominators of the addends (things being added) are the same, apply the equivalence rule by multiplying the numerator and denominator of each fraction by the denominator of the other fraction:

  $\dfrac{a}{b} + \dfrac{c}{d} = \dfrac{ad}{bd} + \dfrac{cb}{db} = \dfrac{ad+bc}{bd}$

Example:

$\dfrac{2}{3} + \dfrac{3}{4} = \dfrac{2 \times 4}{3 \times 4} + \dfrac{3 \times 3}{4 \times 3}$

$= \dfrac{8}{12} + \dfrac{9}{12}$

$= \dfrac{17}{12}$

- **Subtracting fractions:** Follow the same rules as for addition.

- **Multiplying fractions:**

  $\dfrac{a}{b} \bullet \dfrac{c}{d} = \dfrac{ac}{bd}$

  Example:

  $\dfrac{2}{3} \bullet \dfrac{2}{5} = \dfrac{2 \bullet 2}{3 \bullet 5} = \dfrac{4}{15}$

  This equation uses "•" instead of "×". The two are interchangeable.

- **Dividing fractions:** Multiply the first fraction by the reciprocal of the second.

  $\dfrac{a}{b} \div \dfrac{c}{d} = \dfrac{a}{b} \times \dfrac{d}{c} = \dfrac{ad}{bc}$

  Example:

  $\dfrac{2}{3} \div \dfrac{3}{4} = \dfrac{2}{3} \times \dfrac{4}{3} = \dfrac{2 \times 4}{3 \times 3} = \dfrac{8}{9}$

- **Fractions within fractions:** Remember, a fraction is shorthand for division, so,

$$\frac{\frac{a}{b}}{\frac{c}{d}} = \frac{a}{b} \div \frac{c}{d} = \frac{a}{b} \times \frac{d}{c} = \frac{ad}{bc}$$

Example:

$$\frac{\frac{2}{3}}{\frac{4}{5}} = \frac{2}{3} \div \frac{4}{5} = \frac{2}{3} \times \frac{5}{4} = \frac{10}{12} = \frac{5}{6}$$

- **Identity:** $a = \dfrac{a}{1}$. For example, $3 = \dfrac{3}{1}$.

- **In general, $\dfrac{a}{b+c}$ cannot be simplified.**

  Example: There is no way to cancel the 3's in

  $$\frac{3}{3+4} = \frac{3}{7}.$$

- **The sign of the fraction**

Sign	Rule	Example
0	$\dfrac{a}{b} = 0$ if $a = 0$. The denominator, b, can never be 0. What would it mean to divide something into zero parts?	$\dfrac{0}{7} = 0$
−	$\dfrac{a}{b} < 0$ if a and b have different signs (just like the rules for dividing).	$\dfrac{-3}{7} = \dfrac{3}{-7} < 0$
+	$\dfrac{a}{b} > 0$ if a and b have the same sign.	$\dfrac{-3}{-7} = \dfrac{3}{7} > 0$

• **Mixed numbers.** $1\frac{5}{8}$ is shorthand for $1 + \frac{5}{8}$, which equals

$$\frac{8}{8} + \frac{5}{8} = \frac{13}{8}$$

Problems to Watch For

• **You will need to be able to simplify a problem using the equivalence rule again and again throughout the SAT.**

• **Example:** Simplify the expression: $\frac{3}{4} \times \frac{5}{6} \div \frac{7}{3} \div \frac{6}{2} \times \frac{8}{3} \times \frac{1}{4}$

   1. Write the reciprocal of each fraction that follows a ÷

      sign: $\frac{3}{4} \times \frac{5}{6} \times \frac{3}{7} \times \frac{2}{6} \times \frac{8}{3} \times \frac{1}{4}$

   2. Using the formula for multiplication, this equals:

      $$\frac{3 \times 5 \times 3 \times 2 \times 8 \times 1}{4 \times 6 \times 7 \times 6 \times 3 \times 4}$$

   3. Now simplify using the equivalence rule. The first obvious number to divide out of the numerator and the denominator is 3:

      $\dfrac{\cancel{3} \times 5 \times 3 \times 2 \times 8 \times 1}{4 \times 6 \times 7 \times 6 \times \cancel{3} \times 4}$ That's one less multiplication step and about

      10 seconds saved time.

   4. Divide the numerator and denominator by 4. Notice how a 2 is

      left after the 8 is divided by 4: $\dfrac{5 \times 3 \times 2 \times \overset{2}{\cancel{8}}}{\cancel{4} \times 6 \times 7 \times 6 \times 4}$

   5. What's left after all of the possible divisions are done is:

      $$\frac{5}{7 \times 6 \times 2} = \frac{5}{84}$$

• **If two fractions have the same denominator, the fraction with the greater numerator is greater. If two fractions have the same numerator, the fraction with the greater denominator is lesser.**

   Example: We know that $\frac{5}{17} > \frac{3}{19}$ because:

1. $\dfrac{5}{19} > \dfrac{3}{19}$ In two fractions with the same denominator, the one with the greater numerator is greater.

2. $\dfrac{5}{17} > \dfrac{5}{19}$ In two fractions with the same numerator, the one with the greater denominator is lesser.

3. $\dfrac{5}{17} > \dfrac{5}{19} > \dfrac{3}{19}$ Combine statements 1 and 2.

Alternatively, visualize two pies. One pie is cut into 17 pieces and I take 5 of them. The second pie is cut into 19 pieces—each smaller than the pieces from the 17-slice pie—and you take only 3 of them. You've taken fewer pieces, each of which is smaller than mine; so, the total amount of pie you've taken is less than I did.

• **The following facts are used frequently on the SAT:**

$$\frac{1}{2} + \frac{1}{2} = 1 \qquad \frac{1}{4} + \frac{1}{4} = \frac{1}{2} \qquad \frac{1}{8} + \frac{1}{8} = \frac{1}{4}$$

Example: Simplify $1 - \dfrac{1}{1 - \dfrac{1}{2}}$.

1. Simplify the denominator of the larger fraction: $1 - \dfrac{1}{2} = \dfrac{1}{2}$. This leaves $1 - \dfrac{1}{\frac{1}{2}}$.

2. Recognize that $\dfrac{1}{\frac{1}{2}}$ is a reciprocal and equals 2, leaving $1 - 2 = -1$.

- **Word problems often use the word "of" to indicate multiplication.**

  Example: How much more is $\frac{1}{2}$ of $\frac{2}{3}$ than $\frac{3}{4}$ of $\frac{1}{3}$?

  1. $\frac{1}{2}$ of $\frac{2}{3} = \frac{1}{2} \times \frac{2}{3} = \frac{1}{3}$, and

     $\frac{3}{4}$ of $\frac{1}{3} = \frac{3}{4} \times \frac{1}{3} = \frac{1}{4}$.

  2. The first exceeds the second by their difference:

     $\frac{1}{3} - \frac{1}{4} = \frac{4}{12} - \frac{3}{12} = \frac{1}{12}$.

- **The statement $x > \frac{1}{x}$ is not always true.** If $x = 1$ or -1, then $\frac{1}{x} = x$; and, if $0 < x < 1$, then $x < \frac{1}{x}$.

Percentage

Terms and Definitions

- **Percent (%): A fraction whose denominator is 100.**

  Example: $28\% = \frac{28}{100}$.

- **Fun fact (‰):** In Europe, it's not uncommon to hear about per-thousand, which is written as ‰—note the double zero on the bottom. The only place I've seen this done regularly in the U.S. is with batting averages.

Formulas and Guidelines

- **Converting Fractions to Percentages.** To convert a fraction, $\frac{a}{b}$, to a percentage, $x\%$, set up the equation: $\frac{a}{b} = \frac{x}{100}$. Multiplying both sides of the equation by 100, you are left with $x = \frac{100a}{b}\%$.

  Example: 3 is what percent of 5?

  1. Set up the equation: $\frac{3}{5} = \frac{x}{100}$.

  2. Solve for x: $x = \frac{300}{5} = 60$.

  3. So, $\frac{3}{5}$ equals 60%, or 3 is 60% of 5.

- **Converting Percentages to Fractions.** To rename $x\%$ as a fraction, simply write the fraction $\frac{x}{100}$ and simplify it. For example, $.5\% = \frac{.5}{100} = \frac{1}{200}$.

Problems to Watch For

- **x is $y\%$ of z:** This phrase is written mathematically as $x = \frac{y}{100}z$.

- **Percentages need not be between 0 and 100.**

    Example: What percent of 40 is 60?

    1. Set up the equation:

        $$\frac{x}{100} \times 40 = 60.$$

    2. Multiply both sides of the equation by 100 and divide both sides by 40 to get $x =$

        $$\frac{60 \times 100}{40} = 6 \times 25 = 150.$$

    3. 60 is 150% of 40.

- **Memorize** the following equalities that occur often on the SAT:

    $$25\% = \frac{1}{4} \qquad 33\frac{1}{3}\% = \frac{1}{3}$$

Ratios

Terms and Definitions

- **Ratio:** A ratio is a **part-to-part relationship,** analogous to a fraction being a part-to-whole relationship. For example, if one says that an employer matches 50¢ to every dollar an employee invests in a retirement program, one is expressing the match as the ratio 50:100.

Formulas and Guidelines

- **Equivalence rule for ratios:** $x{:}y$ is the same as $ax{:}ay$; you can multiply all parts of a ratio by the same number and the ratio will remain unchanged.

- **Renaming as fractions:** If the ratio of A to B to C is $a{:}b{:}c$, then

    A is $\dfrac{a}{a + b + c}$ of the total, B is

    $\dfrac{b}{a + b + c}$, and so on.

Problem to Watch For

- **When you are given a ratio on an SAT, the problem is apt to test your ability to go from a part-part relationship expressed by a ratio to a part-whole relationship expressed by a fraction.**

    Example: An employer matches 50¢ to every dollar an employee invests in a retirement program. When $1,200 has been saved, what amount is attributable to the employer?

    1. The ratio of employer to employee is 50:100.

    2. The employer's share is

        $$\frac{50}{50 + 100} = \frac{1}{1 + 2} = \frac{1}{3}.$$

    3. The amount the employer has invested is

        $$\frac{1}{3} \times \$1,200 = \$400.$$

Decimals

Terms and Definitions

- **Decimal Point:** A marker that separates the tenths and the units places in a number. For example, the number 123.45 equals 1 hundred, 2 tens, 3 units, 4 tenths, and 5 hundredths.

Formulas and Guidelines

- **Addition and subtraction of decimals:** These operations are just like addition and subtraction with integers. Be sure that you line up the numbers' decimal points.

- **Multiplication of decimals:** Do the multiplication just like you would for integers. To place the decimal point, count the number of digits to the right of the decimal point in each of the numbers to be multiplied. The sum of the number of digits to the right of the decimal points in each of the multipliers is the number of digits there should be to the right of the decimal point in the product.

Example: Find the product of .02 and .5:

.02   Two digits to the right of the decimal point

×.5   One digit to the right of the decimal point

.010   Two + one = three digits to the right of the decimal point

There are three important things to notice about this problem:

1. Even though .010 is more commonly written as .01, don't drop the rightmost zero until after you've placed the decimal point.

2. Because there were only two digits after you finished the multiplication, you needed to add a third one to the left of the 1 before inserting the decimal point.

3. Use commonsense expectations to check your answer. This question is asking what half (.5) of two hundredths (.02) is. Half of two hundredths is one hundredth, .01.

- **To multiply a number by 10, move the decimal point one place to the right.** If there are no digits to the right of the decimal point, add a zero to the right of the last digit. An integer has an implied decimal point after its last digit: $123 \times 10 = 123. \times 10 = 1,230$.

- **To divide a number by 10, move the decimal point one place to the left.** If there are no digits to the left of the decimal point, add a zero before the first digit. For example, $.3 \div 10 = .03$.

- 10^n = **a 1 with n zeros after it.**

  Example: $10^3 = 1,000$.

- 10^{-n} = **a decimal point followed by $(n - 1)$ zeros and a 1.** For example, $10^{-3} = .001$. Another way to look at 10^{-n} is as the reciprocal of 10^n.

  So, $10^{-3} = \dfrac{1}{10^3} = \dfrac{1}{1,000} = .001$.

- **To convert a decimal to a fraction, count the number of digits to the right of the decimal point and call this n:** The numerator will be the number without the decimal point and the denominator will be a 1 followed by n zeros. For example, $2.345 = \dfrac{2,345}{1,000}$. Often, as is true in this case, you will be able to simplify the resulting fraction.

Problem to Watch For

- $.1$ is just another name for $\dfrac{1}{10}$.

PRACTICE PROBLEMS IN FRACTIONS

Answers begin on page 337.

16. One half of the socks in a drawer are brown, $\frac{1}{4}$ of them are black, and $\frac{1}{5}$ of them are blue. If the rest of them are white, what fractional part of the socks are white?

(A) $\frac{19}{20}$

(B) $\frac{3}{11}$

(C) $\frac{1}{20}$

(D) $\frac{1}{11}$

(E) $\frac{8}{11}$

17. How many X cards would have to be taken from pile A and put into pile B for the fractional part of X cards to be the same in both piles?

(A) None

(B) 1

(C) 2

(D) 3

(E) 4

18. In inches, the difference between $7\frac{3}{4}$ feet and $5\frac{5}{6}$ feet is:

(A) 12

(B) 12.5

(C) 18

(D) 23

(E) 25

19. Simplify $\dfrac{1}{\dfrac{1}{a} - \dfrac{1}{b}}$,

($ab \neq 0$ and $a \neq b$).

(A) $\dfrac{ab}{a - b}$

(B) $\dfrac{a - b}{ab}$

(C) $b - a$

(D) $\dfrac{ab}{b - a}$

(E) $\dfrac{b - a}{ab}$

20. If $8 \times .125 = y$, then $y =$

(A) 0

(B) 1

(C) .1

(D) 8.125

(E) .825

21. If $.2^2 = x$, then $x =$

(A) .2

(B) .02

(C) .04

(D) 0.016

(E) .0016

22. If $-0.6(0.4 - p) =$ $1.2(.8p + .7p)$, then $p =$

(A) -5

(B) $-.2$

(C) .2

(D) .5

(E) None of the above

23. If $10n = 3.33333...$ and $n =$ $.33333...$, then n can be rewritten as:

(A) $\dfrac{1}{3}$

(B) $.3^2$

(C) $\dfrac{3}{10}$

(D) $\dfrac{1}{.3}$

(E) None of the above

24. After picking 120 peaches, a woman cans 108 of them. What percent remains?

(A) 10

(B) 30

(C) 50

(D) 70

(E) 90

25. A boy completed 75% of a 12-block trip. How many blocks does he have left to go?

(A) 3

(B) 4

(C) 6

(D) 8

(E) 9

26. A 60-gallon tank is 40% full of water. If the water is poured into a 40-gallon tank, what percent of the 40-gallon tank will be filled?

(A) 24

(B) 40

(C) 60

(D) 96

(E) 100

27. If 30% of a class consists of boys and there are 21 girls in the class, how many boys are in the class?

(A) 30

(B) 9

(C) 60

(D) 42

(E) 10

28. In a scale drawing, 3 inches represent 9 feet. How many inches represent 1 foot 6 inches? (1 foot = 12 inches)

(A) .4

(B) .5

(C) .6

(D) 1

(E) 2

29. If 3:4 is equivalent to a:12, then a =

(A) 1

(B) 9

(C) 11

(D) 12

(E) 14

30. Diane, Gerry, and Katia split the award for a contest in the ratio of 6:2:1, respectively. If the total award was worth $72, then Gerry received

(A) $9

(B) $18

(C) $16

(D) $48

(E) $8

31. In a class of 25 students, 44% are boys. What is the ratio of boys to girls in the class?

(A) 11:1

(B) 11:25

(C) 11:14

(D) 14:11

(E) 25:14

32. The length of a side of an equilateral triangle is what fraction of the perimeter of the triangle?

(A) $\dfrac{1}{6}$

(B) $\dfrac{1}{3}$

(C) 1

(D) $\dfrac{3}{1}$

(E) $\dfrac{60}{1}$

33. A gas tank that is $\dfrac{1}{3}$ full requires 6 gallons to make it $\dfrac{5}{6}$ full. What is the capacity of the tank in gallons?

(A) 2

(B) 12

(C) 36

(D) 48

(E) 24

34. In a town there are fewer than 30 unlicensed dogs. If $\dfrac{2}{5}$ of the unlicensed dogs are male and $\dfrac{3}{8}$ of the unlicensed male dogs are beagles, then how many unlicensed dogs are there in the town?

(A) 20

(B) 25

(C) 30

(D) 40

(E) It cannot be determined from the information given.

35. How many 32-cent stamps can be purchased for d dollars?

(A) $32d$

(B) $\dfrac{d}{32}$

(C) $\dfrac{32}{d}$

(D) $\dfrac{100d}{32}$

(E) $\dfrac{32}{100d}$

The directions for grid-ins are on page 153.

36. If a $\frac{1}{4}$-inch piece of ribbon costs a nickel, how many dollars does 1 foot cost?

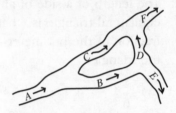

37. The river Paix flows in the directions indicated by the arrows on the map above. If $\frac{5}{8}$ of the water flowing from channel A takes channel B, and $\frac{3}{5}$ of the water from channel B takes channel D, then what fraction of the water from channel A takes channel F?

38. If $\dfrac{5}{x} = \dfrac{15}{9}$, then $x =$

40. 30% of 80 is what percent of 24?

39. Jim paints $\dfrac{1}{3}$ of a fence. Joan paints $\dfrac{1}{2}$ of what is left. What fraction of the fence is left unpainted?

Exponents and Square Roots

In the previous section, we briefly touched on exponents whose base was 10, e.g., $10^2 = 100$. In this section we'll discuss exponents in general, including negative and rational (i.e., can be expressed with a fraction) exponents. The radical is a special case of a rational exponent; specifically $\sqrt[n]{x} = x^{1/n}$. When n is 2, the radical is called a square root ($\sqrt{\ }$). Consequently, any rules that apply to exponents in general also apply to radicals and square roots.

Terms and Definitions

- a^n: When n is an integer, n (the **exponent**) instances of a (the **base**) multiplied together:

$$a^n = \overbrace{a \times a \times \cdots \times a}^{n \text{ times}}$$

- a^{-n}: **The reciprocal of** a^n:

$$a^{-n} = \frac{1}{a^n} = \frac{1}{\underbrace{a \times a \times \cdots \times a}_{n \text{ times}}}$$

- $a^{\frac{1}{n}} = \sqrt[n]{a}$: **The nth root of a.** When n is 2, it's called the square root.

- **Special Cases:**

$$a^0 = 1 \text{ for } a \neq 0$$

$$0^n = 0 \text{ for } n \neq 0$$

$$0^0 \text{ is undefined}$$

$$a^{\frac{1}{2}} = \sqrt{a}$$

$$a^{-1} = \frac{1}{a}$$

$$a^1 = a$$

Formulas and Guidelines

For integer exponents, it's straightforward to visualize a^n as n copies of a multiplied together. The visualization becomes muddled when you throw negatives and fractions into the expression—what does it mean to multiply a by itself $-\frac{3}{8}$ times? I find it easiest to remember rules for positive integer exponents, and convert all problems to ones that use integers.

- $a^n a^m = a^{n+m}$: The bases are equal. Visualize n a's, followed by m a's, for a total of $(n + m)$ a's. For example, $2^3 \times 2^2 = 2^5$.

- $(a^m)^n = a^{mn}$: Visualize n sets of m a's. A special case of this occurs when m and n are reciprocals; for example,

$$\sqrt{a^2} = \left(\sqrt{a}\right)^2 = a$$

- $a^n b^n = (ab)^n$: The exponents are equal. Visualize n a's, followed by n b's. Pair them off and you have n (ab)'s. For example, $3^2 \times 2^2 = (3 \times 2)^2 = 6^2$.

- $a^n \div a^m = a^{n-m}$ and $a^n \div b^n = (a \div b)^n = \left(\dfrac{a}{b}\right)^n = \dfrac{a^n}{b^n}$: The rules for division are analogous to those for multiplication.

- $\sqrt{a}\sqrt{b} = \sqrt{ab}$ and $\sqrt{\dfrac{a}{b}} = \dfrac{\sqrt{a}}{\sqrt{b}}$: This follows directly from the fact that a radical is a special case of an exponent.

- **You can't combine $a^n \pm a^m$ or $a^n \pm b^n$.** For example, you cannot simplify $5\sqrt{x} + x + x^2$.

- $\left(\dfrac{a}{b}\right)^{-\frac{n}{m}} = \dfrac{\sqrt[m]{b^n}}{\sqrt[m]{a^n}} = \dfrac{\left(\sqrt[m]{b}\right)^n}{\left(\sqrt[m]{a}\right)^n}$

$$= \sqrt[m]{\left(\dfrac{b}{a}\right)^n} = \left(\sqrt[m]{\dfrac{b}{a}}\right)^n$$

This is everything thrown together. Make sure you understand why each of these expressions is equal to the others. Although, you wouldn't ever be asked to derive this, one form might be easier to calculate than another. For example, if b is 8 and m is 3, you can

separate and simplify $\sqrt[3]{8}$ to be 2.

- **There are two square roots for every positive number.** If x is the square root of y, then so is $-x$. Generally, there are n n^{th} roots of a number.

- **If a is negative, then a^n is positive when n is even, and a^n is negative when n is odd.** This follows from the fact that multiplying a negative by a negative yields a positive, and multiplying a negative by a positive yields a negative.

- **A negative number has a cube root that is a negative.** For example, $\sqrt[3]{-8} = -2$. Test this by multiplying -2 by itself 3 times.

Problems to Watch For

- **Raising a number to a power does not necessarily increase the number, not even if the exponent is positive.** For example: $\left(\dfrac{1}{2}\right)^2 = \dfrac{1}{4}$.

- **Memorize the fact that $4^n = (2^2)^n = 2^{2n}$.** When it appears in problems, it makes them appear much tougher than they truly are.

Example: Solve for k in the diagram below.

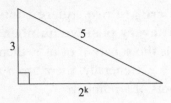

Note: Figure not drawn to scale.

Using the Pythagorean theorem (Need a reminder? See p. 201.) you can set up the equations:

$$\left(2^k\right)^2 = 5^2 - 3^2$$
$$2^{2k} = 4^2$$
$$\left(2^2\right)^k = 4^2$$
$$4^k = 4^2$$
$$k = 2$$

• **Exponents are shorthand for multiplication and consequently follow all of the rules of multiplication.**

Example: When $a = 3$, solve for $\dfrac{a^3 + a^4}{a+1}$.

1. Because exponents follow all the rules for multiplication, you can distribute a^3 in the numerator to get $\dfrac{a^3(1+a)}{a+1}$.

2. $(1 + a)$ and $(a + 1)$ are equal and can be canceled, so you are left with a^3.

3. Substituting 3 for a, you have $a^3 = 27$.

• **Memorize the squares of 1 through 10 and the cubes of 1 through 5** so that when you see a 64 on the exam you immediately recognize that $64 = 8^2 = 4^3$.

Example: Solve for positive x in the equation $(x + 5)^2 = 64$.

1. Because you recognize 64 as a perfect square, you can rewrite the equation to read $(x + 5)^2 = 8^2$.

2. Take the positive square root of both sides to get $x + 5 = 8$.

3. Solve the simple addition to reach $x = 3$.

PRACTICE PROBLEMS IN EXPONENTS AND SQUARE ROOTS

Answers begin on page 340.

41. If $n = -1$, then $n^3 + n^2 =$

(A) -2

(B) -1

(C) 0

(D) 1

(E) 2

42. If $\dfrac{1}{y} = \sqrt{.25}$, then y equals

(A) $\dfrac{1}{4}$

(B) $\dfrac{1}{2}$

(C) 1

(D) 2

(E) 4

43. $4\sqrt{48} - 3\sqrt{12} =$

(A) 5

(B) 10

(C) $\sqrt{3}$

(D) $2\sqrt{3}$

(E) $10\sqrt{3}$

44. $\left(\dfrac{1}{2}x^6\right)^2 =$

(A) x^8

(B) x^{12}

(C) $\dfrac{1}{4}x^8$

(D) $\dfrac{1}{4}x^{12}$

(E) $\dfrac{1}{4}x^{36}$

45. $\sqrt{\dfrac{x^2}{4} + \dfrac{4x^2}{9}} =$

(A) $\dfrac{x}{2} + \dfrac{2x}{3}$

(B) $\dfrac{3x}{5}$

(C) $\dfrac{x\sqrt{5}}{36}$

(D) $\dfrac{5x}{36}$

(E) $\dfrac{5x}{6}$

46. Solve for x in the equation: $50,806 = 5x^2 + 8x + 6$.

(A) 0

(B) 1

(C) 10

(D) 100

(E) $1,000$

47. If $7x - 7y = 20$, then $x - y =$

(A) $\dfrac{20}{7}$

(B) -2

(C) $-\dfrac{20}{7}$

(D) 2

(E) 20

48. For which interval is $x^2 < x$?

(A) $x < 0$

(B) $x < 1$

(C) $-1 < x < 0$

(D) $-1 < x < 1$

(E) $0 < x < 1$

49. A traditional riddle starts, "I met a man with seven wives. Each wife had seven sacks. Each sack had seven cats. Each cat had seven kittens..." How many kittens were there?

(A) 4×7

(B) 5×7

(C) 4^7

(D) 5^7

(E) 7^4

50. Which of the following values is the greatest?

(A) $\left(-\dfrac{1}{2}\right)^{-3}$

(B) $\left(-\dfrac{1}{2}\right)^{-2}$

(C) $\left(-\dfrac{1}{2}\right)^{0}$

(D) $\left(-\dfrac{1}{2}\right)^{2}$

(E) $\left(-\dfrac{1}{2}\right)^{3}$

> The directions for grid-ins are on page 153.

51. If $2^{x+2} = 32$, then x equals

52. If $3x - .3x = 54$, then $x =$

53. Simplify $\sqrt{.0121}$

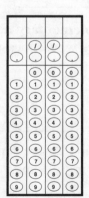

54. Simplify $64^{-\frac{2}{3}}$

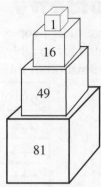

55. The area of one face of each cube is given on that face. What is the height of the stack of cubes?

Geometry

Although most people study only one year of geometry, this topic has accounted for roughly one third of the SAT on past exams. Knowing the information in this section can earn you $200-300$ points.

Symbol	Name	Usage
←—→	Line	←—→
•—•	Line Segment	•—•
•—→	Ray	•—→
∥	Parallel to	$l_1 \parallel l_2$
⊥	Perpendicular to	$l_1 \perp l_2$
∠	Angle	∠A
m∠	Measure of an angle	m∠A = 150°
⌐	Right angle	◣
≅	Congruent to, i.e. having the same measure	$\Delta_1 \cong \Delta_2$
/	Hash marks: Indicate equality. In these pictures, the vertical angles and opposite sides are equal.	

Angles

Terms and Definitions

- **Straight angle:** An angle whose measure is 180°. A line segment forms a straight angle.

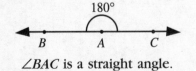

$$180°$$

∠BAC is a straight angle.

- **Supplementary angles:** Two angles whose measures add to 180°.

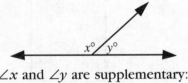

∠x and ∠y are supplementary:
m∠x + m∠y = 180°

- **Right angle (⌐):** An angle whose measure is 90°.

- **Perpendicular (⊥):** Two lines are perpendicular if they form a right angle.

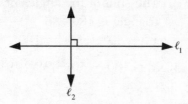

Note that ⌐ indicates a 90° angle. $\ell_1 \perp \ell_2$ means line 1 is perpendicular to line 2.

- **Complementary angles:** Two angles whose measures add to 90°. If you split a right angle into two parts, they are complementary.

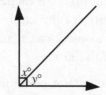

$\angle x$ and $\angle y$ are complementary:
$$m\angle x + m\angle y = 90°$$

- **Vertical angles:** Opposing angles formed by the intersection of two lines.

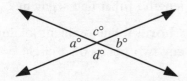

$\angle a$ and $\angle b$ are vertical angles and consequently congruent.

Likewise, $\angle c$ and $\angle d$ are vertical angles and congruent.

- **Parallel lines (∥):** Two lines in a plane (SAT geometry assumes you are working in a plane unless otherwise stated) that never intersect. The distance between parallel lines is constant.

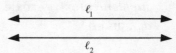

$\ell_1 \| \ell_2$ means line 1 is parallel to line 2.

Formulas and Guidelines

- **Transversal of parallel lines:** A line that intersects two parallel lines.

Given that $\ell_1 \| \ell_2$, ℓ_3 is a transversal.

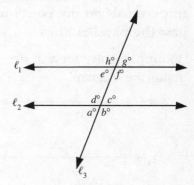

In the previous picture, the eight angles formed by two parallel lines and a transversal adhere to the following rules:

1. $\angle a \cong \angle c \cong \angle e \cong \angle g$

2. $\angle b \cong \angle d \cong \angle f \cong \angle h$

3. Angles a, c, e, and g are *supplementary* to angles b, d, f, and h.

Notice that these rules are consistent with the definitions of vertical, straight, and supplementary angles.

Problems to Watch For

• **Problems involving parallel lines cut by a transversal may appear more difficult when the diagrams include extraneous lines or when the transversals do not continue past the parallel lines.**

Example: Solve for x in the following diagram.

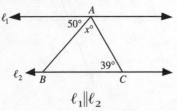

$$\ell_1 \| \ell_2$$

1. $\overline{AB}$ is a transversal, so $m\angle ABC = 50°$.

2. The sum of the angles of a triangle is 180°, so $x° + 50° + 39° = 180°$.

3. $x = 180 - 50 - 39 = 91$.

Circles

Terms and Definitions

• **Circle:** The set of points a given distance from a single point. The single point is called the circle's center. For example, a circle with radius 3 inches is the set of all points 3 inches from the center of the circle. The points inside a circle are not part of the circle.

• **Degrees (°):** A circle is defined to sweep out an angle of 360 degrees.

• **Radius (r):** A line segment joining a circle's center and any point on the circle. Also, the length of that line segment.

• **Chord:** A line segment joining any two points on a circle.

- **Diameter (*d*):** A chord that passes through the center of the circle. Also, the length of that chord. The diameter is the longest chord, with length $d = 2r$.

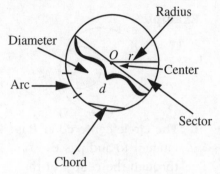

- **Arc:** A contiguous piece of a circle.
- **Sector of a circle:** The pie slice shaped area enclosed by an arc and the radii to the endpoints of the arc.
- **Tangent:** (1) A line that shares exactly one point with a circle. (2) Two circles are tangent if they are tangent to a line at the same point.

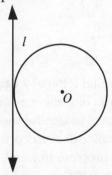

l is tangent to the circle centered at *O*.

- **Inscribed:** A circle is inscribed within a square if each of the sides of the square is tangent to the circle. A square is inscribed within a circle if each of its vertices lies on the circle.

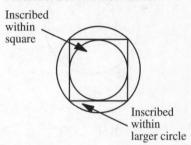

Formulas and Guidelines

- **Pi (π):** $\pi \approx \dfrac{22}{7} \approx 3.14$. The ratio between every circle's circumference and its diameter: $\pi = \dfrac{C}{d}$
- **Circumference (*C*):** The perimeter of a circle. $C = \pi D = 2\pi r$.
- **Area of a circle (*A*):** $A = \pi r^2$.
- **Degrees in an arc:** The number of degrees in an arc is equal to the number of degrees in the angle formed by the radii drawn to the ends of the arc.
- **Length of an arc:** The ratio of the number of degrees in an arc to the number of degrees in a circle, 360, is equal to the ratio of the length of the arc to the

circumference of the circle, $2\pi r$. The circumference is an arc that goes all the way around the circle.

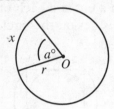

$$\frac{a}{360} = \frac{x}{2\pi r}$$

- **Area of a sector:** The ratio of the number of degrees in an arc to the number of degrees in a circle, 360, is equal to the ratio of the area of the sector the arc defines to the area of the circle, πr^2.

$$\frac{a}{360} = \frac{A}{\pi r^2}$$

Problems to Watch For

- **You must be able to relate the radius, diameter, and circumference of a circle, and approximate the value of π.**

Example:

1. The circle centered at P is tangent to and passes through the center of the circle centered at O. What fraction of the larger circle's circumference best approximates the smaller circle's radius?

(A) $\dfrac{1}{2}$

(B) $\dfrac{1}{3}$

(C) $\dfrac{1}{4}$

(D) $\dfrac{1}{6}$

(E) $\dfrac{1}{12}$

Use capital letters to denote elements of the larger circle and lowercase to denote those of the smaller one. Keep the goal of the problem in mind, to relate r and C.

Step	Equation	Reason
1	$d = R$	You were told that diameter small circle = radius of large circle.
2	$2r = \dfrac{D}{2}$	$d = 2r$ and $R = \dfrac{D}{2}$
3	$2r = \dfrac{C}{2\pi}$	By definition, $D = \dfrac{C}{\pi}$
4	$r = \dfrac{C}{4\pi}$	Divide both sides of the equation by 2.
5	$r \approx \dfrac{C}{12} = \dfrac{1}{12}C$	Approximate π as 3.

The correct answer is (E).

- **Often word problems use this fact: If you say that a wheel is a circle, then the distance the wheel travels in one revolution is equal to its circumference.**

  Example: If a bicycle with wheels 2 feet in diameter were to go around a circular track with diameter 100 feet, how many revolutions would each of the wheels make per lap?

  1. Wheel circumference (C_w) = 2π feet

  2. Track circumference (C_t) = 100π feet

  3. Number of revolutions =

     $$\frac{\text{distance around the track}}{\text{distance covered by each revolution of the wheel}}$$

  4. Number of revolutions = $\dfrac{C_t}{C_w} = \dfrac{100\pi}{2\pi} = 50.$

- **To test your ability to relate rectangular and circular measures, problems often use the fact that tangents to circles are perpendicular to a radius.**

  Example:

  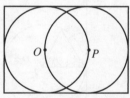

  The circle centered at P passes through O, and the circle centered at O passes through P. If the radius of circle O is 2 centimeters, what is the area, in square centimeters, of the circumscribed rectangle?

1. Because the circles share a radius, $\overline{OP}$, their radii, diameters, circumferences, and other measures are the same.

2. Rectangle length = circle diameter = 4 cm.

3. Rectangle width = 3 × circle radius = 6 cm.

4. Rectangle Area = length × width = 24 cm².

- **Problems with angles and triangles often involve circles because a tangent to a circle conveniently forms a right angle to the radius.** Furthermore, when two radii of a circle are used to form the sides of a triangle, the triangle is guaranteed to be isosceles because all radii of a circle have the same length.

Example:

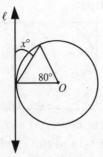

Line ℓ is tangent to the circle with center O. What is x?

1. Notice that the two unknown angles of the inscribed triangle are opposite equal-length sides. Why? Because the two sides are radii of the same circle. Call the degree measure of each of these angles a. The sum of the measures of the angles in a triangle is 180°, so $2a + 80° = 180°$, and subsequently $a = 50°$. **Draw** the angle measures into the figure.

2. Line ℓ is tangent to the circle; consequently it forms a right angle with the radius that intersects it. **Draw** in the right angle.

3. $x + 50 = 90$, the number of degrees in a right angle. So, $x = 40$.

Quadrilaterals

Terms and Definitions

- **Polygon:** A closed, multisided figure in a plane, such as a triangle or quadrilateral.

- **Quadrilateral:** A polygon with 4 sides.

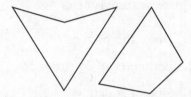

- **Parallelogram:** A quadrilateral whose opposite sides are parallel.

- **Rectangle:** A parallelogram whose 4 angles each measure 90°.

- **Square:** A rectangle whose sides have the same length.

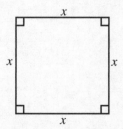

- **Polyhedron:** A closed, multisided figure in *3-dimensional space* such as a pyramid, cone, or cube.

- **Rectangular solid:** Without getting too technical, think of a box. All of the angles formed by the edges are 90°.

- **Cube:** A rectangular solid, all of whose edges have the same length.

Formulas and Guidelines

- **The sum of the angle measures in a quadrilateral is 360°.**

- $A_r = lw$: The area of a **rectangle** is the product of its length and width.

- $A_s = s^2$: For a **square,** the length and the width are the same, so the area is the length of the side squared.

- **The perimeter of an object** is the sum of the lengths of its sides.

- $P_r = 2(l + w)$: For a rectangle, the perimeter is twice the sum of the length and the width.

- $P_s = 4s$: For a square, the perimeter simplifies to 4 times the length of a side.

- V_r = *lwh:* The volume of a rectangular solid (a box) is length × width × height.

- V_c = s^3: The volume of a cube is the length of its edge cubed.

- **Rectangular solids and cubes have 6 faces.**

Problems to Watch For

- **When determining how many rectangular solids of the same dimensions can fit into another, use volumes, not lengths or areas.**

Example: How many 2 × 1 × 3 boxes can fit into a 4 × 5 × 6 box?

1. Volume of large box = 4 × 5 × 6; and, volume of small box = 2 × 1 × 3.

2. The quotient of their volumes is

$$\frac{4 \times 5 \times \cancel{6}}{\cancel{2} \times 1 \times \cancel{3}} = \frac{4 \times 5}{1} = 20$$

- **When a rectangle is inscribed within a circle, the diagonal of the rectangle is a diameter of the circle. (Remember that a square is a type of rectangle.)**

Example: What is the area of a circle circumscribed about a square with perimeter 56?

1. Draw the picture!

2. Perimeter of square = 56.

3. Side of square = 56 ÷ 4 = 14.

4. Diagonal of square = $14\sqrt{2}$.

5. Diameter of circle = $14\sqrt{2}$.

6. Radius of circle = $7\sqrt{2}$.

7. Area of circle = πr^2 = $\pi(7\sqrt{2})^2 = \pi \times 49 \times 2 = 98\pi$.

PRACTICE PROBLEMS IN BASIC GEOMETRY

Answers begin on page 341.

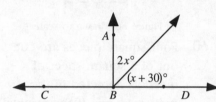

56. $\overline{BA} \perp \overline{CD}$. Solve for x.

    (A) 15

    (B) 20

    (C) 30

    (D) 40

    (E) 50

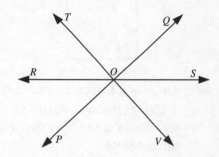

57. Lines $\overleftrightarrow{PQ}$, $\overleftrightarrow{RS}$, and $\overleftrightarrow{TV}$ intersect at O. If $m\angle ROQ = 142°$ and $m\angle TOS = 129°$, find the measure of $\angle POV$.

    (A) 38°

    (B) 51°

    (C) 89°

    (D) 91°

    (E) 189°

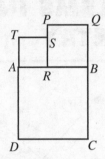

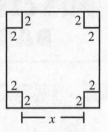

Figure not drawn to scale.

58. *ABCD* is a square whose area is 100. *PQBR* is a square of area 36. What is the area of square *TSRA?*

(A) 2
(B) 4
(C) 16
(D) 25
(E) 36

60. Four square pieces are cut out of a square sheet of metal as depicted in the picture above. If the original area of the metal sheet was $x^2 + 24x$, then what is the area of the sheet without the four pieces?

(A) 1
(B) 4
(C) 6
(D) 9
(E) It can not be determined from the information given.

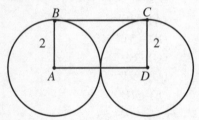

59. From the figure above, *A* and *D* are the centers of two congruent circles. Find the area of rectangle *ABCD* if $\overline{AB}$ and $\overline{CD}$ are both radii of the circles and have length 2.

(A) 1
(B) 2
(C) 4
(D) 6
(E) 8

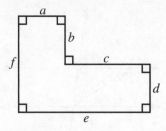

61. The area of the above figure is all of the following EXCEPT

(A) $ab + de$

(B) $af + cd$

(C) $fe - bc$

(D) $af + ed$

(E) $ab + ad + cd$

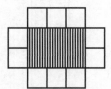

62. From the figure above, if each of the equally sized square tabs is folded up and a lid is put on to form a box, then the volume of the box in terms of s, the side of one of the squares, is:

(A) $10s^2$

(B) $6s^3$

(C) $6s$

(D) $10s^3$

(E) It cannot be determined from the information given.

63. A cylindrical roller is dipped in paint and then rolled for one complete revolution over a piece of paper. If the line of paint is 4 inches long, what is the radius, in inches, of the roller?

(A) $\dfrac{2}{\pi}$

(B) 2

(C) π

(D) 2π

(E) It cannot be determined from the information given.

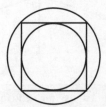

64. One circle is circumscribed around a square with side of length 2, and another circle is inscribed in the same square. Find the ratio of the area of the larger circle to that of the smaller circle.

(A) $4:1$

(B) $\sqrt{3}:1$

(C) $1.5:1$

(D) $\sqrt{2}:1$

(E) $2:1$

65. The volume of a box is 24 cubic inches. If its length is 3 inches and its width is 8 inches, what is its depth in inches?

(A) 0

(B) 1

(C) 2

(D) 3

(E) 4

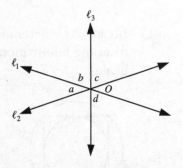

The directions for grid-ins are on page 153.

66. ℓ_1, ℓ_2, and ℓ_3 intersect at O. If $m\angle b = 2 \times m\angle a$, and $m\angle a = \frac{1}{2}m\angle c$, find $m\angle d$.

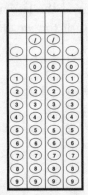

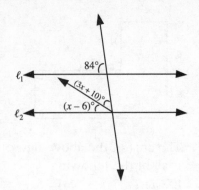

67. If $\ell_1 \| \ell_2$, solve for x.

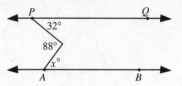

68. If $\overline{PQ} \parallel \overline{AB}$, solve for x.

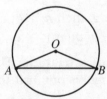

69. The measure of $\angle OAB$ is $20°$. If O is the center of the circle, then what is m$\angle AOB$?

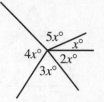

70. From above, what is x?

More Geometry

Many of the formulas in this section are on the test; however, like the problem instructions, the more you memorize now, the smoother test day will be.

Triangles and Trigonometry

Terms and Definitions

- **Triangle (△):** A closed figure in a plane with 3 sides.
- **Equilateral △:** A triangle whose sides and angles are congruent (the same length or measure).

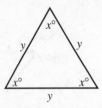

- **Isosceles △:** A triangle, two of whose sides and angles are congruent.

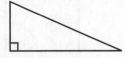

- **Right △:** A triangle with one angle whose measure is 90°.

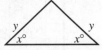

Formulas and Guidelines

- **The sum of the measures of the angles in a triangle is 180°.**

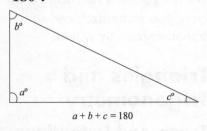

$$a + b + c = 180$$

Note: Figure not drawn to scale.

- **Sides opposite congruent angles are congruent; conversely, angles opposite congruent sides are congruent.**

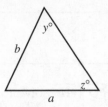

If $y = z$, then $a = b$; likewise, if $a = b$, then $y = z$.

- **If $m\angle y$ is greater than $m\angle z$, then the length of the side opposite $\angle y$ is greater than the length of the side opposite $\angle z$.**

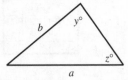

If $y > z$, then $a > b$; likewise, if $a > b$, then $y > z$.

- **Area of a triangle:** The area of a triangle is one half the base times the height: $A = \dfrac{1}{2}bh.$

- **Each of a triangle's three sides can be considered a base.**

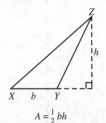 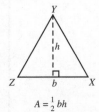

$$A = \tfrac{1}{2}bh \qquad A = \tfrac{1}{2}bh$$

The base is always perpendicular to the height.

- **Pythagorean theorem ($a^2 + b^2 = c^2$):** In a right triangle, the square of the length of the *hypotenuse* (the side opposite the right angle) equals the sum of the squares of the lengths of the legs (the other two sides).

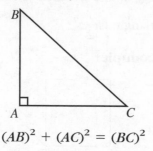

$$(AB)^2 + (AC)^2 = (BC)^2$$

- **30-60-90 Triangle:** A triangle whose angles measure 30°, 60°, and 90°.

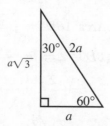

The ratio of the lengths of the sides of a 30-60-90 triangle is $1 : \sqrt{3} : 2$. Put another way, if the length of the side opposite the 30° angle is a, then the length of the side opposite the 60° angle is $a\sqrt{3}$, and the side opposite the right angle is $2a$.

Conversely, if the sides of a triangle are in the proportion a, $a\sqrt{3}$, and $2a$, then the triangle is a 30-60-90 triangle.

Watch out for the case where a, from above, is $\sqrt{3}$, leaving sides of $2\sqrt{3}$, $\sqrt{3}$, and 3.

- **45-45-90 Triangle:** A triangle whose angles measure 45°, 45°, and 90°.

The ratio of the lengths of the sides of a 45-45-90 triangle is $1 : 1 : \sqrt{2}$.

Watch out for the case where each leg has side $\sqrt{2}$, and the hypotenuse has length 2.

Problems to Watch For

- **The area of a right triangle is one half the product of the legs because the legs are the base and height of the triangle.**

Example:

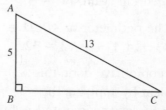

What is the area of $\triangle ABC$?

1. By the Pythagorean theorem, $BC = 12$.

2. Area $\triangle ABC = \left(\dfrac{1}{2}\right)(12)(5)$
   $= 30$

- **Pythagorean Triples:** Sets of integers that satisfy the Pythagorean theorem appear often in SAT questions. These include 3-4-5, 5-12-13, 8-15-17, and 7-24-25. Memorize them so that when you see two out of three numbers from a triple, you'll know the third without having to calculate it.

Example:

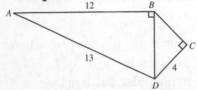

Note: Figure not drawn to scale.

What is the perimeter of *ABCD*?

1. △*ABD* is a right triangle. By the Pythagorean theorem, *BD* = 5.

2. Using the Pythagorean theorem again, *BC* = 3.

3. The perimeter of *ABCD* = 13 + 4 + 3 + 12 = 32.

You could have done this problem by applying the Pythagorean theorem twice, but it is faster to recognize the Pythagorean triples.

- **Triangles whose angles measure 45°, 45°, and 90° occur often on the SAT because they are both right and isosceles triangles, and because one can form them** by splitting a square along its diagonal. Applying the Pythagorean theorem and the formula for the area of the triangle, if the length of a leg of a 45-45-90 triangle is *a*, then the length of the hypotenuse is $a\sqrt{2}$, and the area of the triangle is $\frac{1}{2}a^2$.

Example:

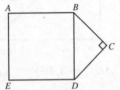

If the area of square *ABDE* is 4 and *BC* = *CD*, what is the area of △*BCD*?

1. Area *ABDE* = 4 ⇒ *BD* = 2.

2. *BD* = 2 ⇒ *BC* = *CD*
$$= \frac{2}{\sqrt{2}} = \frac{2\sqrt{2}}{\sqrt{2}\sqrt{2}}$$
$$= \frac{2\sqrt{2}}{2}$$
$$= \sqrt{2}$$

3. A 45-45-90 triangle with legs of length $\sqrt{2}$ has area $\frac{1}{2}(\sqrt{2})^2 = 1$.

- **Be familiar with 30-60-90 triangles. Memorize the ratio of the lengths of the sides of 30-60-90 triangles.**

  Example:
  What is the area of an equilateral triangle with side of length 4?

  1. Draw the triangle and drop a perpendicular from a vertex to the opposite base.

  2. Due to the symmetry you have formed two 30-60-90 triangles.

  3. The hypotenuse of each is 4, so the leg opposite the 60° angle is $2\sqrt{3}$ and the leg opposite the 30° angle is 2.

  4. The area of each 30-60-90 triangle is
  $$\left(\frac{1}{2}\right)(2)(2\sqrt{3}) = 2\sqrt{3}.$$

  5. The area of the equilateral triangle is
  $$2 \times 2\sqrt{3} = 4\sqrt{3}.$$

Coordinate Geometry

Terms and Definitions

- **Number line:** A *one dimensional*, graphical representation of real numbers in which each point on a straight line corresponds to exactly one number.

- **Coordinate axes:** You can think of the coordinate axes as a two-dimensional number line defining a plane on which each point is represented by a pair of numbers. The first dimension is a horizontal number line called the **x-axis.** The second dimension is a vertical number line called the **y-axis.**

- **x-coordinate:** The first number in a pair, (x, y), that represents a point.

- **y-coordinate:** The second number in a pair, (x, y), that represents a point.

- **Origin:** The point on the coordinate axes represented by the pair (0,0).

- **Positive x-axis:** Those points on the x-axis that are to the right of the origin.

- **Positive y-axis:** Those points on the y-axis that are above the origin.

- **Negative x-axis:** Those points on the x-axis that are to the left of the origin.

- **Negative y-axis:** Those points on the y-axis that are below the origin.

- **Quadrants:** The four sections of the coordinate axes separated by the x- and y-axes. They are numbered from I to IV with Roman numerals as shown in the following diagram.

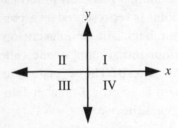

If x is:	And y is:	Then (x,y) is:
positive	positive	in Quadrant I
negative	positive	in Quadrant II
negative	negative	in Quadrant III
positive	negative	in Quadrant IV
0	−	on the y-axis
−	0	on the x-axis
0	0	at the origin

Formulas and Guidelines

- **All points on a horizontal line parallel to the x-axis have the same y-coordinate.**

- **All points on a vertical line parallel to the y-axis have the same x-coordinate.**

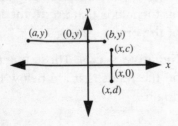

- **The midpoint of two points** (x_1, y_1) and (x_2, y_2) is
$$\left(\frac{x_1 + x_2}{2}, \frac{y_1 + y_2}{2} \right).$$

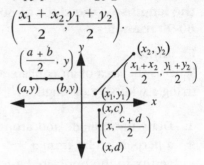

Notice how much simpler the equation is when the points lie on either a horizontal or vertical line.

- **The distance between two points** (x_1, y_1) and (x_2, y_2) is
$$\sqrt{(x_2 - x_1)^2 + (y_2 - y_1)^2}.$$

Notice how the equation simplifies when the points lie on either a horizontal or vertical line. (i.e., $x_1 = x_2$ or $y_1 = y_2$)

- **The slope of a line** describes how steep an angle the line makes with the x-axis. The slope of a line that includes two points (x_1, y_1) and (x_2, y_2) is $\frac{y_2 - y_1}{x_2 - x_1}$, often referred to as the **rise over run**, where the rise is the change in the y value and the run is the change in the x value. It does not matter what two points on the line you choose to compute its slope because a line has a constant slope. The slope of a horizontal line is zero, because all of its points have the same *y*-value. The slope of a vertical line is undefined because all of its points have the same *x*-value, which generates a zero in the denominator of the slope's definition.

Problem to Watch For

- **Squares often appear in problems dealing with coordinate geometry because the equations for the mid-point of two points and the length of a line segment simplify a great deal when the points lie on a horizontal or vertical line.**

Example:

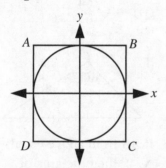

If the circle pictured above has area 16π and is centered at

(0,0) and *ABCD* is a square, find the *x*-coordinate of point *B*.

1. The area of a circle is given by the equation $A = \pi r^2$. Substituting 16π for *A* and solving for *r*, you get $r = 4$. Now you know that every point on the circle is 4 units from the origin.

2. Where the circle crosses the positive *x*-axis, it must have coordinates (4,0). The circle must cross the positive *y*-axis at the point (0,4).

3. *B* is on a line parallel to the *y*-axis at (4,0), so its *x*-coordinate is 4. *B* is on a line parallel to the *x*-axis at (0,4), so its *y*-coordinate is also 4.

4. Putting these together, you determine that the coordinates of point *B* are (4,4).

MORE PRACTICE PROBLEMS IN GEOMETRY

Answers begin on page 343.

71.

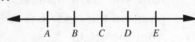

Note: Figure not drawn to scale.

In the figure, B is the midpoint of $\overline{AC}$ and D is the midpoint of $\overline{CE}$. Which of the following statements is necessarily true?

   I. C is the midpoint of $\overline{AE}$.

  II. C is the midpoint of $\overline{BD}$.

 III. The length of $\overline{BD}$ is half the length of $\overline{AE}$.

(A) Statement I only

(B) Statement II only

(C) Statement III only

(D) Statements I and III

(E) Statements I, II, and III

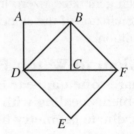

72. *ABCD* and *BFED* are both squares. If square *ABCD* has side 4, then *CF* =

(A) 2

(B) $2\sqrt{2}$

(C) 4

(D) $4\sqrt{2}$

(E) 8

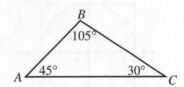

73. If *AB* from above equals $\sqrt{2}$, then the area of $\triangle ABC$ is

(A) $\dfrac{1}{2} + \dfrac{\sqrt{3}}{2}$

(B) $2\sqrt{2}$

(C) $1 + \sqrt{3}$

(D) $\dfrac{1}{2} + \dfrac{\sqrt{6}}{2}$

(E) $\dfrac{\sqrt{2}}{2} + \sqrt{3}$

74. The distance between points (3, 4) and (*a*, *b*) is 5. Point (*a*, *b*) could be any of the following EXCEPT

(A) (0, 0)

(B) (3, 1)

(C) (−2, 4)

(D) (3, 9)

(E) (6, 0)

75. If *x* > *y*, then point (*x*, *y*) can be in all of the following EXCEPT

(A) Quadrant I

(B) Quadrant II

(C) Quadrant III

(D) Quadrant IV

(E) the *x*-axis or *y*-axis

76. If the midpoint of $\overline{AB}$ is (0, 0), and the coordinates of point *A* are (*x*, *y*), then the coordinates of point *B* are

(A) (−*x*, −*y*)

(B) (−*x*, *y*)

(C) (*x*, −*y*)

(D) (*x*, *y*)

(E) None of the above

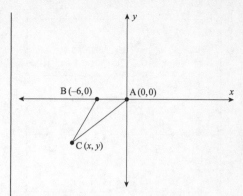

77. If the area of △*ABC* is 12, then the *y*-coordinate of *C* is

(A) −4

(B) 4

(C) −2

(D) 2

(E) It cannot be determined from the information given.

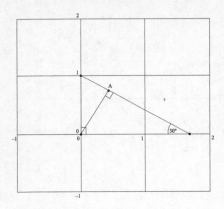

78. In the diagram above, the
x-coordinate of *A* is:

(A) $\dfrac{1}{4}$

(B) $\dfrac{1}{2}$

(C) $\dfrac{\sqrt{3}}{4}$

(D) $\dfrac{\sqrt{3}}{2}$

(E) $\dfrac{3}{4}$

79. A square is drawn inside a
circle in such a way that the
diagonals of the square pass
through the center of the
circle, and the vertices of the
square touch the circle's
edge. If the square has side
$a\sqrt{2}$, then the area of the
circle is

(A) $\dfrac{1}{4}\pi a^2$

(B) $\dfrac{1}{2}\pi a^2$

(C) πa^2

(D) $\sqrt{2}\pi a^2$

(E) $2\pi a^2$

80. Two lines tangent to the
same unit circle intersect at a
60° angle. How far is the
intersection point from the
center of the circle?

(A) 1

(B) $\dfrac{\sqrt{3}}{2}$

(C) $\sqrt{3}$

(D) 2

(E) $2\sqrt{3}$

The directions for grid-ins are on page 153.

81. What is the average degree measure of the angles of a triangle?

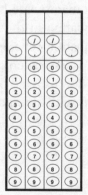

82. A line including the points (x, y) and $(3, 7)$ passes through the origin. What is the value of $\dfrac{y}{x}$?

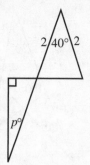

83. From the figure above, find p.

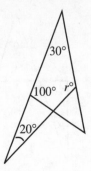

84. From the figure above, $r =$

85. If the distance between $(a, 3)$ and $(b, 9)$ is 10, then $|b - a| =$

Algebra

Algebra in a nutshell: I give you an equation with variables; you determine the value(s) of the variables. Algebraic problems rarely start out in the form $x = 5$, what is x? In fact, they often begin as English descriptions.

Linear Equalities

Terms and definitions

- **Constant:** A value that doesn't change, such as a number.

- **Variable:** A symbol, such as x, that can take on one or more values.

- **Equation or Equality:** A mathematical expression that includes an equals sign. As long as you manipulate both sides of the equation in the same way, the equation remains valid. There's one exception to this rule—don't divide by 0. You can end up with strange results like $0 = 1$.

Formulas and Guidelines

- **Isolate the variable:** To solve an algebraic equation with one variable, collect and isolate the variable on one side of the equation; then solve the expression on the other side of the equation. To isolate the variable, you can apply a few basic manipulations to both sides of an equation:

  1. Add, Subtract, Multiply, or Divide equal amounts from both sides of the equation.

  2. Raise both sides of the equation to the same power. Remember your special cases:

     i. **Square root:** $\frac{1}{2}$ **power**

     ii. **Squaring: 2nd power**

     iii. **Inverting: -1st power**

  3. Distribute a variable into or out of a sum (or subtraction), for example, $2x - 5x = (2 - 5)x = -3x$.

Problems to Watch For

- **Do not mistakenly invert the sum of two fractions. Inversion works only on single fractions.**

  Example:

  Solve for m in the equation: $\dfrac{1}{m} + \dfrac{1}{n} = \dfrac{1}{p}$.

  1. $np + mp = mn$ Multiply both sides by the common denominator mnp.

  2. $np = mn - mp$ Collect the m's on the same side equation by subtracting mp from both sides.

  3. $np = m(n - p)$ Distribute m.

  4. $\dfrac{np}{n-p} = m$ Divide both sides by $(n - p)$.

It would have been wrong to invert both sides of the equation and get $m + n = p$. The SAT tests whether you know this.

- **Always keep in mind what is being asked.** For example: In the previous problem, if you were asked to solve for $\dfrac{1}{m}$, the steps you would take to solve the problem would be much simpler.

- **Recognize that $a - b = -1(b - a)$.**

Example: Solve for w in the equation: $\dfrac{5}{w - 6} + \dfrac{7}{6 - w} = 2$

1. $\dfrac{5}{w - 6} + \dfrac{-7}{w - 6} = 2$ Multiply the numerator and denominator of the second fraction by -1. Remember: multiplying the numerator and denominator of a fraction by the same number does not change the value of the fraction.

2. $\dfrac{-2}{w - 6} = 2$ Add the two fractions, now that they have the same denominators.

3. $-2 = 2w - 12$ Multiply both sides of the equation by $(w - 6)$.

4. $10 = 2w$ Add 12 to both sides.

5. $5 = w$ Divide both sides by 2.

- **Solutions with fractions can have more than one form.** If you're confident of your answer, try altering its form.

Example: $2\dfrac{m}{a} - L = \dfrac{2m - aL}{a}$

- **To get rid of parentheses, apply the distributive rule for multiplication over addition.**

Example: Solve for y in the equation: $6(2y + 3) - 3(y + 1) = 3(y + 1) + 3$.

1. $12y + 18 - 3y - 3 = 3y + 3 + 3$ — Eliminate the parentheses by distribution.

2. $9y + 15 = 3y + 6$ — Collect like terms on both sides of the equation.

3. $6y = -9$ — Subtract $3y$ and 15 from both sides.

4. $y = \dfrac{-9}{6} = -\dfrac{3}{2} = -1.5$ — Divide both sides by 6 and simplify.

Linear Inequalities

When there were "quantitative comparison" questions on the SAT, inequalities were extremely important. In the new test, I expect there will be far fewer problems that involve them.

Terms and Definitions

- **Inequality:** Just like a linear equality except that the statement has either a "less than" sign (<) or a "greater than" sign (>) instead of an equal sign (=).

Formulas and Guidelines

Each of the following rules can be checked with actual numbers, so if you're unsure of a rule during the test, run a quick check; try a negative number, 0, a positive number, and a number between 0 and 1 to cover the major cases.

- **Adding or subtracting a number from both sides of an inequality, whether it is negative or positive, does not change the direction of the sign:** $x < y$ implies ($\Rightarrow$) $x + 5 < y + 5$.

- **Multiplying or dividing by a positive number does not change the direction of the inequality sign:** $x < y \Rightarrow 3x < 3y$.

- **Multiplying or dividing by a negative number changes the direction of the inequality sign:** $x < y \Rightarrow -4x > -4y$.

- **Taking the square roots of both sides of an inequality does not affect the direction of the inequality sign.** But, remember, you cannot take the square root of a negative number: $4 < 9$ and $2 < 3$.

- **The effects of squaring or inverting are indeterminate:**
$-3 < 2$ and $-\dfrac{1}{3} < \dfrac{1}{2}$, but
$2 < 3$ and $\dfrac{1}{2} > \dfrac{1}{3}$.

- **Transitivity: If $a < b$ and $b < c$, then $a < c$.** However, if $a < b$ and $a < c$, you know nothing about the relationship between b and c.

Problems to Watch For

- $p - r < p < p + r$ **for all positive r.**

- $x - y > 0$ **implies and is implied by ($\Leftrightarrow$) $x > y$.** Likewise, $x - y < 0 \Leftrightarrow x < y$.

Odds, Evens, and Remainders

Terms and Definitions

- **Remainder:** When y is divided by x, x divides y a certain whole number of times with some left over that is less than x; the leftover amount is the remainder. For example, when 13 is divided by 5, 5 divides 13 twice to get up to 10, with 3 left over. So 3 is the remainder.

- **Even number:** An integer that is evenly divisible by (leaves no remainder when divided by) 2. Even numbers always end in 0, 2, 4, 6, or 8.

- **Odd number:** An integer that is not evenly divisible by 2. When an odd number is divided by 2, the remainder is always 1. Odd numbers always end in 1, 3, 5, 7, or 9.

Formulas and Guidelines

- **The remainder equation:** If dividing y by x leaves a remainder r, then you can set up the equation $y = nx + r$, where n is some integer and r is the remainder. For example, 13 divided by 5 has remainder 3, so you can set up the equation: $13 = 5n + 3$. In this case, $n = 2$. When y is evenly divided by x, r is 0.

- **E = 2n:** Any even number, E, can be written as the product of 2 and some other number.

- **O = 2n + 1:** Any odd number, O, can be written O = 2n + 1 for some n.

- **2n is always even and 2n + 1 is always odd,** for any integer or expression, n.

• **Arithmetic with odds and evens (modular arithmetic):**

Multiplication & Division	Addition & Subtraction
E × E = E	E + E = E
E × O = E	E + O = O
O × O = O	O + O = E

If during the test you are unsure of one of these rules, take the examples of 0 and 1.

0 is even, and 1 is odd; so, for example, an odd plus an even (0 + 1) is odd, 1.

Problems to Watch For

• **If you can prove the six statements in the modular arithmetic table, you know enough to solve any SAT modular arithmetic problem.**

Example: To prove that O × O = O, let two odd numbers be $2m + 1$ and $2n + 1$.

$$O \times O = (2m + 1)(2n + 1)$$
$$= 4mn + 2m + 2n + 1$$
$$= 2(2mn + m + n) + 1$$
$$= 2(...) + 1$$
$$= \text{an odd number}$$

• **Concepts such as using something a certain number of times with an amount left over are a clue to you, as the problem solver, to try to apply the remainder equation.**

Example: Abby has a box of candy with fewer than 20 pieces of candy in it. If she splits the candy evenly among herself and 3 friends, there is 1 piece left over. If she splits the candy evenly among her 3 friends but excludes herself, there is still 1 piece left over. How many pieces of candy does Abby have?

1. Use the remainder equation twice, once with Abby and once without.

2. With Abby, pieces of candy $= 4n + 1$.

3. Without Abby, pieces of candy $= 3m + 1$.

4. The only number less than 20 that is divisible by both 3 and 4 is 12.

5. So, the number of pieces of candy is 13.

6. Now go back and check your answer: When 13 pieces of candy are split among 3 people, there is 1 left over, and when 13 pieces of candy are split among 4 people, there is 1 left over.

PRACTICE PROBLEMS IN ALGEBRA

Answers begin on page 346.

86. Solve for x in $\dfrac{2x}{3} + \dfrac{5}{6} = \dfrac{x}{6}$

(A) $\dfrac{5}{3}$

(B) -1

(C) $-\dfrac{5}{3}$

(D) 1

(E) -5

87. If $\dfrac{p+q+r}{3} = \dfrac{p+q}{2}$, then $r =$

(A) $q + p$

(B) $2p + 2q$

(C) $\dfrac{p+q}{2}$

(D) 1

(E) 3

88. If $a + b = 3$, then $a + b - 6 =$

(A) -3

(B) 0

(C) 3

(D) 6

(E) 1

89. If $a = b - c$ and $d = c - b$, what is the value of $d - a$ when $b = 4$ and $c = -4$?

(A) 0

(B) 8

(C) -8

(D) 16

(E) -16

90. Solve for v if $\dfrac{3}{u} + \dfrac{4}{v} = 1$

(A) $\dfrac{4u}{u-3}$

(B) $\dfrac{12-4u}{3}$

(C) $7 - u$

(D) $\dfrac{1-4u}{3}$

(E) $\dfrac{3u}{u-4}$

91. If $\dfrac{1}{x} > \dfrac{1}{5}$, then which of the following most accurately describes x?

(A) $x < 5$

(B) $x > 5$

(C) $x \leq 5$

(D) $0 < x < 5$

(E) $0 \leq x \leq 5$

92. If $y \geq 4$, which of the following has the least value?

(A) $\dfrac{4}{y+1}$

(B) $\dfrac{4}{y-1}$

(C) $\dfrac{4}{y}$

(D) $\dfrac{y}{4}$

(E) $\dfrac{y+1}{4}$

93. If $a > b > 0$, then which of the following is *always* true?

(A) $\dfrac{b^2}{a^2} > \dfrac{b}{a}$

(B) $\dfrac{a}{b} > \dfrac{a^2}{b^2}$

(C) $\dfrac{b^2}{a^2} > 1$

(D) $\dfrac{b^2}{a^2} > \dfrac{a^2}{b^2}$

(E) $\dfrac{a^2}{b^2} > \dfrac{a}{b}$

94. If $|2x-1| > 3$, then which of the following could not be a value of x?

(A) 5

(B) 3

(C) -3.5

(D) -1

(E) 24

95. If p and q are both positive, and $q < p$, which of the following is false.

(A) $-4q > -4p$

(B) $\dfrac{q}{2} < \dfrac{p}{2}$

(C) $5 - q < 5 - p$

(D) $\dfrac{-p}{3} < \dfrac{-q}{3}$

(E) $\dfrac{1}{q} > \dfrac{1}{p}$

The directions for grid-ins are on page 153.

96. Solve for y:

$$4(y-3)+1 = 2(y+4)-3$$

97. Solve for x:

$$4x - 6\left(3 - \frac{1}{2}x\right) = 10$$

98. Grid-in a value of x that makes the following statement true:

$$\frac{1}{4} < (1 - x)^2 < 1.$$

99. What is the average of the remainders when 5 consecutive positive integers are divided by 5?

100. Grid-in a number that has remainder 2 when divided by 3, 4, 5, 6, 7, 8, or 10.

More Algebra

This section reviews polynomial arithmetic, quadratic equations, polynomial equations, and two equations with two unknowns.

Polynomial Arithmetic

Terms and Definitions

- **Monomial or Term:** A product, or quotient of numbers and variables, for example, $3x^2y$.

- **Polynomial:** Two or more monomials that are added or subtracted, for example, $3x^2y + 2z$.

- **Coefficient:** A multiplier that precedes a variable. In the expression $3x^2$, 3 is the coefficient.

- **Exponent(s):** The power to which variables in the monomial are raised. In the expression $3x^2y$, there are two exponents, 2 for x and 1 for y, although the 1 is implicit (not written).

Formulas and Guidelines

- **Distributive property:** $a(b + c) = ab + bc$: The distributive law allows you to convert parenthetical expressions to polynomials.

- **Addition and subtraction of polynomials:** When you add two polynomials, consider each of their monomials independently and then add only monomials whose variables are the same, including the power to which they are raised—you can't combine x and x^2. For example, $(2xy + 3x + 3x^2) + (3xy + 4y) = 5xy + 3x + 4y + 3x^2$. There is no way to further simplify this expression.

- **Multiplication of polynomials:** From the distributive property above, you already know how to multiply a monomial by a binomial, $2x(z + w) = 2xz + 2xw$. If you are multiplying a binomial by a binomial, do two distributions:

$$(a + b)(c + d) = (a + b)c + (a + b)d$$
$$= ac + bc + ad + bd$$

- **FOIL (First-Outer-Inner-Last):** If you are multiplying two binomials (a polynomial with two monomials), multiply the first monomial of each binomial together, next the outer two, then the inner two, and finally the last two.

Example: Expand the product $(3a + b)(c - d)$.

1. Write the polynomials side by side and FOIL.

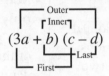

2. Add the partial products, making sure to treat d as a negative: $3ac + (-3ad) + bc + (-bd)$.

3. Get rid of the parentheses and change the signs appropriately. Notice that there are no similar terms; so, you cannot combine any terms: $3ac - 3ad + bc - bd$.

Problems to Watch For

- **Keep the negatives and positives straight when you're doing polynomial math.** It is easy to look at $(x - 5)$ and forget to treat the 5 as negative because it follows a subtraction sign.

- **Example:** Given $x^2 + (x - 5)(3 - x) = 0$, solve for x.

  $x^2 + (3x - x^2 - 15 + 5x) = 0$ FOIL the polynomials.

  $(x^2 - x^2) + (3x + 5x) - 15 = 0$ Collect like terms.

  $8x - 15 = 0$ Simplify.

  $x = \dfrac{15}{8}$ Do the arithmetic.

- **Memorize the following four special cases.** They will tip you off to the short way of doing a problem.

  1. $x^2 - a^2 = (x - a)(x + a)$
  2. $(x + a)^2 = x^2 + 2ax + a^2$
  3. $(x - a)^2 = x^2 - 2ax + a^2$
  4. $(x - a)(x - b) = x^2 - (a + b)x + ab$

  Example: What is $\dfrac{m^2 - n^2}{m + n}$ when $m = 17$ and $n = 15$?

  1. Factor $m^2 - n^2$ into $(m - n)(m + n)$ and rewrite the expression as $\dfrac{(m - n)(m + n)}{m + n}$

2. Since $m + n \neq 0$, you can divide top and bottom by $m + n$, to get $(m - n)$.

3. $m - n = 17 - 15 = 2$

It would have been tedious and time-consuming if you did not recognize the common factors in the fraction and started by squaring 17 and 15.

Polynomial and Quadratic Equations

When you solve linear equations, your goal is to get the unknown on one side of the equation and everything else on the other. This is not possible in an equation such as $x^2 - 4x + 1 = -2$, and in general cannot happen when a variable is raised to a power and then added to itself. Instead, you must factor the polynomial into its linear (not raised to any power) constituents.

Terms and Definitions

- Quadratic Expression: A polynomial expression with one variable, x, of the form $ax^2 + bx + c$, where a, b, and c are constants.
- **Factor or root of a polynomial:** Just as 2 and 4 are factors of 8 because $2 \times 4 = 8$, $(x + 1)$ and $(x - 1)$ are factors of $(x^2 - 1)$ because $(x + 1)(x - 1) = (x^2 - 1)$.

Formulas and Guidelines

- **Zero product rule:** If $ab = 0$, then $a = 0$ or $b = 0$. Applying this to polynomials, if $(x - a)(x - b) = 0$, then $x = a$, or $x = b$.

- **Quadratic Formula:** A quadratic expression of the form $ax^2 + bx + c$, can be factored into:

$$\left(x - \frac{-b - \sqrt{b^2 - 4ac}}{2a} \right) \times$$
$$\left(x - \frac{-b + \sqrt{b^2 - 4ac}}{2a} \right)$$

- **Solving a polynomial equation:**

  1. Get all of the monomials on one side of the equation, and leave a 0 on the other.

  2. Factor the polynomial so you are left with the product of two linear expressions equaling zero.

  3. Using the zero product rule, deduce that one of the

linear expressions must equal 0.

Example: Given $x^2 - 4x + 1 = -2$, solve for x.

1. Collect all of the terms on the left, leaving 0 on the right. This is necessary; otherwise, you won't be able to apply the zero product rule: $x^2 - 4x + 3 = 0$.

2. Factor the polynomial: $(x - 3)(x - 1) = 0$.

3. Using the zero product rule, you know that either $(x - 3) = 0$ or $(x - 1) = 0$.

4. Solving these two linear equations, you get $x = 3$ or $x = 1$.

• **Check your answers!** When you're solving an equation, if you stick your answers back into the original equation it should become a true statement and not something like $4 = 0$.

Problem to Watch For

• **Factoring polynomials:** Remember that $(x - a)(x - b) = x^2 - (a + b) x + ab$. What you know about multiplication with positive and negative numbers can help you factor polynomials. Notice that:

1. The product of the constants a and b in the monomials is the constant in the polynomial.

2. The sum of the constants in the monomials is the opposite (negative) of the coefficient of the first-order term (the term with the variable raised to the first power).

For example, if you were asked to factor $x^2 + 2x - 24$, you would know that the product of the constants in the monomials is -24, and their sum is -2. The factors of -24 are:

-1 and 24	-6 and 4
-2 and 12	-8 and 3
-3 and 8	-12 and 2
-4 and 6	-24 and 1

The only pair that add to -2 are -6 and 4, so $x^2 + 2x - 24 = [x - (-6)](x - 4) = (x + 6)(x - 4)$.

Two Equations with Two Unknowns

Earlier, we reviewed how to solve linear equations. This type of problem is also called one equation (one equal sign) with one unknown (one variable). An extension of this is two equations with two unknowns. There are two methods for solving this type of problem. Sometimes one is easier than the other, but both work all of the time.

Formulas and Guidelines

• **Combination method of solving two equations with two unknowns.** This method works best when the coefficient of one of the unknowns is the same in the two equations.

1. Start with two equations with two unknowns, for example:
$3x + 2y = 33$ and
$4x = 11 + y.$

2. Write the two equations, one on top of the other:
$3x + 2y = 33$
$4x = 11 + y$

3. Manipulate the equations so terms with the same variables line up:
$3x + 2y = 33$
$4x - y = 11$

4. Manipulate the equations so that the coefficients in front of one of the variables are the same or opposite in the two equations. In this example, multiply both sides of the second equation by 2 so that the coefficients in front of y are 2 and -2:
$3x + 2y = 33$
$8x - 2y = 22$

5. If the matching coefficients are opposites, as they are here (-2 and 2), then add the two equations to get a third: $11x + 0y = 55$. If the coefficients were the same instead of opposites you would have subtracted the two equations. *The goal is to get one of the coefficients to become 0.*

6. Now you have one equation with one remaining variable which can be solved straightforwardly. In this case, $x = \dfrac{55}{11} = 5.$

7. But you've only solved half the problem. Now go back and substitute 5 for x in either of the original equations and solve.

For example:

$3(5) + 2y = 33$
$2y = 33 - 15$
$y = \dfrac{18}{2} = 9$

8. You can check your work by plugging the values you found for x and y into the

second equation and confirming it's correct.

- **Substitution method of solving two equations with two unknowns.** This method works best when the coefficient in front of one of the unknowns is 1 or −1.

1. Start with two equations. Again, take the example:
   $$3x + 2y = 33$$
   $$4x = 11 + y$$

2. Solve for one of the variables in terms of the other. Manipulating the second equation you can find y as a function of x:
   $y = 4x - 11$.

3. For every occurrence of y, substitute $4x - 11$ into the first equation:
   $$3x + 2(4x - 11) = 33$$

4. You've replaced all of the y's with x's; so the problem is reduced to one equation with one unknown. In the example, you can solve for x: $3x + 2(4x - 11) = 33$
   $$3x + 8x - 22 = 33$$
   $$11x = 55$$
   $$x = 5$$

5. Again, you substitute the value for x back into either equation to find $y = 9$.

Problem to Watch For

- **When you have two equations and two unknowns and the unknowns are multiplied together, it is often easier and faster to enumerate the factors of their product and guess the values of the unknowns than to solve the problem explicitly.**

Example: The product of two positive numbers is 21 and their difference is 20. What is the greater number?

1. Set up the two equations:
   $$xy = 21$$
   $$x - y = 20$$

2. By factoring 21 you can guess that x and y are either 1 and 21, or 3 and 7.

3. You can quickly compute that $21 - 1 = 20$, so the greater number must be 21.

MORE PRACTICE PROBLEMS IN ALGEBRA

Answers begin on page 349.

101. If $7x - 4y = 7$ and $x = \dfrac{3}{7}y$, then $y =$

(A) -7

(B) -5

(C) -3

(D) 5

(E) 7

102. If $x^2 + y^2 = 25$ and $xy = -5$, then $(x - y)^2 =$

(A) 15

(B) 20

(C) 25

(D) 30

(E) 35

103. If $x + y = 4$, then $x - (5 - y) =$

(A) -1

(B) $\dfrac{5}{9}$

(C) 1

(D) $\dfrac{9}{5}$

(E) 39

104. $y = \dfrac{5}{9}x + 8$. What is y when $y = x$?

(A) 2

(B) $\dfrac{9}{5}$

(C) $\dfrac{5}{9}$

(D) 18

(E) Cannot be determined

105. If $3b - 6 = 2c$ and $6b - 4c = 12$, what is b?

(A) 2

(B) 3

(C) 4

(D) 6

(E) Cannot be determined

106. Asked to solve $\dfrac{x^2-8x+16}{x^2-16}=1$, Albert did the following:

(1) $\dfrac{x^2-8x+16}{x^2-16}=1$ (1) The problem as given.

(2) $\dfrac{(x-4)(x-4)}{(x-4)(x+4)}=1$ (2) Factor the numerator and denominator.

(3) $\dfrac{x-4}{x+4}=1$ (3) Divide $(x-4)$ from the numerator and denominator.

(4) $x-4=x+4$ (4) Multiply both sides of the equation by $(x+4)$.

(5) $-4=4$ (5) Subtract x from both sides of the equation.

In which step did Albert make an error?

(A) 1 − The original problem is ill formed.

(B) 2

(C) 3

(D) 4

(E) 5

107. If $x-y=5$ and $y-x=-5$, what is y?

(A) −5

(B) −1

(C) 1

(D) 5

(E) Cannot be determined

108. $(x+a)(a-x)=$

(A) x^2-a^2

(B) $x^2-2ax+a^2$

(C) a^2-x^2

(D) $-x^2+2ax-a^2$

(E) $-x^2-a^2$

109. If $y = 3x + 6$ and
$x = 3y + 6$, what is y?

(A) -3

(B) -1

(C) 1

(D) 3

(E) Cannot be determined

110. Solve for x in the equation
$(x + 4)^2 - (x - 4)^2 = 16$.

(A) -4

(B) -2

(C) -1

(D) 0

(E) 1

The directions for grid-ins are on page 153.

111. If $a = 96$ and $b = 4$, then
$a^2 - b^2 =$

112. What is a non-negative
solution to $y^4 = 18y^2 - 81$?

113. What is a solution to
$$y - 8 + \frac{15}{y} = 0?$$

114. The difference of the squares of two numbers is 9. The difference of the two numbers is 1. What is their sum?

115. What is the coefficient of x^2 in the product of $(3x^2 + 2x + 6)$ and $(4x^2 + x + 9)$?

Word Problems and Functions

Word Problems

There is no one type of word problem. Word problems can involve concepts from arithmetic to probability. The common thread in all word problems is that first you generate the equation, then you solve the problem. As you are setting up the equation, remember that every equation needs an equals sign. Once you have solved your equation, go back and check the answer. Answers to word problems are usually relatively quick and easy to check.

Four Steps to Solving a Word Problem:

1. Identify what you are solving for and assign it a mnemonic variable name.

2. One phrase at a time, set up the equation(s) that model(s) the problem.

3. Solve the equation(s).

4. Check your answer.

Problems to Watch For

- **The term "increased by" indicates that you should keep the original amount and add an additional amount. Don't forget to keep the original amount.**

Example: Carmen's company had a profit of $900 during its first month of operation. If its profits increased by $66\frac{2}{3}\%$ during the second month of operation, what are its second-month profits in dollars?

1. You are solving for second-month profits.

2. Set up the equation one phrase at a time, recalling that

$$66\frac{2}{3}\% = \frac{2}{3}.$$

3. The profits of the first month are 900.

4. The profits of the second month are:

$$900 \underset{+}{\overset{\text{increased by}}{}} \frac{2}{3}(900).$$

5. Solve: $900 + \frac{2}{3}(900) =$

$900 + 600 = 1,500.$

6. Check your results: Is 1,500 two thirds more than 900? Yes. If you had mistakenly omitted the original $900, your answer would be $600, which is clearly not an increase.

- **One person's age when another person is born is the difference in their ages.**

- **When solving "age problems," give each person his or her own variable.**

Example: A father is four times as old as his daughter. Ten years ago he was only twice as old as his daughter will be in five years. How old was the father when his daughter was born?

1. Name the variables:
   a. **F** for the father's age.
   b. **D** for the daughter's age.
   c. Because the question doesn't ask for *F* or *D*, call the answer *A*.

2. Set up the equations phrase by phrase:

F	A father
$F =$	is
$F = 4D$	four times as old as his daughter.
$F - 10$	Ten years ago he
$F - 10 =$	was only
$F - 10 = 2 (\ldots)$	twice
$F - 10 = 2(D + 5)$	as old as his daughter will be in five years.
$A = F - D$	How old was the father when his daughter was born?

3. Solve the two equations with two unknowns:

$$F = 4D$$
$$F - 10 = 2(D + 5)$$

$4D - 10 = 2(D+5)$	Substitute $4D$ for F in the second equation.
$4D - 2D = 10 + 10$	Distribute the 2 over $(D + 5)$ and collect the D's on one side of the equation.
$D = 10$	Solve for D.
$F = 4D = 40$	Solve for F.
$A = F - D$	Solve for the answer, A.
$\quad = 40 - 10$	
$\quad = 30$	

4. Check your answer:
   ✓ 40 is four times 10;
   ✓ Ten years ago the father was 30, which is twice what the daughter will be in 5 years, 15.

All of the constraints for the problem have been met!

- **Forms of the verb "to be" indicate equality.** In step 2 of the previous example, circle each instance of the verb "to be" (e.g., "is," "was," "will be") and notice how it corresponds to the insertion of an equal sign into the equations.

- **When one person gives something to another, the first person's total goes down *and* the other person's total goes up.**

   Example: Chris and Andrea have $100 together. If Chris gives Andrea $10, she will have $20 more than he will. How much money did Chris start with?

   1. Name the variables:
      a. C: You are asked to solve for the amount Chris started with.
      b. A: The amount Andrea started with.

   2. Set up the equations:

$C + A = 100$	Chris and Andrea have $100 together.
$(A + 10) - (C - 10) = 20$	If Chris gives Andrea $10, she will have $20 more than he will.

   3. Solve the equations:

$A - C = 0$, or $C = A$	Subtract 20 from both sides of the second equation.
$C + C = 100$	Substitute C for A in the first equation.
$C = 50$	Solve for C.

   4. Check your answer:
      ✓ Chris and Andrea each have $50, which sums to $100.
      ✓ If Chris gives Andrea $10, he will have $40 and she will have $60, which is $20 more than his $40.

- **If a person uses $\dfrac{a}{b}$ of something, then $\dfrac{b - a}{b}$ is left over.** Notice that these two fractions added together equal 1. What is used plus what is left over equals the whole. Keep track of whether you want to know how much was used or how much is left over.

Example: Naomi spends $\frac{1}{4}$ of her salary on rent and $\frac{1}{3}$ of what's left over on food. If Naomi's monthly salary is $1,600, how much does she have left over after she pays for rent and food?

1. What's left over after Naomi pays her rent is
$(1 - \frac{1}{4})(1600).$

2. One third of that goes to food; so, what is left over is
$\left(\frac{2}{3}\right)\left(\frac{3}{4}\right)1600.$

3. Simplifying before doing the arithmetic leaves $\frac{1}{2}(1600).$

4. $800 is left over after Naomi pays for food and rent.

Functions

A function is an expression or rule that takes one or more values and generates a new value. Sometimes I imagine an assembly line or food processor—pour the ingredients in and out pops . . . the answer. Functions have names just like variables, $f(x) = x^2$ is a function, f, that takes one value, x, and returns its square. $g(x, y) = x^y$ is a function, g, that takes two values and returns the first raised to the second. Any set of inputs must return exactly one value; however, several different inputs can return the same value. People who work with computers refer to x and y as the **inputs** to the function and the value of the function as its **output** or **return value.** The function is said to **map** its inputs to its outputs.

Terms and Definitions

- **Domain:** The values that the inputs to a function can have. For example, the domain of $f(x) = \sqrt{x}$ is the set of non-negative real numbers.
- **Range:** The values that a function can return. If the domain of $f(x) = x^2$ is the set of integers, then its range is the set of non-negative integers.
- **Polynomial function:** A function whose value can be represented as a polynomial expression. For example, $f(x) = 3x^3 + 2x + 6$. Remember that $6 = 6x^0$ and $2x = 2x^1$.
- **Linear function:** A polynomial function whose highest power is 1. For example, $f(x) = 3x + 2$. The graph of a linear function is a line.
- **Quadratic function:** A polynomial function whose highest power is 2, generally of the form $y = ax^2 + bx + c$.

- **Composite function:** Composing two functions is running them together, and is written $f(x) \circ g(x)$. Functions can be thought of as variables whose values are expressions. Like variables, you can substitute and combine them. If $f(x) = x^2$ and $g(x) = 2x$, then $f(x) \circ g(x) = f(g(x)) = f(2x) = (2x)^2 = 4x^2$. Two important things to remember about composite functions:

  (A) $f(x) \circ g(x)$ does not necessarily equal $g(x) \circ f(x)$. This is the case with the previous example.

  (B) The x's in the two function specifications are different—they are just place holders. Writing $f(x) = 2x$ is no different than writing $f(y) = 2y$.

- **Inverse Function:** If f(x) is a function that **maps** inputs to output, then $f^{-1}(x)$ is the inverse of $f(x)$ if it maps the outputs back to inputs. For example, the inverse of $f(x) = 2x$ is $f^{-1}(x) = \frac{1}{2}x$. Not every function has an inverse.

- **Operator:** A symbol that specifies a function, such as + or ÷. Any symbol that maps inputs to outputs can be an operator. For example, |a| is an operator called absolute value that is defined by the rule, "If $a \geq 0$ return a; otherwise, return $-a$."

- **Model:** A function that describes something occurring in the real world. For example, if t is the time in seconds, then $f(t) = -32t^2 + 1000$ gives the height above ground a penny is after being dropped from a building 1,000 feet high. For this model, we would also need to specify that the range of $f(t)$ is $f(t) \geq 0$, i.e., the penny stops when it hits the ground.

Formula and Guideline

- **Don't be distracted by strange symbols.** Muddle through the problem, carefully following directions without being distracted by the strange symbols.

  Example:

  The symbol $\begin{vmatrix} p & q \\ r & s \end{vmatrix}$ means $ps - rq$. What is the value of $\begin{vmatrix} 2 & 3 \\ 5 & 4 \end{vmatrix}$?

  $$\begin{vmatrix} 2 & 3 \\ 5 & 4 \end{vmatrix} = \overset{p}{(2} \times \overset{s}{4)} - \overset{r}{(5} \times \overset{q}{3)}$$
  $$= 8 - 15 = -7$$

PRACTICE PROBLEMS IN WORD PROBLEMS AND FUNCTIONS

Answers begin on page 350.

116. The inverse of
$f(x) = 2x + 2$ is

(A) $f^{-1}(x) = \dfrac{1}{2}x - \dfrac{1}{2}$

(B) $f^{-1}(x) = x - \dfrac{1}{2}$

(C) $f^{-1}(x) = \dfrac{1}{2}x - 1$

(D) $f^{-1}(x) = x - 1$

(E) $f^{-1}(x) = \dfrac{1}{2}x - 2$

117. Tom has a brother one third his age and a sister three times his age. If the combined age of all three children is five less than twice the oldest, how old is Tom?

(A) 3

(B) 6

(C) 9

(D) 1

(E) 12

118. For all positive integers, if $(p, q) \otimes (x, y) = py - qx$, then $(4, 6) \otimes (8, 2) =$

(A) -40

(B) 56

(C) 40

(D) 44

(E) 20

119. If $f(x) = (x - 1)^2$, then $f\left(\dfrac{3}{4}\right) =$

(A) $-\dfrac{1}{16}$

(B) $\dfrac{1}{16}$

(C) $-\dfrac{49}{16}$

(D) $\dfrac{49}{16}$

(E) None of the above

120. If $x \otimes y = y^2 - 2x^2$, then $2 \otimes (-3) =$

(A) -7

(B) -1

(C) 1

(D) 5

(E) None of the above

121. If $f(x) = 3x$ and $g(x) = \dfrac{1}{3}x$, then $f(x) \circ g(x) =$

(A) 1

(B) x

(C) $3x$

(D) $\dfrac{1}{3}x$

(E) x^2

122. Let $[x]$ denote the greatest integer less than or equal to x. For example, $\lceil 3.4 \rceil = 3$ and $\lceil -1 \rceil = -1$. What is the value of $\lceil -2.3 \rceil + \lceil 2.3 \rceil$?

(A) 0

(B) -1

(C) 1

(D) 2

(E) 4.6

123. If $a \otimes b = a^2 b^3$, then $3 \otimes (-2) =$

(A) -6

(B) 24

(C) -24

(D) 72

(E) -72

124. The operator $\otimes$ is defined by the equation: $x \otimes y = \dfrac{x+y}{xy}$ $(xy \neq 0)$.

I. $a \otimes b = b \otimes a$

II. $(a \otimes b) \otimes c = a \otimes (b \otimes c)$

III. $a \otimes (b + c) = (a \otimes b) + (a \otimes c)$

Of the three properties listed, the ones that are true for all non-zero a, b, and c are:

(A) I only

(B) I and II

(C) II and III

(D) I and III

(E) I, II, and III

125. Which of the following values is NOT in the range of $g(x) = \dfrac{x^2 - 6x + 8}{x - 2}$?

(A) -4

(B) -2

(C) 0

(D) 2

(E) 4

The directions for grid-ins are on page 153.

126. If $f(y) = (y + 1)^2 - (y - 1)^2 + 1$, what is the value of $f(3)$?

127. If $g(p, q) = \left(\dfrac{p - 1}{q + 1}\right)^2$, then what is $g\left(\dfrac{3}{2}, \dfrac{2}{3}\right)$?

128. One quarter of the students at a high school take algebra. One fifth of the students take geometry. The remaining 110 students do not take any math. How many students are there at the school?

129. A man goes to a bank with $4.00 and asks for change. He is given an equal number of nickels, dimes, and quarters. How many of each is he given?

130. If $g(z) = \dfrac{z}{4}$, for what value of z does $g(z) = 3$?

Algebraic Applications

Sequences and Growth

Terms and Definitions

- **Sequence:** An ordered list of objects or numbers.

- **Repeating sequence:** A sequence that can be characterized by a few elements that are repeated in a given order. For example, a decoration is made by hanging colored streamers from a rope. The colors form the pattern red, white, blue, red, white, blue. The colors form a repeating sequence.

- **Consecutive integers:** A sequence of integers, such as 3, 4, and 5, without gaps.

- **Consecutive even integers:** A sequence of even integers, such as -6, -4, -2, and 0.

- **Consecutive odd integers:** A sequence of odd integers, such as -1, 1, 3, and 5.

- **Arithmetic sequence:** A sequence formed by adding a constant value to an element to generate the next element. The nth element is given by the expression $c + kn$, where c is the starting value and k is the amount to be added at each step. For example, 4, 9, 14, 19, 24 ... is an arithmetic sequence that increases by 5 at each step. The nth element is given by $4 + 5n$, where 4 is called the 0th element.

- **Geometric sequence (exponential growth):** A sequence formed by multiplying each element by a constant value to get the next element. The nth element is given by the expression ck^n. For example, $1, \dfrac{1}{2}, \dfrac{1}{4}, \dfrac{1}{8}, ...$ is a geometric sequence that grows by $\dfrac{1}{2}$ at each step. The nth element is given by

$(1)\left(\dfrac{1}{2}\right)^n$, where 1 is called the 0th element.

Formulas and Guidelines

- **Representing consecutive integers:** When a problem refers to unknown consecutive integers, let the smallest one be x, the next one be $x + 1$, and so on.

- **Representing consecutive odd or even integers:** When a problem refers to unknown consecutive even or odd integers, let the smallest one be x, the next one be $x + 2$, the next be $x + 4$, and so on. Notice that you use $x + 2$ for both even and odd integers.

- **n^{th} element rule for repeating sequences:** In a repeating sequence with n elements in the pattern, every element that occupies a position divisible by n is the same as the nth element. For example, given a decoration made by hanging colored streamers from a rope in the pattern red, white, blue, red, white, blue, ...there are 3 colors in the base pattern, so every flag that occupies a position divisible by 3 is blue.

To solve a problem that asks you to find the nth object in a repeating sequence:

1. Count the number of elements in the pattern.

2. Find a number near n that is divisible by the number of elements in the pattern—you know what element that will be from the nth element rule.

3. Count off from the known element to the one you are asked to find.

Example: Determine the color of the 100th flag in the aforementioned streamer.

1. There are 3 elements, and the 3rd element is blue.

2. 102 is divisible by 3 (because $1 + 0 + 2 = 3$), so the 102nd streamer must be blue.

3. Counting backward, the 101st is white, and the 100th is red.

Problems to Watch For

- **If you are comfortable with keeping the meaning of your variables straight during a long problem, it is often easier to let the middle number in a sequence be a variable, say x, and the numbers around it be $x - 1$, $x + 1$, $x - 2$, $x + 2$,...**

Example: The sum of 3 consecutive odd numbers is 33. What is the greatest number?

1. Call the middle number m, the one less than it $m - 2$, and the one greater than it $m + 2$.

2. Setting up the equation with m as the middle number, you get:
   $(m - 2) + m + (m + 2) = 33$.

3. Simplifying, $3m = 33$, or $m = 11$.

4. Go back and find the greatest number, $m + 2$:
   $m + 2 = 11 + 2 = 13$.

- **If you are told that the difference between consecutive numbers in a sequence is constant, you should usually start the problem by determining the constant difference.**

Example: The difference between consecutive numbers in the sequence 3, a, b, and 24 is constant. Find b.

1. It takes 3 steps to get from 3 to 24, and the difference between 3 and 24 is 21, so each step must be 7 long.

2. a is one step after 3, so $a = 3 + 7 = 10$.

3. b is one step after a, so $b = a + 7 = 10 + 7 = 17$.

4. Test the solution: The differences between 3 and 10, 10 and 17, and 17 and 24 are all 7, so you have satisfied the conditions placed by the problem.

- **Doubling or halving every n hours.** When something doubles every k hours, the expression for modeling its value is $y = c2^{\frac{t}{k}}$, where t is the time in hours. Plug in some values: When t is 0, $y = c$. When t is k, $y = 2c$, and when t is $2k$, $y = 4c$. Likewise when something halves every k years, its value can be modeled

$$f(x) = y = c\left(\frac{1}{2}\right)^{\frac{t}{k}}$$

Rates
Terms and Definitions

- **Rate** = $\dfrac{\text{Distance}}{\text{Time}}$: For example, miles per hour or dollars per hour.

- **Distance = Rate × Time**

- **Time** = $\dfrac{\text{Distance}}{\text{Rate}}$

> Although we often talk about *distance* and *time* in rate formulas, in fact rates can be between **any** two units. For example, a telemarketer may be paid at a rate of x dollars per call.

- **Unit:** A standard against which something is being measured. For example, a salary could be 8 dollars per hour, 8 cents per hour, or 8 dollars per minute. Each one is very different.

- **Unit Fraction:** In this case, "Unit" means one. Multiplying by 1 doesn't change the value of a fraction. For example, 12 inches = 1 foot, so $\dfrac{12\text{ inches}}{1\text{ foot}} = \dfrac{1\text{ foot}}{12\text{ inches}}$. To convert 36 inches to feet, multiply by 1:

$$36\text{ inches} \times \dfrac{1\text{ foot}}{12\text{ inches}} = 3\text{ feet.}$$

The inches cancel just like a factor.

Formulas and Guidelines

- **Speed** is a type of rate where the amount is a distance. For example, we talk about miles per hour, $\dfrac{\text{miles}}{\text{hours}}$.

- **Treat speeds as fractions.**

Example: A plane travels x miles during the first 2 hours of a trip and y miles during the last 3 hours of the trip. What was the plane's average speed over the entire trip?

1. The amount (number of miles) the plane covered was $x + y$ miles.

2. The total time it took the plane to cover the distance was $2 + 3 = 5$ hours.

3. The plane's average speed (rate of motion) was $\dfrac{x + y\text{ miles}}{5\text{ hours}}$ or $\dfrac{x + y}{5}$ miles per hour.

Problems to Watch For

- **Rates can involve any ratio of units.** Although we're accustomed to speeds (miles per hour) and pay rates (dollars per hour), it's just as valid for the denominator to be gallons of gasoline as in miles-per-gallon.

- **When units are confusing— should you multiply or divide—include them in the fraction.** Then set up the expression so that you end up with the units you want.

  Example: If the cost of one gallon of gasoline goes up by 5¢, how much extra per year, in dollars, would it cost a driver who averages 12 miles per day in a car that gets 22 miles per gallon?

  1. Consider what you know:
     - 5 cents per gallon extra
     - 12 miles per day
     - 22 miles per gallon

  2. Identify what you want to know: x dollars per year

  3. Set up the expression so that you end up with dollars per year. Choose to multiply or divide so that the units cancel one another:

$$\frac{5 \text{ cents}}{\text{gallon}} \div \frac{22 \text{ miles}}{\text{gallon}} \times \frac{12 \text{ miles}}{\text{day}}$$

$$= \frac{5 \times 12 \text{ cents gallons miles}}{22 \text{ gallons miles days}}$$

$$= \frac{60 \text{ cents}}{11 \text{ day}}$$

4. Multiply by unit fractions to convert cents to dollars and days to years, again choosing to divide or multiply so that the units cancel each other out.

$$\frac{30 \text{ cents}}{11 \text{ day}}$$

$$= \frac{30 \text{ cents}}{11 \text{ day}} \times \frac{365 \text{ days}}{\text{year}} \div \frac{100 \text{ cents}}{\text{dollar}}$$

$$= \frac{30 \times 365}{11 \times 100} \frac{\text{cents days dollar}}{\text{day year cents}}$$

$$= 9.95 \frac{\text{dollars}}{\text{year}}$$

- **When two people can do a task at different rates and you want to know how long it takes them working together, let t be the amount of time they spend, add the part of the task accomplished by each person after time t, and set the sum equal to 1 complete task.**

Example: Ami can paint a room in 4 hours and Joyce can paint the same room in 6 hours. How long would it take them if they worked together?

$$\frac{1 \text{ room}}{4 \text{ hours}} \times t \text{ hours} + \frac{1 \text{ room}}{6 \text{ hours}} \times t \text{ hours} = 1 \text{ room}$$

Set up the equation. Notice how the fractions are set up so the units cancel each other out.

$$t = \frac{24}{10} = 2.4$$

Solve for t. Go back and consider whether this answer makes sense. Their average is roughly one room in five hours and working together they should halve that.

Probability and Statistics

Terms and Definitions

• **Probability of an event P(x): The probability of an event is the number of the times the event can happen divided by the number of times any event can happen.** This is analogous to the part-whole relationship that a fraction represents. For example, if there are 2 blue marbles and 4 red marbles in a bag, then the chance of reaching in and randomly choosing a blue marble is $\frac{2}{6}$, 2 blue marbles divided by 6 marbles total.

• **The probability that two independent events will occur is the product of their individual probabilities (not the sum).** For example, using the same bag of 2 blue marbles and 4 red marbles, the chance of pulling out both blue marbles in succession is $\frac{2}{6} \times \frac{1}{5} = \frac{1}{15}$. Once a blue marble has been selected with probability $\frac{2}{6}$, five marbles remain, one of which is blue. Selecting it occurs with probability $\frac{1}{5}$.

• **Geometric Probability:** The probability of randomly selecting a point in a region of a geometric figure. For example, the probability of selecting a "red point" in a red-black checkerboard is $\frac{1}{2}$ (or 50% or .5).

- **Arithmetic Mean:** A synonym for "average." The arithmetic mean of {0, 1, 1, 0, 0, 0, 1, 3, 8, 6} is 2.

- **Median:** A value for which half the elements are greater and half the elements are less than the value The median of {0, 1, 1, 0, 0, 0, 1, 3, 8, 6} is 1.

- **Mode:** The most commonly occurring value in a set. The mode of {0, 1, 1, 0, 0, 0, 1, 3, 8, 6} is 0.

Formulas and Guidelines

- **Average = Sum ÷ Number of terms**
- **Sum = Number of terms × Average**
- **Number of terms = Sum ÷ Average**

Problems to Watch For

- **When calculating the probability of multiple events, consider if and how they interact.**

Example: A drawer contains 10 black and 10 white socks. If you randomly draw two socks from the drawer, what is the probability that they match?

1. Pick one sock from the drawer.

2. After you've picked one sock, there are 10 socks with the color you didn't pick and 9 socks with the color you did pick.

3. The chance of picking the same color sock is

$$\frac{9}{9 + 10} = \frac{9}{19}.$$

- **Not all problems that deal with averages ask you to solve for the average of a set of quantities.** Often you will have to use the average to compute either the sum of the quantities, the value of an individual quantity, or the number of quantities.

Example: After he took his fourth quiz, Bill's average dropped from 78 to 75. What was Bill's fourth quiz grade?

1. The average of the first three quizzes is 78, so their sum is 78 × 3 = 234.

2. The average of all four of the quizzes is 75, so their sum is 75 × 4 = 300.

3. The difference is the score on the fourth quiz: 300 − 234 = 66.

• **Finding a solution to the problem may not require solving for every variable in** **the problem.** In the previous example you don't know Bill's first three test scores.

PRACTICE PROBLEMS IN ALGEBRAIC APPLICATIONS

Answers begin on page 352.

131. The sum of 5 consecutive odd integers exceeds 3 times the greatest by 6. Find the sum of the integers.

(A) 25

(B) 30

(C) 35

(D) 40

(E) 45

132. What is the average of $2x + 1$, $x + 5$, $1 - 4x$, $3x + 1$?

(A) $2x + 1$

(B) $2x + 4$

(C) $\dfrac{1}{2}x + 2$

(D) $\dfrac{x + 4}{4}$

(E) $\dfrac{2x + 4}{4}$

133. Two members of a basketball team weigh 150 and 175 pounds. A third team member's weight is between the other two. Which of the following cannot possibly be the average weight of the three players?

(A) 159

(B) 161

(C) 163

(D) 165

(E) 167

134. The average of P and another number is A. The other number is:

(A) $A - P$

(B) $\dfrac{AP}{2}$

(C) $2P - A$

(D) $2A - P$

(E) $\dfrac{2A + P}{2}$

135. In a gym class the coach has the students line up and count off by fours. All of the ones are on Team A, the twos are on Team B, the threes are on Team C, and the fours are on Team D. On which team will the 53rd student be?

(A) Team A

(B) Team B

(C) Team C

(D) Team D

(E) Cannot be determined without knowing the total number of students

136. Sarah deposits $1,000 in a college savings account and does not withdraw any money. If she accrues $\frac{1}{2}\%$ interest per month, which expression describes how many dollars she will have after ten years?

(A) $1000 \times .005 \times 120$

(B) $1000 \times 1.005 \times 120$

(C) $1000 \times .5^{120}$

(D) $1000 \times .005^{120}$

(E) 1000×1.005^{120}

137. The first element of a series is 1 and the second element of the series is 2. If each successive element is the *product* of the preceding two elements, which is the first element greater than 1,000?

(A) 6th

(B) 7th

(C) 8th

(D) 9th

(E) 10th

138. *G* girls share the cost of buying *P* pizzas at *D* dollars per pizza. *B* boys decide to join the girls. If no new pizzas are ordered and all of the boys and girls pay an equal share of the total cost of the pizzas, then how much less is each girl's share of the cost than it would have been if the boys hadn't come?

(A) $\dfrac{PDB}{G(B + G)}$

(B) $\dfrac{PD}{B + G}$

(C) $\dfrac{PD}{G}$

(D) $\dfrac{PD(B + G)}{BG}$

(E) $\dfrac{PD}{B}$

139. After the first two quarters at school, Brianne had an 87% average. What is the least average Brianne can have during the third quarter and still be able to have a 90% average for the year?

(A) 83
(B) 86
(C) 87
(D) 93
(E) 96

140. Which of the following expressions might describe the strength of a medicine that loses roughly half of its potency every three hours such that it is completely used up after 12 hours?

(A) $\left(\frac{1}{2}\right)^{\frac{t}{3}}$

(B) $2^{\frac{t}{3}}$

(C) $\left(\frac{1}{2}\right)^{\frac{t}{3}} - \frac{1}{16}$

(D) $\left(\frac{1}{2}\right)^{\frac{t}{12}} - \frac{1}{2}$

(E) $2^{\frac{t}{3}} - 16$

141. If a woman is paid c dollars per hour for every hour she works up to 8 hours and is paid double for every hour she works after 8 hours, how many dollars will she be paid for working 13 hours?

(A) $13c$
(B) $\frac{13}{c}$
(C) $\frac{c}{18}$
(D) $18c$
(E) $\frac{18}{c}$

142. In a race, runner B falls x inches farther behind runner A every y minutes. Express the distance runner B falls behind runner A in feet per hour.

(A) $12xy$
(B) $\frac{x}{2y}$
(C) $\frac{12y}{x}$
(D) $\frac{y}{5x}$
(E) $\frac{5x}{y}$

143. If the cost of a 4-minute telephone call is $0.24, what is the cost of a 15-minute call at the same rate?

(A) $0.60

(B) $0.65

(C) $0.75

(D) $0.90

(E) $1.11

144. A woman buys a pound of steak for $3.00. If the meat loses one fourth of its weight when cooked, what is the cost per pound when it is served at the table?

(A) $2.25

(B) $3.00

(C) $3.75

(D) $4.00

(E) $4.50

145. One pipe can fill a pool in 8 hours, and a second pipe can fill the same pool in 12 hours. If both pipes work together, how many hours will it take to fill the pool?

(A) 4.2 hours

(B) 4.4 hours

(C) 4.6 hours

(D) 4.8 hours

(E) 5.0 hours

The directions for grid-ins are on page 153.

146. Four years ago my age was half of what it will be in eight years. How old am I?

147. In 15 years the ratio of my age to my father's age will be 1:2. Five years ago, the ratio of my age to his was 1:4. How old am I?

148. Ten houses line one side of a street. The average space between the houses is 60 feet more than the average width of the houses. A sidewalk starts 60 feet before the first house and ends 60 feet after the last house. If the total length of the sidewalk is 3,206 feet, find the average width of the houses in feet.

149. Frank travels $2\frac{1}{2}$ kilometers to school; Tom's trip is $1\frac{3}{4}$ kilometers. What is the average distance in kilometers they travel?

150. The sum of 5 consecutive even integers is equal to 3 times the greatest. What is the greatest of the integers?

151. The above diagram shows a bull's-eye made up of four concentric circles with radii 1, 2, 3, and 4. The circles form a center and three rings. If a dart was thrown randomly at the bull's-eye and darts that completely miss the bull's-eye are discounted, what is the probability that the dart will hit the outer ring?

152. A booth at a carnival is set up with a chance game that costs 15 cents to play. The first person to play wins a penny; the second person, a nickel; the third person, a dime; and the fourth, a quarter. The cycle is repeated infinitely with the fifth person winning a penny and so on. After 43 people have played the game, how much money has the booth made as a net profit?

153. Alex leaves New York City, heading north at 35 miles per hour. At the same time, Sam leaves New York City, heading south at 45 miles per hour. In how many hours will they be 640 miles apart?

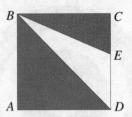

154. *ABCD* is a square, and *E* is the midpoint of $\overline{CD}$. Find the fraction of the square that is unshaded.

155. Gasoline costs $1.50 per gallon. Monday through Friday Ellie travels 12 miles each way to and from work. If Ellie keeps her tires correctly inflated, she gets 24 miles per gallon. If the tires are under-inflated, she only gets 20 miles per gallon. How many dollars per week does she lose if her tires are under-inflated?

Graphs

Graphs are ways of visualizing data, models, and functions.

Graphs of Functions

Terms and Definitions

- **Graph of a function:** If $f(x)$ is a function, then we can graph $y = f(x)$ by drawing every pair of points $(x, f(x))$.

- **Line:** The set of points that can be represented in the form $f(x) = mx + b$.

- **Parabola:** The graph of a quadratic expression, $y = ax^2 + bx + c$. Graphs of quadratic functions look like a $\cup$, or when the coefficient in front of the x^2 is negative, a $\cap$.

- **Proportional** ($\propto$): y is proportional to or varies directly with x, written, $y \propto x$, if $y = kx + c$ for some constants k and c.

- **Inversely proportional:** y varies inversely with x if $xy = c$, or alternatively, $y = \dfrac{c}{x}$ for some constant c. y is inversely proportional to x because the bigger x grows, the smaller y becomes.

Formulas and Guidelines

- **Slope of a line:** The slope of a line is a measure of how steep it is. If the equation for the line is given in the form $f(x) = mx + b$, then m is the slope. The greater the slope (m), the faster $f(x)$ changes for each change in x. If you know *any* two points on a line, (x_1, y_1) and (x_2, y_2), its slope is $\dfrac{y_2 - y_1}{x_2 - x_1}$. Sometimes this is referred to as *rise over* *run*—how much higher the line gets for a horizontal change. A positive slope points up and to the right. A negative slope points down and to the right.

- ***y*-intercept of a line:** The point where a line crosses the *y*-axis. If the equation for the line is given in the form $f(x) = mx + b$, the *y*-intercept is $(0, b)$. Instead of memorizing this, plug in 0 for *x*, and solve: $f(x) = b$.

Problems to Watch For

- **Exponential growth is faster than polynomial growth.** However small the coefficients, exponential functions will always grow faster than polynomial ones in the long run, i.e., when *x* becomes sufficiently large.

  Example: When *x* is a very large positive number, $f(x) = 2x^2 - 2^x$:

  (A) Is a very large positive number

  (B) Is a very small positive number

  (C) Is a very large negative number

  (D) Is a very small negative number

  (E) Does not converge

The correct answer is (C). Because exponentials (i.e., 2^x) grow faster than polynomials (i.e., $2x^2$), the larger *x* is, the bigger the difference between 2^x and $2x^2$.

At some point, the 2^x will completely dwarf the $2x^2$.

- **Look to the extremes.** To understand how a function behaves, consider its values when *x* is a very large negative, 0, and a very large positive.

- **A function grows as fast as its fastest growing term.** For example, when *x* is very big, positive, or negative, the function $f(x) = 5x^3 - 30x^2 - 200x - 4871$ grows proportional to $5x^3$.

Transformations

Formulas and Guidelines

- **Transformations:** Something you do to an expression or graph to convert it to another expression or graph. There are four basic transformations: *shift horizontally, shift vertically, stretch horizontally,* and *stretch vertically.*

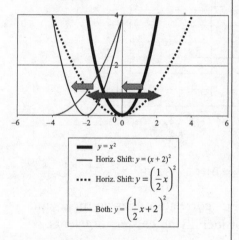

- $y = x^2$
- Horiz. Shift: $y = (x + 2)^2$
- Horiz. Shift: $y = \left(\dfrac{1}{2}x\right)^2$
- Both: $y = \left(\dfrac{1}{2}x + 2\right)^2$

- **Shift Horizontally:** If $y = f(x)$, then substituting $x + c$ for x shifts a graph c units to the left along the x-axis. For example, the point that was at $(a, f(a))$ before the transformation is at $(a, f(a+c))$ afterward.

- **Stretch (or Compress) Horizontally:** If $y = f(x)$, then substituting kx for x compresses the graph to one kth its original size along the x-axis—changes are happening k times as fast.

- **Shift Vertically:** If $y = f(x)$ then adding c to $f(x)$, shifts the graph c units up the y-axis. For example, the point that was at $(a, f(a))$ before the transformation is at $(a, f(a) + c)$ afterward.

- **Stretch (or Compress) Vertically:** If $y = f(x)$, multiplying $f(x)$ by k stretches the graph along the y-axis by a factor of k. For example, the point that was at $(a, f(a))$ is transformed to $(a, kf(a))$.

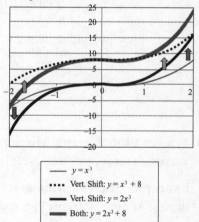

- $y = x^3$
- Vert. Shift: $y = x^3 + 8$
- Vert. Shift: $y = 2x^3$
- Both: $y = 2x^3 + 8$

Data Representation and Interpretation

Graphs often correlate rows and columns. This section presents different types of graphs you might be asked to interpret.

Terms and Definitions

- **Histogram (Bar Chart):** A graph where each column or bar is a distinct event and the rows are the number of times the event occurs.

Example:

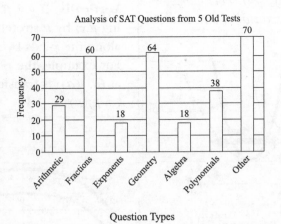

Analysis of SAT Questions from 5 Old Tests

Question Types

- **Scatter Plot:** A graph where points correlate values on the *x*- and *y*-axes. Scatter-plots are useful for identifying clusters of events.

Example: The following graph shows temperature samples taken during August. A trend line has been added to show the "average" or best fitting line to the graph. Given this graph, you should be able to recognize that (a) it peaks between 3 p.m. and 4 p.m.; and (b) the data suggests an inverted parabola or a function proportional to $-x^2$.

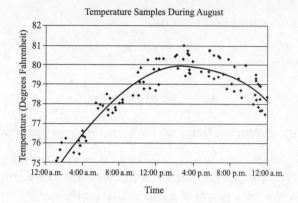

Temperature Samples During August

• **Matrix or Table:** A two-dimensional table with rows and columns. Each row and each column converge at some value. The graph will usually have a title, which explains the significance and units of where the rows and columns meet.

Example: Consider the following table.

Average Fuel Economy by Vehicle Type (miles per gallon)			
	Hybrid	*SUV*	*Pickup*
City	60	20	24
Hwy	56	24	29

When gasoline costs $2.00 per gallon, approximately how much would a driver who commutes 1,000 city miles per month save per year by switching from a pickup to a hybrid vehicle?

1. SUV Cost $= 1,000 \dfrac{\text{miles}}{\text{month}} \times 12 \dfrac{\text{months}}{\text{year}} \times 2 \dfrac{\text{dollars}}{\text{gallon}} \div 20 \dfrac{\text{miles}}{\text{gallon}}$

$= (24,000 \div 20) \dfrac{\text{dollars}}{\text{year}}$

$= 1,200 \dfrac{\text{dollars}}{\text{year}}$

2. Hybrid Cost $= (24,000 \div 60) \dfrac{\text{dollars}}{\text{year}}$

$= 400 \dfrac{\text{dollars}}{\text{year}}$

3. Savings $= 1,200 - 400 = \$800$ per year

If the units are confusing here, go back and review fractions beginning on page 165.

- **Quantitative:** Able to be measured numerically. For example, the maximum value in a graph is a quantitative measure.

- **Qualitative:** Describing the quality or property of something without measuring it precisely. For example, the slope of a graph being positive.

Problems to Watch For

- **A problem based on the following graph is apt to ask a question about the batting average of a specific game or to compare a series of games.**

  Example: In which game did the Beavers' batting average drop the most?

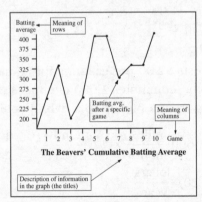

Glancing quickly across, you will see that the steepest drop is from game 2 to 3; so in game 3 the Beavers' average dropped the most.

PRACTICE PROBLEMS IN GRAPHS

Answers begin on page 355.

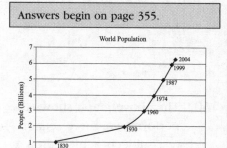

World Population

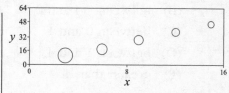

156. The above graph shows the world population over the last 200 years. Roughly how much faster was the population growing in 1993 than in 1880?

(A) 2 times

(B) 4 times

(C) 8 times

(D) 16 times

(E) 32 times

157. Which statement best describes the above graph?

(A) y is proportional to x and proportional to the size of each point.

(B) y is proportional to x and inversely proportional to the size of each point.

(C) y is proportional to $-x$ and inversely proportional to the size of each point.

(D) y is inversely proportional to x and proportional to the size of each point.

(E) y is inversely proportional to x and inversely proportional to the size of each point.

158. The slope of the line that connects the points in the previous graph is:

(A) less than −4

(B) between −4 and 0

(C) between 0 and 1

(D) between 1 and 4

(E) greater than 4

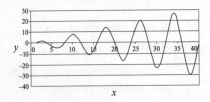

159. In the graph above, as x increases, which of the following is true about y?

(A) y becomes a large positive number.

(B) y becomes a small positive number.

(C) y becomes a small negative number.

(D) y becomes a large negative number.

(E) None of the above

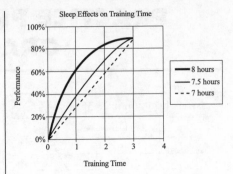

160. The above graph shows the performance three sets of test subjects achieved on a sample task as a function of the amount of training they received. The test subjects were grouped by the average number of hours they sleep per night: 7 hours, 7.5 hours, or 8 hours. How long does it take for a person who gets 7 hours of sleep to attain the same proficiency level as a person who has had 8 hours of sleep and 1 hour of training?

(A) 1 hour

(B) 1.5 hours

(C) 2 hours

(D) 2.5 hours

(E) 3 hours

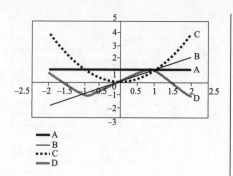

— A
— B
···· C
▨▨▨ D

161. Which of the curves on the graph to the left cannot be expressed in the form x^n for some n?

(A) A

(B) B

(C) C

(D) D

(E) All can be written in the form x^n.

Calling Plan	Monthly	Evenings & weekends per minute	Daytime per minute
Unlimited	$ 55.00	unlimited	unlimited
Weekends	$ 40.00	unlimited	$ 0.10
Best of Times	$ 20.00	$ 0.05	$ 0.10
Simplicity	$ 10.00	$ 0.08	$ 0.08
Per Call	$—	$ 0.10	$ 0.10

162. The above chart shows the cost of five telephone calling plans. Which of the following expressions describes the cost of the Weekends Plan, if e represents evening minutes and d represents daytime minutes?

(A) 40

(B) $40 + e + d$

(C) $40 + e + .1d$

(D) $e + .1d$

(E) $40 + .1d$

163. Referring to the telephone rate chart, Sarah is trying to save money. How many minutes would she have to spend on the phone per month to make the Simplicity Plan a better deal than the Per Call plan?

(A) 80

(B) 100

(C) 125

(D) 200

(E) 500

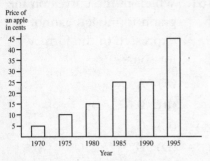

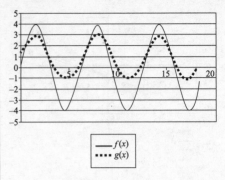

— $f(x)$
···· $g(x)$

164. Which 5-year period in the above graph showed the greatest percentage increase in apple price?

(A) 1970–1975

(B) 1875–1980

(C) 1980–1985

(D) 1985–1990

(E) 1990–1995

165. If $f(x) = \dfrac{3x - 2}{5}$, then $f^{-1}(x) =$

(A) $\dfrac{5}{3x - 2}$

(B) $\dfrac{2 - 3x}{5}$

(C) $\dfrac{5}{2 - 3x}$

(D) $\dfrac{5x + 2}{3}$

(E) $\dfrac{5x - 2}{3}$

166. In the graph above, if the solid line is a graph of $f(x)$, then the dashed line could be a graph of:

(A) $\dfrac{1}{2}f(x) + 1$

(B) $\dfrac{1}{2}f(x) + 3$

(C) $\dfrac{1}{2}f(x) - 1$

(D) $\dfrac{3}{4}f(x) - 1$

(E) $\dfrac{1}{4}f(x) + 3$

The directions for grid-ins are on page 153.

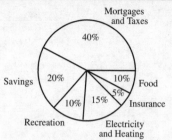

Mortgages and Taxes 40%

Savings 20%

Food 10%

5%

Recreation 10% 15% Insurance

Electricity and Heating

167. The pie chart shows Della's monthly budget as percentages. If her monthly income is $5,000, how many dollars would she save each month if the electric and heating bills were decreased by 20%?

168. A line includes the three points (0, 32), (100, 212), and (x, 77). What is the value of x?

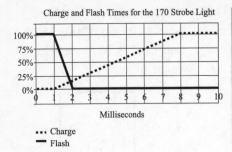

Charge and Flash Times for the 170 Strobe Light

··· Charge
— Flash

Test No.	% Correct
1	90%
2	75%
3	95%
4	90%
5	85%

169. The above graph shows the time it takes for a strobe light to charge and to flash. What is the maximum number of flashes per second assuming that the bulb must completely charge before flashing?

170. The above table shows the percent correct Evan received on each of five 60-question tests. What was the total number of questions Evan answered correctly during the five tests?

THE PRACTICE SAT

 Are you on schedule?

Check the PLAN OF ATTACK on pages vi–viii.

As you know, only College Board officials know the exact specifications of the new test that will debut in spring 2005. I've decided that that is amazingly unimportant. These test segments will be very close to the real thing, and ALL practice with SAT-type questions is valuable. Make a few mistakes? No problem! Those are mistakes you will NOT make on Test Day.

So . . . get out your timer, the No. 2 pencils, and scratch paper. Go to a quiet place where you won't be disturbed. Try to imitate actual test conditions as closely as possible, and read all directions carefully. If others in your class are working with this book, you could ask a teacher to help all of you create an SAT MORNING, followed by an analysis of your right and wrong answers.

Record your answers on the answer sheets at the back of the book.

Compute your best-guess score with the charts on p. 364.

| SECTION 1 | TIME—25 MINUTES | WRITTEN ESSAY |

Directions: Consider the following comments and the assignment below it. Then plan and write an essay that explains your ideas as persuasively as possible. Keep in mind that the support you provide—both reasons and examples—will help make your view convincing to the reader.

"Never let it be forgotten that glamour is not greatness; applause is not fame; prominence is not eminence. The person of the hour is not apt to be the person of the ages. It is what the unimportant do that really counts and determines the course of history. The world would soon die but for the fidelity, loyalty, and consecration of those whose names are unhonored and unsung."

Adapted from remarks by John R. Sizoo,
a former U.S. Intelligence officer.

Assignment: What is your view of Mr. Sizoo's remarks? Do "unimportant" people actually determine the course of history? If they are "unhonored" and "unsung," did they make such a difference after all? In an essay, support your position by discussing an example (or examples) from literature, the arts, science and technology, current events, or your own experience or observation.

(Note: Be sure to set the timer for 25 minutes. Write on your own paper, as legibly as possible.)

Stop!

If you finish before your timer rings, check your work on this section only. Do not turn to any other section in the test.

Note: Save your essay to take to an English teacher along with the College Board's scoring rubric, so that you can estimate a score for your test essay or try Peterson's online essay service at www. petersons.com/satessayedge.

SECTION 2   TIME—25 MINUTES   20 QUESTIONS

Directions: In this section, solve each problem, and then choose the most appropriate answer from the choices given.

1. The cost of a 25¢ candy bar is raised 20 percent. What is the new cost of the candy bar?

   (A) 45¢
   (B) 40¢
   (C) 30¢
   (D) 25¢
   (E) 20¢

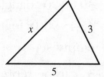

Note: Figure not drawn to scale.

2. Which of the following best describes x?

   (A) $3 < x < 5$
   (B) $x = 2$
   (C) $x = 4$
   (D) $2 < x < 8$
   (E) $2 < x < 5$

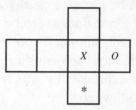

3. The above pattern can be folded into all of the following cubes EXCEPT

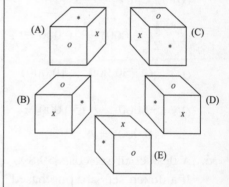

4. If $\dfrac{1}{2} + \dfrac{1}{8} - \dfrac{1}{4} - \dfrac{1}{6} = \dfrac{1}{x}$, then $x =$

   (A) 0
   (B) 1
   (C) $1\dfrac{1}{2}$
   (D) $\dfrac{5}{24}$
   (E) $4\dfrac{4}{5}$

5. A $50,000 inheritance has been left after a man has died. Before the money may be divided up, $10,000 must be paid on outstanding debts. Of what is left, half is to be given to charity and the remainder is to be split evenly among 4 cousins. The amount each cousin receives is expressed by which of the following?

(A) $\frac{1}{2}(50,000 - 10,000) \div 4$

(B) $\left[\frac{1}{2}(50,000) - 10,000\right] \div 4$

(C) $\frac{1}{2}(50,000) - 10,000 \div 4$

(D) $\frac{1}{2}(4)(50,000 - 10,000)$

(E) $50,000 - \frac{1}{2}(50,000 - 10,000) \div 4$

6. A desk-chair set costs $9.89. If a dozen sets are purchased at once, the cost is reduced to $9.14 per set. A school needs to buy 1 gross (12 dozen) sets. How much does it save by buying the sets by the dozen instead of singly?

(A) $9.00

(B) $18.00

(C) $19.03

(D) $24.00

(E) $108.00

7. What number goes in the blank space above to form a geometric sequence?

(A) 3

(B) 4

(C) 5

(D) 6

(E) 7

8. The intersection of the set of right triangles and the set of isosceles triangles is the set of

(A) equilateral triangles

(B) isosceles triangles

(C) 30-60-90 triangles

(D) 45-45-90 triangles

(E) empty set

9. $|x| > 3$ can be represented graphically as:

(A) ←———⊕———⊕———⊕———→
　　　　　−3　　0　　3

(B) ←———⊕———⊕———●———→
　　　　　−3　　0　　3

(C) ←———○———●———○———→
　　　　　−3　　0　　3

(D) ←———⊕———⊕———●———→
　　　　　−3　　0　　3

(E) ←———○———⊕———○———→
　　　　　−3　　0　　3

10. When $x \neq 2$, $\dfrac{-3x^2 + x + 10}{2 - x}$ can be simplified to be

(A) $3x + 5$

(B) $-3x + 5$

(C) $3x - 5$

(D) $\frac{3}{2}x + 5$

(E) $-\frac{3}{2}x + 5$

11. $\left(\sqrt{2}+\sqrt{3}\right)^2 =$

   (A) 5
   (B) 6
   (C) $5+\sqrt{5}$
   (D) $5+\sqrt{6}$
   (E) $5+2\sqrt{6}$

12. If y is proportional to x and y is inversely proportional to z^2, then,

   (A) x is proportional to z
   (B) x is inversely proportional to z
   (C) x is proportional to z^2
   (D) x is inversely proportional to z^2
   (E) x is proportional to z^3

13. The range of f(x) is y, such that $-1 < y < 3$. What is the range of 2f(x) + 3?

   (A) $-2 < y < 6$
   (B) $1 < y < 9$
   (C) $-1 < y < 6$
   (D) $-1 < y < 9$
   (E) $1 < y < 6$

14. Where do the lines defined by $y = 3x + 6$ and $y = 3x - 6$ cross?

   (A) (0, 6)
   (B) (2, 0)
   (C) (−2, 0)
   (D) (0, 0)
   (E) They do not cross.

15. If 1 is added to each of the digits of 3,642, then the resulting number is

   (A) 1 more than 3,642
   (B) 4 more than 3,642
   (C) 1,000 more than 3,642
   (D) 1,111 more than 3,642
   (E) 4,753 more than 3,642

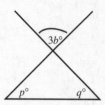

16. From the diagram above, the sum of p and q, in terms of b, equals

   (A) $2b$
   (B) $3b$
   (C) $180 - b$
   (D) $180 - 2b$
   (E) $180 - 3b$

17. Over what interval(s) is the statement $x^3 > x^2$ true?

   (A) All x
   (B) $x > 0$
   (C) $x > 1$ or $x < -1$
   (D) $-1 < x < 1$
   (E) $x > 1$

18. If $y = \dfrac{1}{x+1}$, then what is x in terms of y?

(A) $\dfrac{1}{1+y}$

(B) $\dfrac{1}{y-1}$

(C) $\dfrac{1}{y}$

(D) $\dfrac{1-y}{y}$

(E) $\dfrac{1}{y} - y$

19. The instructions on a can of orange juice concentrate state that the water should be mixed with the concentrate in the ratio of 3 to 1. If 12 liters of orange juice are needed, how many liters of concentrate need to be bought?

(A) 3

(B) 4

(C) 6

(D) 36

(E) 48

20. $(a - b)(b - a) =$

(A) $a^2 - 2ab + b^2$

(B) $a^2 - b^2$

(C) $a^2 + 2ab + b^2$

(D) $a^2 + 2ab - b^2$

(E) $-a^2 + 2ab - b^2$

Stop!

Do not go on to the next section of the test until you have set your timer.

SECTION 3	TIME—35 MINUTES	54 QUESTIONS

Directions: Questions 1 through 15 test your knowledge of grammar, usage, diction (choice of words), and idiom. Some sentences are correct. No sentence contains more than one error. If you find an error, it will be underlined and lettered. Elements of the sentence that are not underlined will not be changed. In choosing answers, follow the requirements of standard written English. If there is an error, select the one underlined part that must be changed to make the sentence correct, and fill in the corresponding oval on your answer sheet. If there is no error, fill in answer oval E.

1. I think that that hat looks well
   (A)   (B)
   on her, don't you? No error
   (C)   (D)   (E)

2. Many students, even though

   they attend school regularly,
   (A)
   know scarcely nothing about
                  (B)
   the problems that school
                  (C)
   administrators face. No error
                  (D)   (E)

3. Except Molly and I, everyone
                  (A)
   was on time for the first notes
   (B)   (C)
   of the play's overture. No error
                  (D)   (E)

4. Raoul had already started the
                  (A)
   car's engine when Amelia
   (B)
   had gotten into the car and
   (C)
   said, "Let's go." No error
          (D)   (E)

5. "Well, the dog's house is just
        (A)   (B)
   plain gone," says Steve, and he
                          (C)
   sat down heavily at the
                          (D)
   kitchen table. No error
        (D)   (E)

6. Four yapping, friendly dogs,
                  (A)
   several mangy, stray cats, and a
   (B)
   parrot called Nancy constitute
                  (C)   (D)
   our home menagerie. No error
                              (E)

7. A half mile farther down the
                  (A)
   river, past that ledge of rocks
                  (B)
   and those old fir trees, lie the
                              (C)
   waterfall that we absolutely
                  (D)
   must avoid. No error
                  (E)

8. Liza and Emily were inspired to
$\overline{\hspace{2cm}}$
(A)
become a medical doctor
$\overline{\hspace{2cm}}$
(B)
after attending a lecture series
$\overline{\hspace{2cm}}$
(C)
on medicine and its challenges
$\overline{\hspace{2cm}}$
(D)
in the Third World countries.

No error
$\overline{\hspace{1cm}}$
(E)

9. Concerned about a variety of
$\overline{\hspace{2cm}}$
(A)
modern ecological dilemmas,
$\overline{\hspace{2cm}}$
(B)
our new text addresses each
$\overline{\hspace{2cm}}$
(C)
problem in a discrete, fact-filled
$\overline{\hspace{2cm}}$
(D)
chapter. No error
$\overline{\hspace{1.5cm}}$
(E)

10. Our town's elderly citizens

tell of the days when the canal
$\overline{\hspace{1cm}}$
(A)
was being dug by crews of men
$\overline{\hspace{2cm}}$
(B)
which had brought along their
$\overline{\hspace{2cm}}$
(C)   (D)
favorite mules as both workers

and friends. No error
$\overline{\hspace{2cm}}$
(E)

11. "You ought to pay attention

to me, and set your worries
$\overline{\hspace{1cm}}$ $\overline{\hspace{1cm}}$
(A)   (B)
aside," Marlin insisted, adding

that he was undoubtably
$\overline{\hspace{2cm}}$
(C)   (D)
correct. No error
$\overline{\hspace{1cm}}$
(E)

12. When unprotected skin
$\overline{\hspace{2cm}}$
(A)
is exposed to the sun, it can
$\overline{\hspace{2cm}}$
(B)
not only be damaged, but it
$\overline{\hspace{1cm}}$ $\overline{\hspace{1cm}}$
(C)   (D)
significantly increases the risk
$\overline{\hspace{2cm}}$
(D)
of melanoma, a serious skin

cancer. No error
$\overline{\hspace{1cm}}$
(E)

13. Because of dangers from a
$\overline{\hspace{1cm}}$ $\overline{\hspace{1cm}}$
(A)   (B)
variety of snakes, each member
$\overline{\hspace{1cm}}$
(B)
of our wildlife hiking group was

reminded to keep their eyes on
$\overline{\hspace{1cm}}$ $\overline{\hspace{1cm}}$
(C)   (D)
the path. No error
$\overline{\hspace{1cm}}$
(E)

14. We all believed that the story
$\overline{\hspace{1cm}}$
(A)
submitted by a freshman

reporter was incredulous, but
$\overline{\hspace{1cm}}$ $\overline{\hspace{1cm}}$
(B)   (C)
we turned it in to our editor

anyway. No error
$\overline{\hspace{1cm}}$
(D)   (E)

15. One would think that ushering
$\overline{\hspace{1cm}}$
(A)
is easy, since all you have to
$\overline{\hspace{1cm}}$
(B)
do is make sure the audience
$\overline{\hspace{1cm}}$
(C)
is seated before the play begins.
$\overline{\hspace{1cm}}$
(D)
No error
$\overline{\hspace{1cm}}$
(E)

Directions: The following questions ask you to improve some aspects of early-draft paragraphs. Some questions focus on organization and development of the paragraph (its structure), while others ask you to improve sentence structure or even word choice. In selecting an answer, follow the conventions of standard written English.

Questions 16–19 refer to the following passage:

(1) Parts of Pennsylvania have always been coal country, where work in winter began and ended in the dark, even if you were only six or seven years old. (2) Breaker boys were supposed to be twelve, of course, according to an 1885 law, and fourteen to work in the mines themselves. (3) But breaker boys simply sat on benches at the bottom of the coal chutes and picked out the refuse, so perhaps they didn't need to be exactly twelve. (4) So, apparently, went the thinking of the mine owners, because it wasn't a very demanding job.

(5) But consider that job. (6) The boys, some as young as five, sat in clouds of coal dust as the shining black coal thundered toward them, down the chutes. (7) Within seconds they were coal-black themselves, and would have choked on the dust had they not worn handkerchiefs over their mouths. (8) They kept moist mouths by chewing on cuds of tobacco. (9) Smoking tobacco was not allowed, just chewing.

(10) Hunched over, separating the slate and rock from the clean coal, the breaker boys began work at seven in the morning amid the thick black dust and deafening machinery. (11) If they were working at full capacity, quitting time came at six or six-thirty. (12) All that time, hunched over on a wooden bench.

(Information obtained from *Growing Up in Coal Country*, 1996, by Susan Campbell Bartoletti)

16. Which of the following choices best revises sentence 4?

    (A) Revise to avoid all those commas.

    (B) Rewrite as: "After all, being a breaker boy wasn't a very demanding job."

    (C) Rewrite as: "Apparently it's an easy job, according to the mine owners."

    (D) Rewrite as: "At least that's what the mine owners thought about being a breaker boy, which wasn't a very demanding job in their eyes."

    (E) Revise for wordiness to read: "It is an easy job."

17. A new paragraph begins with sentence 5. In this sentence, the primary function of the word "job" is to

    (A) emphasize the idea that very young boys are working

    (B) be the direct object of the verb "consider"

    (C) act as a transition, repeating a word used in the last sentence of the prior paragraph

    (D) focus the reader's attention on the job of breaker boy

    (E) continue the relaxed, conversational style of writing

18. Of the following choices, which would be the best revision for sentences 8 and 9?

    (A) Although smoking tobacco was forbidden, the boys kept their mouths moist by chewing cuds of tobacco.

    (B) While they weren't allowed to smoke, the boys kept their mouths moist by chewing on cuds of tobacco.

    (C) Mouth moistening being a problem, they chewed on cuds of tobacco. They couldn't smoke it, of course.

    (D) Keeping the mouth moist was a problem. The boys chewed tobacco for this, although they were not allowed to smoke it.

    (E) To keep their mouths moist, the boys chewed tobacco, although smoking tobacco was forbidden.

19. Reread the last paragraph. In revision, one of the best ways to improve this paragraph would be to

(A) repair the last sentence (12), which is a fragment

(B) combine sentences 11 and 12

(C) add material emphasizing the extreme length of the breaker boys' work day

(D) add a concluding sentence that echoes the irony in sentence 4, "it wasn't a very demanding job."

(E) add interesting information, such as when the boys ate lunch, or took breaks, if breaks were allowed

Questions 20–22 refer to the following passage:

(1) Swifter than racehorses, the fastest dog in the world is the Greyhound. (2) He's a long-legged, deep-chested dog typically bred by sportsmen for racing or coursing hares and other wild game. (3) Ancient Egyptians left behind eloquent pictographs that showed men releasing their hounds to chase hares, using a collar amazingly similar to the ones used now at race meets. (4) Even before King Canute, in the eleventh century, gentlemen in Britain treasured their Greyhounds, partly, one suspects, because only a "gentleman" could keep one. (5) Today, these popular "long dogs," still race for the entertainment of spectators, yet their years on the track are limited. (6) A necessary business has sprung up, as a result, and many animal lovers happily share their lives with their stately, "retired" Greyhounds.

20. The problem in sentence 5 is best corrected by which of the following revisions?

(A) Remove the comma after "long dogs."

(B) Divide this long sentence into two sentences.

(C) Remove the word "still."

(D) Divide this sentence into two sentences in order to add information about how the racing meets are conducted.

(E) Change the last clause from passive voice to active voice.

21. Revising for clarity and logical flow, which of the following revision choices works best for sentence 6?

(A) A necessary business has sprung up—dog adoption services—as a result, which lets many animal lovers share their lives with these stately, "retired" Greyhounds.

(B) As a result, a necessary business has come about, which lets the stately, "retired" Greyhounds move into homes.

(C) As a result, a necessary pet adoption service has evolved that places the stately, "retired" Greyhounds in homes with eager owners.

(D) Thus, many animal lovers now happily share their lives with the racing Greyhounds, newly retired, and still stately and polite, as are all of their breed.

(E) A much-needed service has developed, in consequence, that places these wonderful "retired" Greyhounds in homes with eager owners.

22. The structure of sentence 2 could best be improved by which of the following revisions?

(A) Removing the word "typically"

(B) Substituting "A Greyhound is" for the opening pronoun contraction "He's"

(C) Removing the phrase "by sportsmen"

(D) Adding the preposition "for" before "coursing hares"

(E) No revision is needed for this sentence.

Directions: In choosing answers, pay attention to grammar, choice of words, sentence construction, and punctuation. In each of the following sentences, part of the sentence or the entire sentence is underlined. Beneath each sentence you will find five ways of phrasing the underlined part. Choice A repeats the original; the other four are different. Choose the answer that best expresses the meaning of the original sentence. If you think the original is better than any of the alternatives, choose it; otherwise, choose one of the others. Your choice should produce the most effective sentence—clear and precise, without awkwardness or ambiguity.

23. Clubs often teach a person to be both a pal and courteous.

    (A) to be both a pal and courteous

    (B) to be friendly and a courteous person

    (C) both to be a pal and a courteous one

    (D) to be both friendly and courteous

    (E) both to be friendly and courteous

24. Seeing that the town did not have a library, a campaign was begun by Sara and Leonard Wringer to raise funds for the building of one.

    (A) a campaign was begun by Sara and Leonard Wringer to raise funds

    (B) a campaign to raise funds was headed by Sara and Leonard Wringer

    (C) funds were raised in a campaign by Sara and Leonard Wringer

    (D) Sara and Leonard Wringer began a campaign to raise funds

    (E) Sara and Leonard Wringer had campaigned to raise funds

25. By selling the remainder of the building sites over the weekend, the determined Realtors kept the dream of a new subdivision alive, <u>that had been the hope of everyone in the adjacent small town.</u>

(A) that had been the hope of everyone in the adjacent small town

(B) that was what everyone in the adjacent small town had hoped

(C) because that was the hope of everyone in the adjacent small town

(D) a hope of everyone in the adjacent small town

(E) which had been the hope of everyone in the adjacent small town

26. Emigrants from England, Ireland, and other north European countries poured into the new land called America, somewhat ahead of immigrants from central Europe, <u>while these groups competed for jobs in the prosperous new country.</u>

(A) while these groups competed for jobs in the prosperous new country

(B) although these groups competed for jobs in the prosperous new country

(C) which inevitably led to competition for jobs in the prosperous new country

(D) which meant that all of these groups were forced to compete for jobs in the prosperous new country

(E) and while these groups competed for jobs, it was a prosperous new country

27. <u>Many classic songs have been rearranged</u> and newly recorded by famous modern composers, some acknowledged favorites have not.

(A) Many classic songs have been rearranged

(B) Although many classic songs have been rearranged

(C) Many a classic song has been rearranged

(D) In spite of many classic songs that have been rearranged

(E) Never mind that many classic songs have been rearranged

28. The traffic roundabout is common in England, <u>where cars drive at a steady pace around a center island</u> in the roadway, shooting off in a variety of directions, avoiding the tedium of waiting at lengthy stoplights.

(A) where cars drive at a steady pace around a center island

(B) which is a place where cars drive at a steady pace around a center island

(C) the cars drive at a steady pace around a center island

(D) in their roads, so that cars can drive at a steady pace around a center island

(E) when cars can drive at a steady pace around a center island

29. Destruction resulting from a massive flood can be measured not only in the damage to property but <u>it has a residual emotional</u> effects on people.

(A) it has a

(B) it likewise has a

(C) also the

(D) the similar damage in

(E) also in the

30. One common error made by beginning teachers is overestimating how much work students can comprehend <u>in a day, another that occurs</u> nearly as often is underestimating students' abilities.

(A) in a day, another that occurs

(B) daily; another that occurs

(C) in a day; another one that occurs

(D) , and another error that keeps occurring

(E) daily, while one more error that occurs

31. While Mark Twain proved himself capable of earning large sums of money from writing and <u>lecturing, he lost most of it</u> through unwise investments.

(A) lecturing, he lost most of it

(B) lecturing, then he lost most of it

(C) giving lectures, he soon lost most of it

(D) his lectures, he went on to lose most of it

(E) lecturing; he lost most of it

32. Roughly two out of every five male children <u>born with color blindness</u> which must be compensated for as they grow older.

    (A) born with color blindness

    (B) having been born with color blindness

    (C) being born with color blindness

    (D) are born with color blindness

    (E) , unfortunately born with color blindness,

33. Piano tuners recognize that the finer a piano is tuned, the <u>finer the sound for the tone of the instrument.</u>

    (A) finer the sound for the tone of the instrument

    (B) more fine the tone will be of the instrument

    (C) nicer the sound of its tone

    (D) finer its tone will be

    (E) better will be the resulting tone of the instrument

34. Since the original turkeys found in North America were wily <u>birds, that's why they were difficult</u> prey for colonial hunters.

    (A) birds, that's why they were difficult

    (B) birds, they were difficult prey

    (C) birds, were also difficult prey

    (D) birds; that's why they were difficult prey

    (E) birds and they were also difficult prey

Directions: The following questions ask you to improve some aspects of early-draft paragraphs. Some questions focus on organization and development of the paragraph (its structure), while others ask you to improve sentence structure or even word choice. In selecting an answer, follow the conventions of standard written English.

Questions 35 and 36 refer to the following passage:

(1) Although admired by many teenage students, writer Zora Neale Hurston is not as well known to the larger world, according to many literary critics. (2) Hurston's second novel is *Their Eyes Were Watching God*, the story of an African-American woman who learns who she is by "going tuh God," and by learning how to live for herself. (3) This

book was written in the late 1930s at the time of the Harlem Renaissance. (4) Severely criticized at the time by African-American males for not writing literature in the protest tradition, Ms. Hurston would probably be amazed at the success of her poetic novel in the last three decades. (5) After all, her book had languished out of print for thirty years, until it was "discovered" by African-American college instructors who knew the worth of their discovery. (6) Their devotion to the art of Zora Neal Hurston is captured by Alice Walker's quote on the front cover of current paperback reprints: "There is no book more important to me than this one."

35. In the first three sentences of this paragraph, a writer should do which of the following to improve transition, clarity, and coherence?

    (A) Delete sentence 3.

    (B) Omit the theme of the novel.

    (C) Rewrite sentences 2 and 3 as follows: Perhaps the most popular novel is Hurston's second one, *Their Eyes Were Watching God*, written in the late 1930s at the time of the Harlem Renaissance. It is the story of an African-American woman who learns who she is by "going tuh God" and learning how to live for herself.

    (D) Omit the information about teenage students' admiration in sentence 1.

    (E) Rewrite as follows: Sadly unknown to much of the world, writer Zora Neale Hurston is well known to college and high school students, who admire her poetic novel, *Their Eyes Were Watching God*. Written in the late 1930s at the time of the Harlem Renaissance, it is the story of an African-American woman who learns who she is by "going tuh God" and by learning how to live for herself.

36. Considering diction, which of the suggested changes improves sentence 6 the most?

(A) Change "captured" to "nailed down"

(B) Change "devotion to" to "respect for"

(C) Change "captured by Alice Walker's quote" to "this comment by Alice Walker"

(D) Change "art" to "writing"

(E) Change "Their devotion" to "The college professors' devotion"

Questions 37–39 refer to the following passage:

(1) The blue crab, called *callinectes sapidus* by scientists, didn't need William Warner's prize-winning book, *Beautiful Swimmers*, to make a name for themselves. (2) He's been a diet staple for Native Americans and all the immigrants who followed for centuries, as old piles of shells can testify. (3) Termed "middens," these piles tell archaeologists that blue crabs have been dietarily and economically important for ages. (4) Clearly, Blue crabs are North Carolina's most valuable fishery. (5) At the peak of crabbing success in 1997, North Carolina alone had over 2200 crabbers. (6) As recently as 2002, about 1700 crabbers landed 36,401,781 pounds of tasty crab worth over $29 million. (7) Knowing that some crabbers fish as many as 700 pots, scientists are casting intelligent eyes on the crab population, wondering how long the numbers will hold up. (8) Now the state is down to a core group of some 1300+ folks whose living depends on setting pots to catch crabs.

37. Which sequence of sentences suggested below would result in a more coherent, logical order for this paragraph?

(A) No change needed. The paragraph is clear and logical as is.

(B) Sentence order 4, 6, 5, 7, and 8

(C) Sentence order 4, 5, 8, 6, and 7

(D) Sentence order 5, 6, 4, 8, and 7

(E) Sentence order 5, 4, 6, 7, and 8

38. In revision, which error in the first sentence would need to be corrected?

(A) Remove commas around "called *callinectes sapidus* by scientists"

(B) Remove commas around *Beautiful Swimmers*

(C) Remove italics on Beautiful Swimmers

(D) Change "called" to "termed"

(E) Change "themselves" to "himself"

39. Of the following choices, which change in diction benefits sentence 7 the most?

(A) Change "intelligent" to "wary"

(B) Change "intelligent" to "distraught"

(C) Change "Knowing" to "Aware"

(D) Change "casting" to "viewing"

(E) Change "population" to "critters"

Directions: Questions 40 through 54 test your knowledge of grammar, usage, diction (choice of words), and idiom. Some sentences are correct. No sentence contains more than one error.

If you find an error, it will be underlined and lettered. Elements of the sentence that are not underlined will not be changed. In choosing answers, follow the requirements of standard English.

If there is an error, select the one underlined part that must be changed to make the sentence correct, and fill in the corresponding oval on your answer sheet. If there is no error, fill in answer oval E.

40. Every one of the sailors aboard
(A)   (B)
the ship, with the exception of
(C)
the boilerman's apprentice,

were rescued after the storm.
(D)
No error
(E)

41. In the early morning, before the
(A)
canoeists' arms got tired, the
(B)
only sounds heard on the

river are the songs and laughter
(C)
of people on vacation. No error
(D)   (E)

42. "Working as carefully and

    as slowly the way Mr. Jones
       (A)   (B)
    does, is the way to train a good
     (C)   (D)
    hunting dog," my dad told us.

    No error
     (E)

43. Because of new store policies,
          (A)
    many of the sales force don't
      (B)   (C)
    want to work in it any longer.
      (C)   (D)
    No error
     (E)

44. Mel only scrubbed floors in his
      (A)   (B)
    diner and cheerfully ignored the
     (B) (C)
    walls and the often grimy
                (D)
    woodwork. No error
           (E)

45. I didn't realize it when I met
           (A)
    him, but he had formally been
            (B)
    principal of our high school,
     (C)
    back when my brother's class

    were students. No error
     (D)   (E)

46. If only you could of been there,
     (A)   (B)
    my sister said, you would've
               (C)
    enjoyed the play immensely.
     (C)   (D)
    No error
     (E)

47. "Why don't you just delegate
        (A)   (B)
    the work to Bailey and I, and
               (C)
    we'll plan the picnic," Sally
          (D)
    said. No error
        (E)

48. We will certainly give all the
             (A)
    returning vets their well-earned
          (B)
    hero's welcome when the
     (C)
    war is finally over. No error
     (D)   (E)

49. Wishes of hospital patients are
             (A)
    frequently overlooked

    in the planning of patient
          (B)
    facilities nor visiting hours.
         (C)   (D)
    No error
     (E)

50. I believe there going to that
          (A)
    campsite simply because it's the
          (B)   (C)
    closest one to the boat dock.
        (D)
    No error
     (E)

51. Don't say that your making
        (A)   (B)
    plans for only one firepit when
          (C)
    the camp plainly needs at least
              (D)
    three. No error
        (E)

52. Looking at the magnificent

cathedrals in Europe, the past
$\overline{}$
(A)
seems to come alive for me—a
$\overline{}$
(B)
past profoundly different from
$\overline{}$ $\overline{}$
(C) (D)
my own time. No error
$\overline{}$
(E)

53. Feel free to go ahead and give
$\overline{}$ $\overline{}$
(A) (B)
the package to whomever
$\overline{}$
(C)
comes to the door. No error
$\overline{}$ $\overline{}$
(D) (E)

54. After we'd gone away to school,
$\overline{}$
(A)
Mom sent us, Jim and I, a huge
$\overline{}$ $\overline{}$
(B) (C)
box of snacks to share with

everyone on our floor. No error
$\overline{}$ $\overline{}$
(D) (E)

Stop!

If you finish before your timer rings, check your work on this section only.
Do not turn to any other section in the test.

Section 4   Time—25 Minutes   20 Questions

Directions: In this section, solve each problem, and then choose the most appropriate answer from the choices given.

1. The solution set of the equation $\sqrt{x} = x$ includes

    I. -1

    II.   0

    III.   1

    (A)   II only

    (B)   III only

    (C)   I and III only

    (D)   II and III only

    (E)   I, II, and III

2. A cylinder is formed in such a way that a sphere of radius 2 can just fit inside. What is the volume of the cylinder?

    (A) π

    (B) 2π

    (C) 4π

    (D) 8π

    (E) 16π

3. In a certain state one must pay a state income tax of 5%. The federal income tax instructions say that one may deduct 75% of the amount of one's state income tax. If a man was able to deduct $900 from his federal income tax because of his state income tax, what was his income?

    (A) $3,375

    (B) $6,000

    (C) $7,200

    (D) $13,500

    (E) $24,000

4. Margaret has d dimes and n nickels totaling \$3.00. If she has 40 coins altogether, which of the pairs of equations could be used to solve for the number of nickels and dimes Margaret has?

(A) $\begin{cases} x(d) + (40 - x)n = 300 \\ n + d = 40 \end{cases}$

(B) $\begin{cases} 300 - d = n \\ n + d = 40 \end{cases}$

(C) $\begin{cases} 5n + 10d = 300 \\ n + d = 40 \end{cases}$

(D) $\begin{cases} 40 - (n + d) = 300 \\ n + d = 40 \end{cases}$

(C) $\begin{cases} 2n + d = 300 \\ n + d = 40 \end{cases}$

5. In a prehistoric village, rocks, stones, and pebbles were used as money. The relative values of the "coins" were:

$$1 \text{ rock} = 7 \text{ stones}$$
$$1 \text{ rock} = 49 \text{ pebbles}$$

If a man used 6 rocks to purchase a hide that cost 5 rocks, 2 stones, and 3 pebbles, how much change was he owed?

(A) 1 rock, 5 stones, 4 pebbles

(B) 5 stones, 4 pebbles

(C) 4 stones, 4 pebbles

(D) 5 stones, 5 pebbles

(E) 6 stones, 5 pebbles

6. All of the following are implied by the equation $\dfrac{a}{b} = \dfrac{c}{d}$ EXCEPT

(A) $ad = bc$

(B) $\dfrac{a}{c} = \dfrac{b}{d}$

(C) $\dfrac{a - b}{b} = \dfrac{c - d}{d}$

(D) $\dfrac{a + b}{a - b} = \dfrac{c + d}{c - d}$

(E) $\dfrac{ad}{c} = \dfrac{bc}{d}$

7. The set S contains the integers 1 through 9 inclusive. What is the value of the number of even numbers in S minus the number of odd numbers in S?

(A) -2

(B) -1

(C) 0

(D) 1

(E) 2

8. Four equilateral triangles are placed so they form one big equilateral triangle. How many times as great as the perimeter of a small equilateral triangle is the perimeter of the big equilateral triangle?

   (A) 2

   (B) $2\frac{1}{2}$

   (C) 3

   (D) $3\frac{1}{2}$

   (E) 4

9. A 21-inch by 56-inch piece of material is to be cut up into equal squares. What is the greatest length that the sides of the squares may be so that there is no extra material?

   (A) 1

   (B) 3

   (C) 7

   (D) 14

   (E) 21

10. A job can be done in 25 hours by 6 people. How many people would be needed to do the same job in 8 or fewer hours?

   (A) 16

   (B) 17

   (C) 18

   (D) 19

   (E) 15

Grid-In Questions

Directions for Student-Produced Response Questions

Each of the remaining 10 questions requires you to solve the problem and enter your answer by marking the ovals in the special grid, as shown in the examples below.

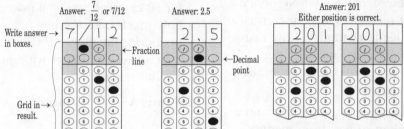

Answer: $\frac{7}{12}$ or 7/12

Answer: 2.5

Answer: 201
Either position is correct.

Write answer → in boxes.

←Fraction line

←Decimal point

Grid in → result.

Note: You may start your answers in any column, space permitting. Columns not needed should be left blank.

- Mark no more than one oval in any column.
- Because the answer sheet will be machine-scored, **you will receive credit only if the ovals are filled in correctly.**
- Although not required, it is suggested that you write your answer in the boxes at the top of the columns to help you fill in the ovals accurately.
- Some problems may have more than one correct answer. In such cases, grid only one answer.
- No question has a negative answer.
- **Mixed numbers** such as $2\frac{1}{2}$ must be gridded as 2.5 or 5/2.

  (If $\boxed{2 \; 1 \; / \; 2}$ is gridded, it will be interpreted as $\frac{21}{2}$, not $2\frac{1}{2}$.)

- **Decimal Accuracy:** If you obtain a decimal answer, **enter the most accurate value the grid will accommodate.** For example, if you obtain an answer such as 0.6666 . . . , you should record the result as .666 or .667. **Less accurate values such as .66 and .67 are not acceptable.**

Acceptable ways to grid $\frac{2}{3}$ = .6666 . . .

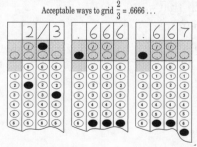

11. A 64-ounce bottle of concentrated detergent costs $7.20. The same size bottle of regular detergent costs $4.88. If one needs half an ounce of concentrated detergent or a whole ounce of regular detergent to wash a load of laundry, how many cents does one save per wash using the concentrated detergent?

12. If a car can go 30 miles on a gallon of gas, how many gallons are required to go 100 miles?

13. The average height of three students is between 5 foot 8 inches and 5 foot 10 inches. If two of the students are exactly 6 feet tall, what is a possible height of the third student, in inches?

14.

2	a	b
c	d	3
e	1	f

A 3 × 3 table is filled in, as pictured above, such that each of its rows, columns, and diagonals sum to 15. What is the sum of all 9 entries in the table?

15. The points $(0,0)$, $(a,3)$, and $(3,b)$ all lie on a line. What is the value of ab?

16. Chicken is selling for $1.50 per pound. If Elizabeth buys two pounds with a coupon for 50 cents off the total price, how much does she pay per pound for the chicken? Give your answer in dollars without the dollar sign.

Column A	Column B

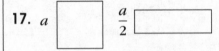

17. a $\dfrac{a}{2}$

The above square and rectangle have the same area. Denote the perimeter of the square P_s and the perimeter of the rectangle P_r. If $P_s = nP_r$, what is n?

18. What is the least positive number that may be represented in an SAT I/PSAT grid?

19.

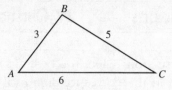

A circle is formed by spinning triangle ABC around point A. If its area is πx, what is x?

20.

$N = \{2, 4, 6\}$
$D = \{3, 6, 9\}$

What is the positive square root of the difference between the greatest and least fractions that can be formed by choosing one number from set N to be the numerator and one number from set D to be the denominator?

Stop!
If you finish before your timer rings, check your work on this section only. Do not turn to any other section in the test.

SECTION 5   TIME—25 MINUTES   29 QUESTIONS

Directions: For each question in this section, select the best answer from among the choices given and fill in the corresponding oval on your answer sheet. Each sentence needs a word or words to complete its meaning.

1. Life on La Digue, one of the smaller islands in the Seychelles group, goes on at a _____ pace; transport there is by ox cart, bicycle, or foot.

   (A) leisurely
   (B) jaunty
   (C) relentless
   (D) timeless
   (E) remarkable

2. Captain Jack's prompt, _____, and intelligent reactions were often necessary to save his ship and crew from disaster on their long voyage.

   (A) wise
   (B) decisive
   (C) swift
   (D) evasive
   (E) hereditary

3. The soft, rhythmic _____ of an owl's wings at night belies its _____ skill as a ruthless predator.

   (A) flap..definite
   (B) beat..dubious
   (C) motion..unknown
   (D) whir..formidable
   (E) singing..scheming

4. Leukemia is a long and weary process of disease, _____ for a fortunate number of people, marching _____ toward death for a few.

   (A) vanquished..inexorably
   (B) mitigated..vainly
   (C) conquered..peacefully
   (D) doomed..swiftly
   (E) foretold..inevitably

5. Once an enemy's true nature is _____, an opponent has some chance to _____ the situation and perhaps gain the upper hand.

   (A) superimposed..recreate
   (B) exposed..arbitrate
   (C) disguised..ameliorate
   (D) veiled..understand
   (E) manifest..improve

6. The complexity of Doris Lessing's philosophical speculations sometimes obscures the _____, the clear purpose and vision, of her prose.

   (A) abstraction
   (B) singularity
   (C) irregularity
   (D) intricacy
   (E) lucidity

7. An oil painting that is offered as genuine must be _____ by reputable and acknowledged art historians before it is put up for sale in the best galleries.

   (A) authenticated
   (B) credited
   (C) coordinated
   (D) authorized
   (E) analyzed

8. To consolidate his reign Tsar Ivan the Terrible created the *oprichniki,* a ruthless palace guard loyal only to himself; they were the _____ of the nobility who always threatened his _____ rule.

   (A) pride..vindictive
   (B) worst..illegal
   (C) scourge..tyrannical
   (D) founders..benign
   (E) betrayers..vulnerable

9. Unlike its original meaning, the word *sophistry* has acquired a negative _____, suggesting a _____ argument resulting from deceitful tactics artfully employed.

   (A) feeling..famous
   (B) significance..debatable
   (C) denotation..mature
   (D) meaning..forensic
   (E) connotation..specious

10. Although he appeared _____ and timorous to his fellows, the rabbit Fiver in *Watership Down* proved his value to their community with repeated, _____ predictions.

   (A) pompous..unwarranted
   (B) contentious..fallacious
   (C) unstable..unerring
   (D) untoward..vague
   (E) audacious..vacillating

11. Because this new edition of the ecology text offers _____ notes on recent experiments, we're assuming that the field has _____ considerably more knowledge.

    (A) external..accumulated

    (B) meretricious..exhibited

    (C) relatively few..avoided

    (D) copious..amassed

    (E) repetitive..assumed

12. His habitually negative attitude has at last become _____—harmful to his business life as well as to his personal one.

    (A) deleterious

    (B) chronic

    (C) devastating

    (D) derogatory

    (E) embarrassing

13. The educational community _____ the local paper for covering the career of a local teenage singer in depth while _____ to celebrate the achievements of their high school debate team.

    (A) commended..forgetting

    (B) applauded..opting

    (C) derided..intending

    (D) condemned..overlooking

    (E) castigated..neglecting

14. A gifted orator, Marion Wright Edelman is capable of delivering a(n) _____ graduation address that _____ common truths with passion and insight.

    (A) impenetrable..utters

    (B) ringing..infuses

    (C) intriguing..demolishes

    (D) attenuated..delivers

    (E) original..addresses

15. Reacting to his friend's offering of champagne as he lay on his deathbed, the penniless, outcast playwright Oscar Wilde is reputed to have said. "I am dying beyond my means," perhaps a(n) _____ comment.

    (A) reticent

    (B) irreversible

    (C) apocryphal

    (D) acerbic

    (E) provincial

Directions: The passages below are followed by two questions per passage. Answer each question based on what is stated or implied in the passage.

Questions 16 and 17 refer to the following passage:

While Europe has traditionally drawn visitors to admire its monuments along with its age-old customs, individual states in North America are only recently seeing the commercial advantages in heritage tourism. In southern states, in particular, where history is alive and kicking, the advantages of marketing the past are clearly attractive. Just recently Kitty Hawk, North Carolina, was flooded with tourists celebrating the birth of flight. Come, see, and spend is the idea.

16. Of the following choices, which answer best describes the rhetorical purpose(s) of the last sentence?

   (A) for amusement— although this sentence is somewhat simplistic

   (B) ending the paragraph on a lighthearted note

   (C) encapsulating the paragraph's material in an amusing way

   (D) reiterating the importance of tourist dollars

   (E) emphasizing the importance of historical sites

17. A writer mindful of the need to write in a precise, vivid way would revise this passage in primarily which one of the following ways?

   (A) Revise to be more humorous

   (B) Revise to add descriptive adjectives and adverbs

   (C) Revise for succinctness

   (D) Replace weak verbs with active ones

   (E) Replace the long sentences with short, punchy ones

Questions 18 and 19 refer to the following passage:

(1) The artistic term "cubism" refers to the style of an early twentieth-century school of painters who represented surfaces and figures—even light, shade, and tints of color—by means of a wide variety of cubical and/or geometrical shapes. (2) Painter Henri Matisse dubbed the work "cubism" in 1908, and he was not in a flattering mood at the time. (3) Nonetheless, this abstract style based on realism but divorced from it, has endured, leading the way to what we call modern art. (4) Its major exponents include Fernand Leger, Georges Braque, Andre Derain, and the even better-known Pablo Picasso.

18. The tone in sentence 2 is best termed

(A) acidic

(B) negative

(C) factual

(D) reportorial

(E) ironic

19. In sentence 4, the word exponent is used to mean

(A) someone who is above the rest of a group

(B) one who interprets or exemplifies

(C) someone who achieves highly

(D) one who flouts a convention

(E) a harbinger, one who goes before the crowd

The following passage is a conversation between a young actress and a friend of hers. The time is the 1890s and the place is New York City. The actress, Carrie, has had some success in the theater and is about to become a celebrity.

Line   The music ceased and he arose, taking a standing position before her, as if to rest himself.

"Why don't you get into some good, strong comedy-drama?" he said. He was looking directly at her now, studying her face.

5   Her large, sympathetic eyes and pain-touched mouth appealed to him as proofs of his judgment.

"Perhaps I shall," she returned.

"That's your field," he added.

"Do you think so?"

10   "Yes," he said; "I do. I don't suppose you're aware of it, but there is something about your eyes and mouth which fits you for that sort of work."

Carrie was thrilled to be taken so seriously. For the moment, loneliness deserted her. Here was praise which was keen and

15   analytical.

"It's in your eyes and mouth," he went on abstractedly. "I remember thinking, the first time I saw you, that there was something peculiar about your mouth. I thought you were about to cry."

20   "How odd," said Carrie, warm with delight. This was what her heart craved.

"Then I noticed that that was your natural look, and tonight I saw it again. There's a shadow about your eyes, too, which gives your face much this same character. It's in the depth of

25   them, I think."

Carrie looked straight into his face, wholly aroused.

"You probably are not aware of it," he added.

She looked away, pleased that he should speak thus, longing to be equal to this feeling written upon her countenance. It

30   unlocked the door to a new desire.

She had cause to ponder over this until they met again— several weeks or more. It showed her she was drifting away from the old ideal which had filled her in the dressing rooms of the Avery stage and thereafter, for a long time. Why had she lost it?

35   "I know why you should be a success," he said, another time, "if you had a more dramatic part. I've studied it out—"

"What is it?" said Carrie.

"Well," he said, as one pleased with a puzzle, "the expression in your face is one that comes out in different things. You

40 get the same thing in a pathetic song, or any picture which moves you deeply. It's a thing the world likes to see, because it's a natural expression of its longing."

Carrie gazed without exactly getting the import of what he meant.

45   "The world is always struggling to express itself," he went on. "Most people are not capable of voicing their feelings. They depend upon others. That is what genius is for. One man expresses their desires for them in music; another in poetry; another one in a play. Sometimes nature does it in a face—it makes the

50 face representative of all desire. That's what has happened in your case."

He looked at her with so much of the import of the thing in his eyes that she caught it. At least, she got the idea that her look was something which represented the world's longing. She took

55 it to her heart as a creditable thing, until he added:

"That puts a burden of duty on you. It so happens that you have this thing. It is no credit to you—that is, I mean, you might not have had it. You paid nothing to get it. But now that you have it, you must do something with it."

60   "What?" Carrie asked.

"I should say, turn to the dramatic field. You have so much sympathy and such a melodious voice. Make them valuable to others. It will make your powers endure."

Carrie did not understand this last. All the rest showed her

65 that her comedy success was little or nothing.

"What do you mean?" she asked.

"Why, just this. You have this quality in your eyes and mouth and in your nature. You can lose it, you know. If you turn away from it and live to satisfy yourself alone, it will go fast

70 enough. The look will leave your eyes. Your mouth will change. Your power to act will disappear. You may think they won't, but they will. Nature takes care of that."

He was so interested in forwarding all good causes that he
sometimes became enthusiastic, giving vent to these preachments.
75 Something in Carrie appealed to him. He wanted to stir her up.

"I know," she said, absently, feeling slightly guilty of neglect.

"If I were you," he said, "I'd change."

The effect of this was like roiling helpless waters. Carrie
troubled over it in her rocking chair for days.

80 "I don't believe I'll stay in comedy so very much longer," she
eventually remarked to Lola, her friend.

"Oh, why not?" said the latter.

"I think," she said, "I can do better in a serious play."

"What put that idea in your head?"

85 "Oh, nothing," she answered; "I've always thought so."

Still, she did nothing—grieving. It was a long way to this
better thing—or seemed so—and comfort was about her; hence
the inactivity and longing.

20. Which of the following is the
most plausible inference to
make based on the statement
in lines 5-6?

(A) The speaker is intelligent but somewhat
conceited.

(B) Carrie is trying to
beguile the speaker
with her good looks.

(C) The speaker is clearly
revealing his own
self-deception.

(D) Carrie has suffered
some personal anguish
caused by the speaker.

(E) Carrie and the speaker
are both rehearsing a
scene from a play.

21. Carrie feels the speaker's
comments to be "keen and
analytical" (lines 14-15)
primarily because

(A) she is accustomed to
hearing excellent
criticism of her work

(B) she knows she is
speaking with a highly
educated and informed
professional

(C) the speaker's comments
confirm her own
opinions about the
quality of her work

(D) her innocent vanity is
flattered by such
favorable judgments

(E) her own ambition and
drive need this kind of
positive support in
order for her to succeed

22. Carrie's real talent as an actress that so appeals to the speaker is apparently her ability to project an image of

    (A) threatened innocence and virtue

    (B) a seductive beauty and temptress

    (C) a highly skilled manipulator

    (D) towering pride and achievement

    (E) universal qualities of kindness and generosity

23. Which of the following best states what Carrie's "heart craved" (line 21)?

    (A) Sincere attention from an attractive man

    (B) Assurance that she would never fail

    (C) Intelligent public relations and promotion

    (D) Better opportunities and offers to perform

    (E) Admiration and strong ego support

24. The man speaking to Carrie assumes that she

    (A) needs him to be her agent and manage her career

    (B) lacks the necessary self-knowledge to create opportunities for herself

    (C) will be easy to take advantage of when his chance arrives

    (D) is impressed with his power of critical intelligence

    (E) really wants only to get married and have a family

25. The "feeling written upon her countenance" (line 29) is best described as one of

    (A) glamour and sophistication

    (B) grief and abandonment

    (C) pathos and vulnerability

    (D) ambition and willfulness

    (E) languor and self-satisfaction

26. The man implies that unless Carrie cultivates those artistic talents he sees in her (lines 67–72), she will

   (A) grow restless and eventually leave the theater

   (B) suffer increasingly nasty reviews from her critics

   (C) be in defiance of nature and become vulnerable to God's anger

   (D) lose control over her own future

   (E) lose her talents altogether

27. In line 78, the word "roiling" most nearly means

   (A) heating excessively

   (B) turning around

   (C) stirring up

   (D) poisoning

   (E) purifying

28. The author's chief purpose in the passage is to

   (A) evoke sympathy for the energetic and thoughtful man

   (B) clarify and highlight one particular trait of Carrie's

   (C) subtly reduce Carrie's image to that of a lonely, alienated woman

   (D) portray a potential romantic relationship between two young people

   (E) depict a bully engaged in humiliating an innocent young woman

29. Carrie's final response to the man's suggestions for her future career (lines 80–86) implies that she is

   (A) an indecisive person with little self-confidence and faith in her future

   (B) totally reliant on friends and coworkers for advice and support

   (C) the most astute judge of her prospects and talents

   (D) a very disciplined, reflective person who will take only known risks

   (E) an unintelligent, indolent person who lives only in the present

Stop!
Do not go on to the next section of the test until you have set your timer.

| SECTION 6 | TIME—20 MINUTES | 20 QUESTIONS |

Directions: In this section, solve each problem, and then choose the most appropriate answer from the choices given.

1. A number that is divisible by both 6 and 8 is also divisible by

   (A) 5
   (B) 9
   (C) 11
   (D) 16
   (E) 24

2. On a certain island there are liars and truth-tellers. Liars must always lie and truth-tellers must always tell the truth. A visitor comes across a native and asks him if he always tells the truth. The native responds, "I always tell the truth." The native could be

   (A) a truth-teller
   (B) a liar
   (C) either a truth-teller or a liar
   (D) neither a truth-teller nor a liar
   (E) None of the above

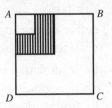

3. The three squares pictured above share a common vertex at *A*. The interior squares each have another vertex at the center of another one of the squares. What is the ratio of the area of the shaded region to the area of the unshaded region?

   (A) 3:4
   (B) 3:8
   (C) 3:12
   (D) 3:13
   (E) 3:16

4. On a long street the houses are numbered in jumps of 6. That is, the first house has a street number 6, the second 12, and so on. What is the sum of the last digits of the street numbers of the 83rd, 84th, 85th, 86th, and 87th houses?

(A) 15
(B) 20
(C) 25
(D) 85
(E) 90

5. A man can paint m meters of fence in h hours and 15 minutes. What is his average speed in meters per hour?

(A) $h\left(1 + \dfrac{1}{4}\right)m$

(B) $\dfrac{m}{h + 15}$

(C) $\dfrac{m}{h + \dfrac{1}{4}}$

(D) $\dfrac{h + 15}{m}$

(E) $\dfrac{h + \dfrac{1}{4}}{m}$

6. A car is driven 2 miles across town. If the radius of a wheel on the car is 1 foot, how many revolutions has the wheel made?

(5,280 feet = 1 mile)

(A) $\dfrac{5,280}{\pi}$

(B) $\dfrac{10,560}{\pi}$

(C) $\dfrac{2,640}{\pi}$

(D) 5,280

(E) 10,560

7. The operation $\boxed{x}$ indicates that one should subtract 2 from x and then multiply the result by 2. The operation $\widetilde{x}$ indicates that one should multiply x by 2 and then subtract 2 from the product. $\widetilde{x} - \boxed{x} =$

(A) -2
(B) 0
(C) 2
(D) 4
(E) It cannot be determined from the information given.

8. $\left(x - \dfrac{1}{x}\right)^2 + 4 =$

(A) 4

(B) 5

(C) $x^2 - \left(\dfrac{1}{x}\right)^2 + 4$

(D) $x^2 + \left(\dfrac{1}{x}\right)^2$

(E) $\left(x + \dfrac{1}{x}\right)^2$

9. On a street corner there are two flashing lights, a red one and a blue one. The red one flashes three times per minute, and the blue one flashes twice per minute. If the lights start off flashing at the same time, how often do they flash together?

(A) once every 6 seconds

(B) once every 10 seconds

(C) once every minute

(D) once every 2 minutes

(E) once every 6 minutes

10.

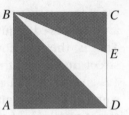

In this figure, ABCD is a square with area 2. If $\overline{DE}$ is twice as long as $\overline{EC}$, what is the area of $\triangle BED$?

(A) 1

(B) $\dfrac{1}{3}$

(C) $\dfrac{2}{3}$

(D) $\sqrt{2}$

(E) $\dfrac{\sqrt{2}}{3}$

The directions for grid-ins are on page 287.

11. A bath tub measures 5 feet by 1 foot by 18 inches. If it takes 6 minutes to drain the water out of a half full tub, how fast is the water flowing in cubic feet per minute?

12. It costs $2,000 per year to operate a boiler that is 60% efficient (60% of the gas is turned in to heat). How many dollars could one expect to save annually, if one replaced the boiler with one that is 90% efficient? (Do not code the dollar sign in your answer.)

13. If $f(x) = \frac{2}{3}x + 2$ and

$g(x) = \frac{3}{2}x + 15$, for what

value of a does $f(a) = g(-a)$?

14. Solve for *positive x* in the equation: $5x^2 + 6x = 560$.

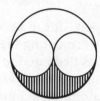

15. In the figure above, two circles are drawn inside a larger circle with radius 4 such that the two circles intersect at the center of the larger circle, and each circle is tangent to the others. If one randomly picks a point in the large circle, what is the probability it will be in the shaded section?

16. How many revolutions will a 28-inch diameter bicycle wheel make during a 11-mile ride? ($\pi \approx \frac{22}{7}$, 1 mile = 5280 feet, and 1 foot = 12 inches).

17. What is the probability of correctly guessing the last two digits of a number known to be even?

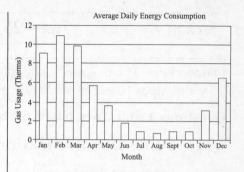

Average Daily Energy Consumption

18. A family uses natural gas to heat its house, heat water, dry clothes, and cook. The above graph shows the family's average daily natural gas usage measured in therms during each month of the year. Assume that all activities except heating the house require the same amount of gas year round, and the family does not heat the house in the summer. Within 2 therms, estimate how much gas the family uses to heat its house per year.

$$4 \leq a \leq 14$$
$$7 \leq b \leq 12$$

19. Given the above constraints, what is the minimum value of $\frac{b}{a}$?

20. The minimum SAT math score is 200 and the maximum is 800. If there are 60 questions, what is the average amount each correct question contributes to one's score?

| SECTION 7 | TIME—25 MINUTES | 27 QUESTIONS |

Directions: The passage below is followed by two questions. Answer the questions based on what is stated or implied in the passage.

Questions 1 and 2 are based on the following passage:

1945–1960: Decolonization

The Second World War had a decisive effect upon African development and change. The wave of Asian independence during the 1940s together with the founding of the United Nations dedicated to equal rights and self-determination combined to enhance the position of the emergent groups in African society and to transform them into powerful political movements. Opposition to alien influence was not, of course, a new phenomenon in Africa. Indeed, protest groups had from time to time during the previous half century expressed resentment and resistance to Christianity, to Western education, and to the disruption of traditional economic practices.

1. Based on the prose presentation and the writer's style, we can infer that this piece of writing is most likely

   (A) a bit of newspaper journalism
   (B) part of a personal letter
   (C) a portion of a history textbook
   (D) part of an official government report
   (E) a portion of a speech

2. Which of the following statements best expresses the theme of this paragraph?

   (A) The Second World War changed Africa forever.
   (B) WWII and other external forces fueled Africa's drive for independence.
   (C) Africa had a history of resisting Western thought.
   (D) Before World War II, Africa had been a more docile continent.
   (E) Opposition to alien influence erupted after the Second World War.

Directions: For each question in this section, select the best answer from among the choices given and fill in the corresponding oval on your answer sheet. Each sentence needs a word or words to complete the meaning.

3. Many team members were abrupt, even _____ at times, about responding to suggestions from their young, inexperienced swimming coach.

   (A) pleasant
   (B) curt
   (C) uninterested
   (D) hesitant
   (E) unaware

4. The size and simplicity of an Indian tepee or wigwam lead us to conclude that it was built more for _____ than for _____.

   (A) tradition..feasibility
   (B) liveability..comfort
   (C) custom..efficiency
   (D) practicality..ostentation
   (E) pretense..appearance

5. In general, _____ behavior on the part of administration aggravates an already tense worker problem rather than _____ it.

   (A) humorless..worsening
   (B) responsible..soothing
   (C) autocratic..alleviating

   (D) diplomatic..condoning
   (E) meretricious..maximizing

6. Ignoring the power and _____ of domineering, even occasionally despotic, foreign governments could _____ the demise of our own.

   (A) pride..continue
   (B) ambition..herald
   (C) thrust..forestall
   (D) prestige..enhance
   (E) colonialism..enjoin

7. While certain herbicides appear _____ to farmers deeply concerned with profit and loss, their effect has been to _____ the bird population dependent on formerly weedy hedgerows and ditches.

   (A) beneficial..decimate
   (B) applicable..augment
   (C) attractive..dishearten
   (D) prohibitive..enhance
   (E) mandatory..restructure

8. "I'm sure Jackie didn't intentionally _____," his older sister said quickly, "because he rarely even _____!"

   (A) prognosticate..hurries
   (B) castigate..bothers
   (C) equivocate..categorizes
   (D) prevaricate..fibs
   (E) deliberate..hesitates

9. Lawmakers eager to promote a piece of legislation no doubt feel _____ whenever their bill _____ committee.

   (A) thwarted..languishes in
   (B) exasperation..races through
   (C) uplifted..bogs down in
   (D) satisfaction..is deposited in
   (E) exhilaration..is studied in

10. Known for _____ rather than garrulity, Mrs. Brown was nonplussed when nominated to be president, a position that frequently demanded _____.

   (A) amiability..gravity
   (B) fastidiousness..precision
   (C) reticence..eloquence
   (D) obsequiousness..courtesy
   (E) incoherence..clarity

11. Though purists say it is _____ to suggest "splitting" an infinitive with an adverb, e.g., *to radically alter,* we need to _____ each inherited grammatical guideline to decide whether or not it suits our evolving language.

   (A) redundant..evaluate
   (B) distasteful..peruse
   (C) heresy..scrutinize
   (D) expeditious..establish
   (E) incongruous..ponder

12. Long, elegant skirts, flowery speech, and a more formal life style seemed _____ with the imposing, elaborate, often _____ architectural style favored in America in the late 1800s.

   (A) to contrast..expensive
   (B) at odds..preservationist
   (C) archaic..Grecian
   (D) to proliferate..romantic
   (E) compatible..baroque

Directions: The passages below are followed by questions based on their content. Answer each question based on what is stated or implied in the passage.

Questions 13–18 are based on the following passage:

Line   The central mystery of the Celtic religion, and the ceremonial
rituals which embodied its essence, will always be elusive. For
many the Celtic mystique, with its romantic emphasis on the fairy
and the spirit-world, has obscured the spirituality of these warrior
5   peoples and the fact that they even had a religion. The ancient
oral tradition that perpetuated the laws, legends, and the tribal
teachings, through the trained memories of a group of poets and
priests, made the act of writing unnecessary. And, much like the
prohibitions laid on the Celtic warrior heroes, which predestined
10   their lives and actions, the taboo on writing continued as long as
the old religion lasted.

The earliest remnants of Celtic culture in Central Europe are
usually dated between 800 and 450 B.C. and assigned to the
Hallstatt culture, after the metal artifacts found in a cemetery at
15   Hallstatt in Austria, a centre for salt and copper mining. The later
Celtic phase, the La Tène, named after a village site in Switzer-
land, continued in Continental Europe until Roman times. The
style of ornament associated with the La Tène culture, with its
wild, imaginative but formalized decoration of floral patterns and
20   abstract symbols, was still the dominant characteristic of Celtic
metalwork, stonecarving, and manuscript illumination in Britain
and Ireland a thousand years later.

The Celts emerged from the Rhinelands of Central Europe as
a distinctive group of clans or tribes between 1000 and 500 B.C.
25   Their language, religion, social organization, and customs were
different from those in the Mediterranean south, or further east by
the Danube. In general the Celts seem to have many affinities
with Indo-European warrior groups who had overrun the Indus
Valley civilizations a millennium or so earlier. A number of archaic
30   linguistic forms, such as *raja,* king (Latin *rex,* Irish *ri,* and Gallic
-rix) or *rigu,* queen, as well as many others connected with
sacred customs and social organizations, are shared by Indo-

European languages in Asia and Europe. Cultural affinities
between the Celts and India can be also traced in the animal
35   rituals in which the spirit of the new king or queen is rendered
incarnate with that of a bull or horse; in the act of fasting to gain
recognition for a grievance; in the position of women and the fact
that they were accorded parity with men (Boadicea in Britain and
the legendary Maeve in Ireland) in the warrior class; in metric
40   forms, which in the *Rig Veda,* oldest and most important of the
sacred books, are similar to some early Irish and Welsh verse; and
in the close relationship between teacher and pupil, which is still
such a feature of Indian religious life and which was an essential
part of the Celtic oral tradition.

13. The passage is primarily
concerned with the

(A) artifacts left by various
Celtic cultures

(B) oral tribal teachings of
two separate but related
Celtic cultures

(C) dominant characteristics
of Celtic art

(D) similarities between
Indo-European warrior
groups and the Celts

(E) elusive ceremonial
rituals of the Celtic
people

14. The passage suggests that
Celtic culture is "elusive"
(lines 1–2) primarily because

(A) there are relatively few
artifacts of the Celts

(B) Celtic traditions were
mingled with those of
Wales and Ireland

(C) other related groups of
warrior peoples added
their beliefs to those of
the Celts

(D) few archaeologists and
historians have been
properly trained to sift
the available material
for facts

(E) the Celts left no written
records

15. In line 13, the phrase
"assigned to" most nearly
means

(A) allotted for

(B) set apart for

(C) designated as

(D) ascribed to

(E) transferred to

16. The word *raja* is mentioned in line 30 as an example of a linguistic form that

    (A) has influenced modern linguistic forms despite its antiquity

    (B) is similar in Latin, Gallic, and Irish

    (C) is shared by some Asian and European languages

    (D) was used by Indo-European warrior groups in the Indus Valley

    (E) was used by the Celts but not by their neighbors to the east and south

17. Which one of the following is NOT mentioned in the passage as a cultural affinity between the Celts and India?

    (A) The position of women

    (B) Animal rituals involving a bull or horse

    (C) Ceremonial feasts as acts of recognition

    (D) Forms of language

    (E) Metric forms

18. It can be inferred that the Celtic verse mentioned in lines 39–41 differs from such Indian sacred texts as the *Rig Veda* in that the Celtic verse

    (A) is older than the Indian sacred texts

    (B) was passed down orally while the Indian sacred texts were written

    (C) contains fewer archaic Indo-European linguistic forms than do the Indian sacred texts

    (D) displays less complex schemes of rhyme and rhythm than do the Indian sacred texts

    (E) does not concern itself with religious or spiritual themes

Questions 19–27 are based on the following passage:

Line   Ruins of Greek construction abound in the Mediterranean region,
        but as a matter of perspective one must realize that all written
        records of ancient Greece are exceedingly scarce. It is difficult to
        estimate how much Greek literature has survived in any form, but
5   it almost certainly must be less than 1 percent. Very few of the
        surviving works are in their original form, almost all are corrupted
        by careless copying over many centuries, and few contain much
        information that would permit dating them even indirectly.
        Nevertheless, it is clear that ancient Greece was the scene of
10   much geological thinking . . . and that many of the seminal ideas
        eventually found their way into printed books.
            The fragmentary kaleidoscope of Greek science records
        isolated glimpses of important geological understanding. In the
        sixth century B.C., the Pythagoreans were the first to teach that
15   the Earth was round because it cast a round shadow on the moon
        in eclipses. Eratosthenes (ca. 276–ca. 195 B.C.), the second
        director of the Museum Library in Alexandria, devised a method
        of measuring the diameter of the Earth's sphere. He observed that
        on the summer solstice, the longest day of the year, the sun stood
20   at an angle of one-fiftieth of a circle from vertical in Alexandria,
        but was directly overhead in Syene (now Aswan). He had no
        accurate way of measuring the north-south distance between the
        two places (the length of the meridian), but he made a reasonable
        estimate and calculated a remarkably accurate value for the
25   Earth's diameter. Later commentators have pointed out the
        obvious sources of error in his estimate, but that does not
        diminish the brilliant simplicity and fundamental grandeur of the
        experiment. There is some uncertainty about the units he used,
        but his result appears to be only about 20 percent larger than
30   modern determinations.
            Extending his calculations to include some doubtful sun-
        angle determinations and rough distance estimates, Eratosthenes
        then attempted to establish a coordinate grid for the whole
        ancient world. The result was a distinct improvement in the
35   world map of the day, but the unreliability of the data was
        recognized and severely criticized by the astronomer Hipparchus

of Bithynia (?–after 127 B.C.). In categorically rejecting conclusions
based on inadequate data, Hipparchus was being very scientific,
but in failing to concede that an inspired guess is better than no
40   information at all he set geography back a fair distance. It was
this same Hipparchus who pioneered the quantitative approach to
astronomy and developed the precession of the equinoxes.
Almost all of his original writings are lost and his work is known
mostly from references to it in Ptolemy's *Almagest,* written about
45   three centuries after Hipparchus died.

      Herodotus of Halicarnassus (?484–?425 B.C.), the great histo-
rian of Greek antiquity, concerned himself mainly with political
and military history, but he had traveled as far as the Black Sea,
Mesopotamia, and Egypt and made accurate geological observa-
50   tions. He was aware that earthquakes cause large-scale fracturing
and thus may shape the landscape. . . . He noted the sediment
carried by the Nile and estimated the amounts of deposition
from the annual floods in the Nile Valley and the growth of the
great delta. "Egypt . . . is an acquired country, the gift of the
55   river," he wrote, and throughout those discussions he displayed
a remarkable understanding of the vastness of geologic time.

19. The reference to the "ruins of Greek construction" in line 1 serves primarily to

(A)   provide a concrete example of the ancient Greeks' technical abilities

(B)   introduce the relationship between Greek architecture and Greek geology

(C)   highlight the influence of Greek culture throughout the Mediterranean region

(D)   establish a contrast between the large number of ruins and the scarcity of written documents

(E)   show that the ancient Greeks' intellectual legacy has endured better than have their physical monuments

20. The author calls ancient Greek geological ideas "seminal" in line 10 to suggest that these ideas

(A) contained the seeds of later development

(B) were fragmented or incomplete

(C) seem amorphous or unformed

(D) revealed primitive thought

(E) displayed the Greeks' carelessness

21. The passage as a whole is primarily concerned with explaining

(A) the differences in methodology between two Greek geologists

(B) how ancient Greek geology has affected modern geological thinking

(C) some of the remarkable achievements of early Greek geologists

(D) why the written records of ancient Greek science are so fragmentary

(E) why the ancient Greeks were fascinated with geology

22. The author views the achievements of Eratosthenes with

(A) professional detachment

(B) slight skepticism

(C) respect and qualified admiration

(D) amusement and deep interest

(E) condescension

23. It can be inferred from the passage that the astronomer Hipparchus was NOT

(A) scientific in his approach

(B) particularly flexible or intuitive

(C) pioneering in his approach

(D) published in his time

(E) critical of other scientific studies

24. Which of the following is cited in the passage as being true of the work of Hipparchus?

(A) It helped to establish that the Earth was round.

(B) It was criticized in its day by Eratosthenes of Alexandria.

(C) It was primarily concerned with astronomy rather than with geology.

(D) Its conclusions were nearly always based on accurate and reliable data.

(E) Its existence is corroborated in a work written centuries after Hipparchus's death.

25. Which of the following is most likely to have been an objection raised by Hipparchus to Eratosthenes's research?

(A) Eratosthenes could not accurately measure the distances between the sites of his sun-angle measurements.

(B) Eratosthenes failed to take the precession of the equinoxes into account in making his calculations.

(C) Eratosthenes used estimated values when he should have taken accurate measurements.

(D) Eratosthenes's coordinate grid was based on a measurement of the Earth's diameter that was too large.

(E) Eratosthenes's calculations were faulty.

26. According to the passage, Greek geological information was

I. almost all lost

II. of little value for today's scientists

III. surprisingly accurate and often grand in scope

IV. acquired after much thought and calculation

V. carefully dated and logically explained

(A) I, III, and V

(B) II and IV

(C) III and V

(D) I, III, and IV

(E) I, II, and V

27. In calling Egypt "an acquired country" (line 54), Herodotus was referring to the way in which

   (A) Herodotus had added Egypt to the list of countries whose geography he had studied

   (B) earthquakes had changed Egypt's natural borders to increase its territory

   (C) Egypt's military might have enabled it to annex parts of other countries

   (D) the Nile's predictable floods enabled Egypt's economic prosperity

   (E) the Nile had added sediment to the great delta to increase Egypt's land mass

Stop!

Do not go on to the next section of the test until you have set your timer.

Directions: The two passages below are followed by questions based on their content and on the relationship between the two passages. Answer the questions on the basis of what is stated or implied in the passages and in any introductory material that may be provided.

The passages below are about the Maori people of New Zealand. The first passage, written in 1770, is from the log of Captain James Cook, who explored the southern Pacific around that time. The second is a general account of the Maoris written by another Englishman about 1900, more than a century later.

Passage 1

Line The natives of this country are a strong, raw-boned, well-made active people rather above than under the ordinary size, especially the men. Those who do not disfigure their faces by tattooing and scarifying have in general very good features. The men
5 generally wear their hair long, combed up and tied upon the crown of their heads; some of the women wear it long and loose upon their shoulders, old women especially.

They seem to enjoy a good state of health and many of them live to a good old age. Many of the old and some of the middle
10 aged men have their faces marked and tattooed with black, and some few we have seen have had their backs and thighs and other parts of their bodies marked, but this is less common.

The women have very soft voices and may by that alone be known from the men. The making of cloth and all other domestic
15 work is wholly done by them, and the more laborious work such as building boats, houses, and tilling the ground, fishing, etc. by the men.

Whenever we were visited by any number of them that had never heard or seen anything of us before, they generally came
20 off in the largest canoes they had, some of which will carry 60, 80, or 100 people. They always brought their best clothes along with them which they put on as soon as they came near the ship. In each canoe were generally an old man, in some two or three; these used always to direct the others, were better clothed and
25 generally carried a halberd or battle ax in their hands or some

such like thing that distinguished them from the others. As soon as they came within about a stone's throw of the ship, they would lay by and call out to us to come ashore with them so they could kill us with their spears which they would shake at us.

30   At times they would dance the war dance, and at other times they would trade and talk to us and answer such questions as were put to them with all the calmness imaginable. Then again, they would begin the war dance, shaking their paddles and spears and making strange contortions at the same time. As soon as they

35   had worked themselves up to a proper pitch, they would begin to attack us with stones and darts and oblige us, whether we would or no, to fire upon them. Musketry they never regarded unless they felt the effect, but great guns they did because these threw stones farther than they could comprehend. After they found that

40   our arms were so much superior to theirs and that we took no advantage of that superiority, and a little time given them to reflect upon it, they ever after were our good friends.

The Maoris are far happier than we Europeans; being wholly unacquainted not only with the superfluous but the necessary

45   conveniences so much sought after in Europe, they are happy in not knowing the use of them. They live in a tranquillity which is not disturbed by the inequality of condition: the Earth and sea of their own accord furnish them with all things necessary for life. They covet not magnificent houses, house-hold stuff, etc.; they

50   live in a warm and fine climate and enjoy a very wholesome air, so that they have very little need of clothing and this they seem to be fully sensible of, for many to whom we gave cloth, etc., left it carelessly upon the sea beach and in the woods as a thing they had no manner of use for. In short, they seemed to set no value

55   upon anything we gave them.

Passage 2

Among the most industrious of Polynesian races, the Maoris have always been famed for wood-carving; and in building, weaving, and dyeing they had made great advances before whites arrived. They are also good farmers and bold seamen. In the Maori wars

60   they showed much strategic skill, and their knowledge of fortification was very remarkable. Every Maori was a soldier, and war was the chief business and joy of this life. Tribal wars were incessant. The weapons were wooden spears, clubs, and stone

tomahawks. The women were allowed a voice in the tribe's
65 affairs, and sometimes accompanied the men into battle.

Ferocious as they were in war, the Maoris are generally
hospitable and affectionate in their home life, and a pleasant
characteristic, noticed by Captain Cook, is their respect and care
of the old. They buried their dead, the cemeteries being orna-
70 mented with carved posts. Their religion was a nature worship
intimately connected with the veneration of ancestors. There was
a belief in the soul, which was supposed to dwell in the left eye.
They had no doubt as to a future state, but no definite idea of a
supreme being.
75   While they had no written language, a considerable oral
literature of songs, legends, and traditions existed. Their priest-
hood was a highly trained profession, and they had schools which
taught a knowledge of the stars and constellations, for many of
which they had names.
80   Many Maoris are natural orators and poets, and a chief was
expected to add these accomplishments to his prowess as a
warrior or his skill as a seaman. They have been called the Britons
of the south, and their courage in defending their country and
their intelligence amplify the compliment. By the New Zealanders,
85 they are cordially liked.

1. Which of the following is the
   most apt reading of the
   phrase "above than under"
   (line 2)?

   (A) more than less
   (B) nearer than farther
   (C) taller than shorter
   (D) heavier than lighter
   (E) stronger than weaker

2. Which of the following
   phrases is assumed, and not
   written, between "fishing,
   etc." and "by the men" (lines
   16–17)?

   (A) is assigned
   (B) and such actions
   (C) or war-making
   (D) is mostly done
   (E) not women, but

3. The natives' behavior when first encountering the European seamen appeared to the seamen to be

   (A) puzzling and contradictory
   (B) clever and humorous
   (C) sinister and malevolent
   (D) heroic and gallant
   (E) friendly and hospitable

4. The author implies that the Maoris became "good friends" of the seamen because the Maoris

   (A) had a judicious sense of reality
   (B) needed the seamen's knowledge
   (C) admired the seamen's energy
   (D) were forced to obey the seamen
   (E) admired the generosity of the seamen

5. The author suggests the Maoris are happier than Europeans because they

   (A) are healthier and stronger
   (B) lack guns and cannon
   (C) seem not to be acquisitive
   (D) have made war into a sport
   (E) have no commerce or money

6. In line 47, the phrase "inequality of condition" most nearly means

   (A) differences in inherited talents
   (B) social, class, and economic distinctions
   (C) physical variations in health
   (D) different historical and geographical backgrounds
   (E) degrees of wealth and poverty

7. In line 71, "veneration" most nearly means

   (A) flattering explanation of
   (B) deep reverence for
   (C) biological preservation of
   (D) easy appreciation for
   (E) supernatural fear of

8. The phrase "a future state" (line 73) is best understood to mean

(A) modern England

(B) colonial New Zealand

(C) an advanced culture

(D) protracted states of war

(E) life after death

9. The phrase "amplify the compliment" (line 84) is best interpreted to mean

(A) makes the Maoris as fine a society in their way as the Britons are in their own way

(B) extends the worth of the Maoris' natural aggressiveness and tendencies to make war

(C) enlarges the meaning of their ceremonies for the dead and their ancestor worship

(D) that, compared with the Maoris, the Britons are deficient in courage and intelligence

(E) that, though respected by the New Zealanders, the Maoris are a threat to British law and ethics

10. Passage 1 differs from Passage 2 primarily in which of the following aspects?

(A) The extent to which logical analysis is employed

(B) The persuasive goals of the authors

(C) Subject matter and facts

(D) Style of language and tone

(E) Authors' assumptions about culture

11. Compared to Passage 2 in terms of style, Passage 1 is

(A) sentimental and lyrical

(B) pointed and persuasive

(C) a closely reasoned argument

(D) an urgently stated sermon

(E) relaxed and discursive

12. The information about the Maoris in Passage 1 would seem to be more reliable than the information in Passage 2 because

    (A) Passage 1 is longer than Passage 2

    (B) the author of Passage 2 is not as friendly as the author of Passage 1

    (C) the author of Passage 1 was with the Maoris when he wrote about them

    (D) the author of Passage 2 offers fewer facts than does the author of Passage 1

    (E) the author of Passage 2 was writing at a later date than was the author of Passage 1

Directions: The following brief passages are followed by two questions each. Answer questions based on material stated or implied in the passage.

Questions 13 and 14 are based on the following passage:

When June arrives, so do the red-brown beetles known as June bugs. These hearty, inch-long bugs crash into screens and windows and whirl away as if unfazed by the encounter, probably thanks to their heavily-armored shells. But before they could fly around and party, these bugs spent the winter underground, hatching into white, soft-bodied grubs only after the ground warmed up. As grubs they ate your parents' grass, corn, potatoes, and strawberries. Long ago, the grubs themselves were eaten as a treat by the Greeks and Romans, and today they're consumed by many in Asia, Africa, and South America. Our own modern dogs love the grubs, too. But frankly, I'd rather have a hamburger.

13. Given the style of this passage, we can infer that the intended audience is most probably

    (A) college students

    (B) retired people

    (C) academics

    (D) young people

    (E) the newspaper readership

14. The writing style of this passage can best be described as

    (A) didactic, yet hilarious

    (B) breezy and informal

    (C) somewhat dull and instructional

    (D) ponderous, yet interesting

    (E) uninspired

Questions 15 and 16 are based on the following passage:

Line Long ago, before the world was quite finished, the swine were in charge of all animal activities because they were so much smarter than the rest of man's animals. They ruled the land, and the whales ruled the seas. They were content on land as were the

5 behemoths in the seas. In contrast, men fought with other men and held great councils—smoking many pipes and drinking much legonde, the ancient intoxicating beverage—as they struggled to find a way to live in peace as the animals did. The swine debated among themselves about whether to enlighten the men on the

10 proper management of civilization, but decided in the end to let mankind discover the way for themselves.

15. Based on the writing style, this excerpt is most probably an example of which literary genre?

    (A) science fiction or fantasy

    (B) mythology

    (C) gothic romance

    (D) historical fiction

    (E) folklore or fable

16. In line 5, the word "behemoths" is used to mean

    (A) the swine

    (B) the men, who were forever at war

    (C) the whales

    (D) all the sea creatures

    (E) all the land creatures

Stop!
If you finish before your timer rings, check your work on this section only.

ANSWER SECTION

Answers to Practice Critical Reading Questions

Practice Critical Reading 1
(pp. 60–65)

1. **The correct answer is (C).** The phrase "Transported to the Indies" modifies the noun phrase that comes right after it, "his live blood."

2. **The correct answer is (D).** See lines 6–11, especially "interior vitality," line 16.

3. **The correct answer is (C).** See lines 7–8, "those summers had *dried up* all his physical superfluousness."

4. **The correct answer is (B).** See the description in lines 12–15.

5. **The correct answer is (A).** You could substitute this phrase for "endued with" in the passage.

6. **The correct answer is (A).** The author describes Starbuck in positive terms but is aware of Starbuck's weaknesses.

7. **The correct answer is (E).** The other seamen are contrasted with Starbuck.

8. **The correct answer is (D).** See lines 27–34.

9. **The correct answer is (B).** See the second paragraph, especially lines 35–38.

10. **The correct answer is (D).** Starbuck seems to have learned to be cautious (lines 44–49) from these deaths.

11. **The correct answer is (E).** See lines 58–64.

12. **The correct answer is (E).** See lines 58–64.

13. **The correct answer is (C).** If you have any doubt, reread the last paragraph.

14. **The correct answer is (D).** The author has shifted from the particular man Starbuck to men in general.

Practice Critical Reading 2
(pp. 65–71)

1. **The correct answer is (B).** You have to read the whole paragraph to determine that the author considers being old and ignorant a "critically important" misery.

2. **The correct answer is (C).** See lines 2–4.

3. **The correct answer is (D).** See lines 4–5.

4. **The correct answer is (E).** See lines 7–9.

5. **The correct answer is (A).** Examples of figures of speech: the mind as a treasury in line 12; "foolish old age" as "a barren vine" and as a fool's university in lines 13–14; life as sweet as a summer day in lines 21–23.

6. **The correct answer is (D).** Antisthenes is saying that his studies taught him to talk with himself—that having something to think about is like having someone to talk to.

7. **The correct answer is (E).** See lines 16–17.

8. **The correct answer is (B).** See lines 43-50.

9. **The correct answer is (A).** See lines 52-56.

10. **The correct answer is (D).** See lines 49-50.

11. **The correct answer is (B).** Forging "the anchors of the mind" (line 67) is the more rigorous or logical work of the mind, while "spinning the gossamers" is more delicate or creative.

12. **The correct answer is (E).** In line 70, being "full of life and fire" is contrasted to being a "stunted ascetic."

13. **The correct answer is (C).** Both authors are writing about education, the way to knowledge and learning.

14. **The correct answer is (C).** See particularly lines 4-7, 15-16, and 20-27 in Passage 1 and the final paragraph of Passage 2.

15. **The correct answer is (B).** Both authors reveal the strength of their opinions in the first paragraphs of their passages.

Practice Critical Reading 3
(pp. 71-74)

1. **The correct answer is (A).** The first paragraph discusses the simple nervous systems of simple animals in order to set up the discussion of the workings of more complex neural systems, which is the subject of the passage as a whole.

2. **The correct answer is (D).** See lines 20-23, which explain the opposite actions of axons and dendrites.

3. **The correct answer is (D).** Read the last sentence of the passage.

4. **The correct answer is (B).** The axon membranes are exposed to the "extracelluar medium"—the surrounding environment outside the cell.

5. **The correct answer is (B).** Note lines 26-30, which explain the contrast between vertebrate and invertebrate glial cell sheaths.

Practice Critical Reading 4
(p. 74)

1. **The correct answer is (D).** This concept is explained in sentence 2.

Practice Critical Reading 5
(pp. 75-79)

1. **The correct answer is (B).** Wars did not change the landscape for Native Americans, but their settling of the land did as they tilled fields, set fires, etc. See the final paragraph.

2. **The correct answer is (C).** "Intrepid" and "dauntless" are excellent synonyms.

3. **The correct answer is (E).** Reread that last paragraph. Authors often plant the thought they most want readers to remember at the end—in the major stress position.

4. **The correct answer is (B).** Reread lines 23-27.

5. **The correct answer is (C).**

6. **The correct answer is (A).** While answer choice (B) may be true, it is too sweeping a claim—too broad. The author repeatedly says that so many changes occurred at so many different times that an accurate description of early western North America is not possible.

7. **The correct answer is (D).** Note that authorities are cited here, which always adds credibility.

8. **The correct answer is (D).** Fires to clear land typically affect smaller animals, not megafauna. Also, much of the megafauna became extinct in earlier millennia, before humankind.

9. **The correct answer is (D).** This is by far the most logical choice.

Practice Critical Reading 6
(pp. 79–81)

1. **The correct answer is (D).** M. Renard addresses the "Judge" (line 8) and speaks of his "witnesses" (line 18).

2. **The correct answer is (A).** At Mme. Renard's first outburst, M. Renard spoke to himself but not to her (line 6). When he teased her and she got angry, he was again silent (line 17). He also says he "felt" her final comment, though he did nothing (line 30).

3. **The correct answer is (A).** They felt indignant because the "little man" had stolen their fishing spot and wounded because he was catching what they considered to be their fish.

4. **The correct answer is (B).** See lines 24–25, 27–29, and 33–35.

5. **The correct answer is (D).** M. Renard is wordy, but he conveys his feelings movingly. Choice (C) might draw you, but note that M. Renard recounts events in precise chronological order.

Practice Critical Reading 7
(pp. 81–82)

1. **The correct answer is (B).** Reread the second sentence. Knight is the one who says that sociology is "the science of talk" and he thinks that it includes bad talk, as well as good talk.

2. **The correct answer is (D).** The entire paragraph supports this choice, but no other.

Answers to Practice Sentence Completions

Practice Sentence Completions 1
(pp. 88–90)

1. **The correct answer is (D).** inestimable (This word is defined after the blank.)

2. **The correct answer is (B).** ambivalent. .diversity (Everything after the semicolon shows that James is of two minds about joining a fraternity, and the first blank must describe this state; only answer (B) and possibly answer (A) fill this requirement. The second blank must offer a contrast to being with people just like James—like-minded, in other words. The question is of people types, not education, so answer (A) does not work.)

3. **The correct answer is (C).** compromise. .disparate (Logic points to *disparate* for the second blank; the first blank must be filled by a word describing how people with differences can meet and solve problems. Answer (D) is way off the mark.)

4. **The correct answer is (B).** credulous. .succumb to (The first blank narrows the choice to (A) or (B); *credulous* means *gullible, easily fooled.* One can't *adhere to* a scheme, so that leaves (B) *succumb to,* or *give in to.*)

5. **The correct answer is (B).** a volatile (The word chosen must be a direct opposite of the name *Patience;* note *at odds with her name,* plus the entire predicate.)

6. **The correct answer is (B).** incompatible. .witty repartee (Logic requires a negative word for the first blank, because this sentence contrasts the attitude of a serious artist with that of people who give endless parties. Idiomatic usage then requires *witty repartee* for the second blank, as the people are being *regaled* (delightfully entertained).)

7. **The correct answer is (C).** paradox. .inhibited (This sentence requires an understanding of the word *paradox,* which the sentence goes on to illustrate. The second blank demands a negative word; thus, answer (B) may be tempting, but it is not as precise as answer (C), nor does it work idiomatically.)

8. **The correct answer is (C).** chaotic. .tranquillity (The first blank needs a negative word to contrast with a positive word that goes with *and peaceful* in the second blank. Only answer (C) offers that contrast.)

9. **The correct answer is (E).** susceptible. .efficacy (A sentence of contrast: the first blank narrows the choices to (C) and (E), but *inevitability* isn't a logical choice of word to refer to *miracles.*)

10. **The correct answer is (A).** terseness. .profusion (This sentence contrasts literary styles, the lean versus the fat. Other answers may be momentarily tempting, but none set up the exact contrast except answer (A).)

Practice Sentence Completions 2
(pp. 90–92)

1. **The correct answer is (B).** enriched (The rest of the sentence provides an implied definition. Note the word *distinguished.*)

2. **The correct answer is (E).** lax. .bribed (The kind of security that makes escapes common could only be (C), (D), or (E). Guards who are easily *converted* or *investigated* wouldn't necessarily help someone escape, but those who are easily *bribed* (E) certainly would.)

3. **The correct answer is (B).** incongruous (This sentence of stark contrasts joined in one person requires a word that describes this odd state, not a judgment call as offered by answers (C), (D), and (E).)

4. **The correct answer is (C).** canny. .acumen (Contrast requires that the first blank be filled by an opposite of *young, ingenuous;* the second blank must explain why opponents are often *surprised.* Answer (A) is weak all around.)

5. **The correct answer is (A).** attest. .unabated (Sentence sense and general knowledge require answer (A).)

6. **The correct answer is (D).** prehensile. .precocious (The first clause points to a word meaning *to grasp quickly and well,* for which *prehensile* is the perfect choice; the word required in the second blank is extremely similar, and it is defined in the sentence.)

7. **The correct answer is (B).** dearth. .inundated with (Contrast requires a negative word in the first blank, especially called for by the verb *suffered;* the second blank must complete the meaning of *reams of information.* Answer (E) is weak, off the mark.)

8. **The correct answer is (E).** altruism. .narcissism (The first blank must be a word that coordinates well with *generosity,* because the two words are joined by *and;* the contrast, however, requires an opposite in the second blank, and *narcissism* is the most specific, given the phrase *in her own name.* Her new charity is an extremely selfish-looking thing to her associates.)

9. **The correct answer is (C).** ascetic. .avaricious (Only answers (A), (B), and (C) can be considered for the first blank, and, of those choices, only answer (C) has a negative word in the second blank, and it's the perfect word, as it must be an opposite to *no need of worldly goods.*)

10. **The correct answer is (E).** obsolescent. .myopic (Logic requires a word meaning *old, outdated,* or *obsolete* in the first blank; only answer (E) is possible. *Myopic,* meaning nearsighted, completes the contrast.)

Practice Sentence Completions 3
(pp. 93–95)

1. **The correct answer is (C).** problem-solving skills (Answer (B) merely repeats *logic* in the sentence and is not as specific as answer (C).)

2. **The correct answer is (E).** didactic (Definition of required word in sentence.)

3. **The correct answer is (A).** lackluster. .incapable (Sentence logic requires two negative words.)

4. **The correct answer is (B).** mollified (*Mollified* means *placated* and refers to someone whose anger or insult has been alleviated, as by an apology.)

5. **The correct answer is (D).** sanguinity. .debacle (Comparison requires a word meaning *optimism* in the first blank and a word referring to the effect of investments going sour in the second blank. Answer (A) shows a weak word, *process,* in its second slot.)

6. **The correct answer is (B).** catholic. .demagogue (Contrast requires an antonym of *parochial* (narrow, limited) in the first blank. The second blank is followed by a definition of *demagogue,* pointing to it as the perfect answer choice.)

7. **The correct answer is (A).** combat. .isolation (Sentence logic and idiomatic usage allow only the word *combat* in the first blank; the words *alone* and *solitary* mandate choosing *isolation.*)

8. **The correct answer is (C).** reluctant. .inaccurately reflect (The word *although* sets up a sentence with contrasting clauses, further emphasized by the verb *feared.* Answer (C) is the only logical choice.)

9. **The correct answer is (E).** fortuitous (This word is what the sentence goes on to define.)

10. **The correct answer is (B).** a formidable. .revolutionizing (Another sentence of contrast: The first blank requires a negative word and the second, a positive one. Only (B) and maybe (D) meet this requirement, and *revolutionizing* is a much better way of describing what a "remarkable machine" does than is *codifying.*)

Practice Sentence Completions 4
(pp. 95–97)

1. **The correct answer is (B).** a modest (Key words: *viewers did not flock/only*)

2. **The correct answer is (D).** demanding (Key words: *economics textbook/yet/ read attentively*)

3. **The correct answer is (D).** distort (Key words: *rather than/just so that*)

4. **The correct answer is (C).** truth (Key words: *Although* (sets up contrast)/ *honestly*)

5. **The correct answer is (E).** metamorphosis. .ruthless (Key words: *considerate* (requires sharply contrasting word for second blank)/*underwent a total/bent on evil*)

6. **The correct answer is (A).** harsh reality. .idealistic goals (Key words: *moral good/imagination*)

7. **The correct answer is (D).** relentless. .tenacity (Key words: *determination/ conquer*)

8. **The correct answer is (D).** an enigma (Key words: *to puzzle*)

9. **The correct answer is (D).** innate. .cultivate (Key words: *in a structured environment/wasteful* (sets up contrast))

10. **The correct answer is (B).** modicum. .chimera (Key words: *more than/not/ but/an actual man*)

15. **The correct answer is (D).** distort (Key words: *rather than/just so that*)

16. **The correct answer is (C).** truth (Key words: *Although* (sets up contrast)/ *honestly*)

Answers to Practice Writing Questions

Practice Identifying Sentence Errors 1
(pp. 104–105)

1. **The correct answer is (A).** An error in diction. The little sister should behave *respectfully* in church—in a manner that shows respect. To say that you gave awards to Bob and Jeannie *respectively* means that you awarded Bob first, and Jeannie second, *in that order*. Dressing *respectably* means dressing in a sensible (not lewd) manner.

2. **The correct answer is (A).** An error in verb tense. The verb "would have" is conditional, and is used to indicate something that possibly could happen. In this sentence, after the word "if," you must use the past perfect tense. If you had notified me (*but you didn't*, so what follows is put into conditional tense), I would have done something.
   Note: Look sharp. This common verb tense error is sure to appear on the test.

3. **The correct answer is (C).** Error in pronoun agreement. Each member is a singular phrase, requiring a singular pronoun that refers back. Thus, each member of the tour was warned to keep his (or her) camera ready.

4. **The correct answer is (B).** Error in diction. Dad was worried about rising costs. We raise children. You raise your head (lift it) up off the pillow. Costs, like bread, rise.

5. **The correct answer is (C).** Error in subject-verb agreement. The subject is films (plural), so the sentence should read: Here are the films you ordered.
   Note that some words in this common sentence are elided (left out). The full meaning of the sentence is, Here are the films that you ordered, or The films that you ordered are here.
   Note: If you feel grammatically challenged, rearrange words in a sentence to make the meaning absolutely clear.

6. **The correct answer is (C).** Error in pronoun choice. This sentence needs a subject and verb (who is) for its adjectival clause. One and a half inches means a lot to someone who's wishing to grow taller.
   Whose is possessive. Whose clothes are these? Whose car is that?
   One and a half inches is a unit of measurement here—akin to six days, fourteen pounds, two cups—which takes a *singular verb*. It's one thing.
   When the amount in the unit is thought of as separate, distinct entities, then use a *plural verb*. E.g., Five new quarters are in my coin collection.

7. **The correct answer is (E).** No error.

8. **The correct answer is (B).** Diction error. Sentence should read "fewer people than she had expected" because you can *count* people.
   Use few with all things you can count (trees, ideas, statues) and less with things you cannot count (butter, water, jelly). The latter are called *mass nouns*.

9. **The correct answer is (B).** Error in subject-verb agreement. When both items linked by or are singular nouns, the verb must be singular to agree. A puppy with bad habits or a kitten that scratches seems (think "either one seems") like trouble on foot.

10. **The correct answer is (E).** No error.
    Note: If you missed number 1, 4, or 8, then you should review the words and phrases in the Diction and Idiom Glossary, pp. 142–148.

Practice Identifying Sentence Errors 2
(pp. 105–106)

1. **The correct answer is (C).** Error in verb tense. The delay will occur in the future, if it occurs, and therefore requires will be as a future tense verb. Would is a conditional verb. E.g., I would go to the concert if I were you.

2. **The correct answer is (A).** Error in idiom. The phrases kind of a and sort of a are slang, not standard English.

3. **The correct answer is (B).** Error in pronoun case. The subject of the clause— that she could depend on the prom committee and me—is she. Its verb is could depend on and its two direct objects are prom committee and me, an object pronoun.
    Note: "Wordy" verbs like depend on are common. Think of burn up or burn down, act up or act out, put up with, etc. Grammarians refer to these as particle constructions.
    Myself is either a reflexive or intensive pronoun and can NEVER be an object. Watch for this common error on your test!
    e.g., Please do that for Mona and me. (Object of preposition for)
    I hit myself with the hammer. (Reflexive use—reflects back to subject)
    I baked that cake myself. (Intensive use—emphasizes the other pronoun; sometimes a noun)

4. **The correct answer is (E).** No error. Either the girls or the coach calls time out. . . .
    The *subject nearer the verb* determines whether the verb is singular or plural in *either-or* constructions.

5. **The correct answer is (C).** Pronoun error. In this independent (main) clause, you need both a subject and a verb. . . . it's (it is) somewhat tricky to put the apostrophe in its (possessive pronoun) place.

6. **The correct answer is (B).** Error in subject-verb agreement. The subject is troop. The prepositional phrase of Boy Scouts acts as an adjective to describe troop. Think: Many a troop . . . has spent, and you'll choose the singular verb to match troop.

7. **The correct answer is (A).** Pronoun error. This clause requires a subject and verb, you are, not a possessive pronoun, your. Think: I'm sure (that) you are bound to take offense. . . .

8. **The correct answer is (C).** Pronoun error. Separate the who/whom clause from the rest of its sentence. . . . who/whomever wrote the funniest essay. The clause needs a subject, who, for the verb wrote. Always ignore the rest of the sentence when deciding who/whom questions. Use either the objective case (whom) or the subject case (who) *depending solely on its use within the clause.*

9. **The correct answer is (A).** Error in idiom. Standard English says I see that. The slang phrase I see where is unacceptable because the words following I see will almost always be the direct object in the sentence. E.g., I see that we all need grammatical help (clause as direct object).

     Correct use of I see where would be I see where he went, or another similar sentence in which where will always be an adverb.

10. **The correct answer is (D).** Error in diction. The snacks are healthful snacks (to promote good health). The adjective healthy applies to animals, people, or things in good physical condition.

Practice Improving Sentences 1
(pp. 108–110)

1. **The correct answer is (B).** Error: Awkward phrasing and wordiness. Always eliminate the fact that.

2. **The correct answer is (D).** Error: Unclear reference. The pronoun that has to refer to a specific noun. Here, that noun must be pharmacy, which had not appeared in the sentence.

3. **The correct answer is (C).** Error: Lack of parallel structure. The three parallel verb phrases are begin their own theater, write their own plays, and thereby discover their own creativity.

4. **The correct answer is (B).** Error: Comma splice. This error creates a run-on sentence.

5. **The correct answer is (E).** Error: Incorrect conjunction. This is a cause and effect sentence. The ants survived because they were resistant to pesticides.

6. **The correct answer is (A).** Correct.

7. **The correct answer is (C).** Error: Misplaced modifier. The prepositional phrase about every two weeks acts as an adverb modifying gives. Keep adverbial modifiers close to their verbs for sentence sense.

8. **The correct answer is (D).** Error: Pronoun reference. The pronoun they is plural, and cannot correctly refer back to a singular anyone. Beware of pronouns! They cause more trouble than any other part of speech.

9. **The correct answer is (E).** Error: Vague pronoun. The it is a lone pronoun, standing for an unspecified concept. The readers wonder what the it means. Don't depend on weak pronouns like it and this. Use specific nouns instead.

10. **The correct answer is (D).** Errors: Shift in verb voice and dangling modifier. I biked is in the active voice, whereas the houses could be seen is in passive voice. The opening clause, As I biked along the quiet street must refer to the first noun in the main clause. You know that the houses cannot bike along the street.

Practice Improving Sentences 2
(pp. 111–114)

1. **The correct answer is (D).** Error: Lack of parallelism. All three things heard about the movie in this sentence need to be expressed in parallel form for clarity and grace in writing. Here, those three things are the *direct objects* of <u>had heard</u> and therefore must be *noun clauses* as in answer (D).

2. **The correct answer is (B).** Error: Comma splice. Two complete ideas are expressed, so punctuation needs to show that. (A semicolon before <u>consequently</u> works, too.)

3. **The correct answer is (E).** Error: Tense shift. The underlined portion has a verb in past tense, yet the other verbs are present tense. The guts of the sentence are

           subject verb predicate   noun
   (The) <u>trouble</u> is that we <u>owe</u> more thanks

   Because the verb <u>owe</u> appears in present tense, the past tense verb <u>was</u> makes no sense.

4. **The correct answer is (C).** Error: Missing pronoun antecedent. No noun exists in this sentence to which <u>it</u> can refer back. Watch out for the vague <u>it</u> and <u>this</u>. A measly pronoun cannot serve as a meaningful word for any foregoing, large, *unstated* concept or for a *missing noun.* (See sentence 2, Practice 1.) Examine all pronouns with a suspicious eye!

5. **The correct answer is (D).** Error: Incorrect subordination. The conjunction <u>and</u> links ideas that are equal. This sentence has a main idea—<u>Rachel Carson wrote eloquent essays</u>—and a subordinate idea—<u>that communicate the need for respecting our fragile world.</u>

6. **The correct answer is (C).** Error: Dangling modifier. A beginning participial phrase must modify a noun that follows directly after it. <u>Blowing across the sands</u> cannot modify <u>boy</u>.

7. **The correct answer is (E).** Error: Faulty punctuation. The semicolon separates two complete thoughts (independent clauses) that could stand alone as sentences. (Or a semicolon separates many items in a list that may have commas within them.) A dependent clause like <u>which was a dream come true</u> cannot masquerade as a sentence.

8. **The correct answer is (B).** Error: Wordiness. The most succinct sentence wins out here.

9. **The correct answer is (A).** No error. The introductory past participial phrase modifies <u>house</u>—the first noun that follows it—as it is supposed to do.

10. **The correct answer is (C).** Lack of clarity/shift in voice. <u>To attend</u> and (you) <u>must reserve</u> are now both in active voice. Adding a subject is critical. Readers need to know that a person will be attending the games, not just the seats.

Practice Improving Paragraphs 1
(pp. 117–122)

1. **The correct answer is (E).** Errors: Poor organization. Wordiness/redundancies. You can usually cut both from a sentence. Here, biography is also unnecessary. Answer (E) is structurally the most sound, given the other choices, and it suits a straightforward historic essay. Its *subject-verb-object* structure is also the most traditional/common.

2. **The correct answer is (B).** Errors: Lack of smooth flow; the original two sentences read like items in a list. Answer (B) is the result of sentence combining and its three prepositional phrases are nicely parallel.

3. **The correct answer is (D).** Error: Loose, rambling structure of three independent clauses linked with "and."
   When revising, ignore the structure of the original sentence yet keep the sense of it in as few words as possible, especially when asked to revise for *succinctness*, as here.

4. **The correct answer is (C).** Errors: Extraneous material. Fragmented structure. No other place in this paragraph discusses Napoleon's father, so it's best to consider him elsewhere, and keep the unity of the paragraph—a vital goal. Also, this material is a fragment, not a sentence.

5. **The correct answer is (B).** Error: Diction error sets wrong tone. Avoid slang words like humongous in serious essays. Slang jars the reader's ear because it is out of tone with the other words. Also, whenever you can avoid the weak verb forms of to be, do it. This revision shows a good place for a stunner word—here, the word prodigious.

6. **The correct answer is (A).** Errors: Diction. The wrong conjunction skews the logic of the sentence. Also, voice switches from passive to active.
   The wrong conjunction, because, messes up the logic of this sentence. Napoleon wasn't ill-tempered and over-bearing BECAUSE he was patriotic! Also, why use the passive voice, saying "was considered to be"?

7. **The correct answer is (A).** Errors: Abrupt ending. Use of weak "it is" as sentence-starter. Both sentences are dull, boring. The question asks for a more *graceful* ending to the paragraph.
   Answer (B) rambles in run-on fashion, and uses "it is."
   Answer (C) is factually inaccurate. The notebooks concern Napoleon's military education, not his patron.
   Answer (D) is extremely wordy (verbose) and boring.
   Answer (E) begins the sentence with information the reader doesn't have, which is confusing. This section must lead up to the notebooks, explaining how they came to be; they have to be placed at the end of a sentence, in the stress position.

Practice Improving Paragraphs 2
(pp. 123–127)

1. **The correct answer is (C).** The writing style in the first paragraph establishes the tone of the work, which should remain consistent throughout. You can determine tone by word usage and sentence structure. Textbooks typically have a more formal tone, as befits instruction. Magazine pieces are more informal—even chatty. Diary writing is personal in tone, and may be highly idiosyncratic, as befits the writer.

   Also, the opening paragraph of a short essay (not necessarily a longer one) typically makes a thesis statement, giving readers the main idea.

2. **The correct answer is (D).** This paragraph focuses on one significant use of chufa, the major ingredient in a highly successful product, horchata. The essay must show why chufa is an economically significant plant, in order to meet the assignment.

3. **The correct answer is (E).** The main purpose of this transitional phrase is to move (transition) from the discussion of one use of chufa, the drink called horchata, to a different use—food for animals that could be used to attract wild animals to one place for viewing, a popular form of ecotourism. While answers (A), (B), (C), and (D) are basically correct, they are not the major reason this phrase appears where it does.

4. **The correct answer is (B).** Paragraphs 3 and 4 give further support to the thesis, which maintains that chufa is an economically important plant. The support appears in several examples, facts, and a quote. The job of the middle paragraphs of any essay is to buttress the thesis. Use specific examples that are visual, concrete, or appealing to the senses. Broad, general claims are worthless.

5. **The correct answer is (A).** Read the sentences in this order: 5, 7, 6, and 8. Given these four sentences, this arrangement represents the most logical progression of information. A picky writer might suggest removing sentence 7 altogether, for the sake of unity, as this particular topic is never pursued.

6. **The correct answer is (E).** The error we need to fix is called a <u>pronoun shift</u>. The first-person pronouns, <u>I and me</u>, appear for the first time in the final sentence, a jarring experience for any reader, and one that can easily be avoided.

7. **The correct answer is (B).** This choice echoes information from the opening—always an appealing idea in closing—while keeping the writer's original idea that chufa would fit in well at Thanksgiving, one of the most significant meals eaten by Americans. The idea in the last two paragraphs is that this plant from the world's past can be culturally and economically valuable today in America.

   Note that the tone of answer choice (E) is formal and stilted—wrong for this essay.

Answers to Math Questions

Practice Problems in Arithmetic (pp. 162–164)

1. **The correct answer is (C).** Whatever x is, $-x + x = 0$.

2. **The correct answer is (C).** Start with 1 and, using the tests for divisibility, enumerate all of the possible factors:

    $1 \times 24 = 24$
    $2 \times 12 = 24$
    $3 \times 8 = 24$
    $4 \times 6 = 24$

    5 is not a factor of 24. You needn't check any numbers greater than 6, because any number greater than 6 would divide 24 fewer than 4 times, and you've already enumerated all of the positive integers less than 4.

3. **The correct answer is (B).** The equation becomes $19 - (-12) = 19 + 12 = 31$.

4. **The correct answer is (C).** All integers divisible by 4 are divisible by 2.

5. **The correct answer is (C).** 2 is the only even number that is prime. All other evens are divisible by 2.

6. **The correct answer is (C).** Region I has all positive integers, Region V has all the negative integers, and region III has one element, 0.

7. **The correct answer is (A).** $|x - y| = |y - x|$ = the difference between x and y.

8. **The correct answer is (E).** Your Venn diagram should look like:

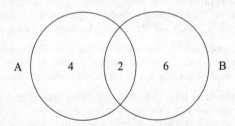

9. **The correct answer is (C).** Absolute values are always non-negative, so you can square both sides of the inequality without changing the direction of the inequality.

10. **The correct answer is (C).** The factors of 24 are 3 and 2^3, so $p \times 9 \times 10 \times 11$ must include these factors. The 9 and the 10 cover the 3 and one of the 2's; so, p must include the other two 2's. The only response that includes two 2's as factors is (C), 4.

11. **The correct answer is (10).** $620 \div 60 = 62 \div 6 = 31 \div 3$, which is 10 with a remainder of only 1.

12. **The correct answer is (20).** $2 \times 3 = 6$, and $6 \times 7 = 42$, so dividing each side of the equation by these factors leaves $a = 4 \times 5 = 20$.

13. **The correct answer is (10).** Notice that $1 + 20 = 2 + 19 = \ldots = 10 + 11 = 21$. Grouping the expression this way leaves $10(21) = 21x$.

14. **The correct answer is (50).** Imagine the even numbers lined up over the odd numbers:

$$2+4+6+\ldots+98+100$$
$$-(1+3+5+\ldots+97+\ 99)$$
$$\overline{\ 1+1+1+\ldots+\ 1\ +\ 1\ }$$

15. **The correct answer is (54.5).** The average number of 'yes' votes is

$$\frac{43+17+32+17}{2} = 54.5$$

Practice Problems in Fractions (pp. 174–179)

16. **The correct answer is (C).** The brown, black, blue and white socks together make up all of the socks; so, the sum of their fractional parts must be 1. Algebraically, this is stated: $\frac{1}{2}+\frac{1}{4}+\frac{1}{5}+w=1$. Multiplying both sides of the equation by 20 gives you $10+5+4+20w=20$ or $w=\frac{1}{20}$.

17. **The correct answer is (D).** Do this problem one card at a time. After taking one X card from pile A and putting it in pile B, the fractional part of X cards in pile A is $\frac{3}{5}$ and the fractional part of X cards in pile B is $\frac{1}{7}$. Notice that the "size" of the whole changes when you move cards. After moving the third X card, the fractional part of X cards in pile A is $\frac{1}{3}$ and in pile B is $\frac{3}{9}$. Since $\frac{1}{3}=\frac{3}{9}$, 3 is the answer.

18. **The correct answer is (D).** $7\frac{3}{4}$ feet $= 7\times12 + \frac{3}{4}\times12$ inches $= 93$ inches, and $5\frac{5}{6}$ feet $= 5\times12 + \frac{5}{6}\times12$ inches $= 70$ inches.

The difference is $93 - 70 = 23$ inches.

19. **The correct answer is (D).** $\dfrac{1}{\dfrac{1}{a}-\dfrac{1}{b}} = \dfrac{ab}{\dfrac{ab}{a}-\dfrac{ab}{b}} = \dfrac{ab}{b-a}$

20. **The correct answer is (B).** Either you can rename the decimal as a fraction and then do the multiplication, or you can just do the multiplication with decimals. Doing the multiplication with decimals looks like

$$\begin{array}{r} .125 \\ \times\ \ 8 \\ \hline 1.000 \end{array}$$

21. **The correct answer is (C).** $.2^2 = .2 \times .2 = .04$.

22. **The correct answer is (B).** $-0.6(0.4 - p) = 1.2(.8p + .7p)$

$$-.24 + .6p = 1.8p$$
$$-.24 = 1.2p$$
$$-.2 = p$$

23. **The correct answer is (A).** By subtracting the second equation from the first, you cause all of the 3s after the decimal point to subtract out, so you are left with $9n = 3$. Dividing both sides by 9 and then simplifying leaves you with $n = \dfrac{1}{3}$.

24. **The correct answer is (A).** The number remaining is $120 - 108 = 12$.

25. **The correct answer is (A).** $D = \dfrac{75}{100} \times 12$ is the distance the boy has walked. By dividing the numerator and the denominator first by 25 and then by 4, you can simplify the equation to $D = 9$. Subtracting 9, the distance already walked, from 12, the total distance, leaves 3 blocks to go.

26. **The correct answer is (C).** The first statement, "60-gallon tank is 40% full of water," can be written as $P = \dfrac{40}{100} \times 60 = 24$. Don't stop here and mark answer (A). Ask what percent 24 is of 40. Algebraically, it is written

$$24 = \frac{c}{100} \times 40 \text{, or}$$

$$c = \frac{24 \times 100}{40} = 60$$

27. **The correct answer is (B).** Problems involving boys and girls usually leave out one important unstated fact: the number of boys plus the number of girls equals the total number of people. Call the number of people in the class x. This means the number of boys is 30% of x or $\dfrac{30x}{100}$. Since the number of boys added to the number of girls equals the total number of people in the class, you can set up the equation $\dfrac{30}{100}x + 21 = x$. Solving for x, you get $x = 30$; that is, there are 30 people in the class. Subtracting 21, the number of girls in the class, leaves 9, the number of boys in the class.

28. **The correct answer is (B).** The word "represents" implies that a ratio is being used. We can assume that the ratio is constant throughout the drawing; so, we can set up the equation: $\dfrac{3 \text{ inches}}{9 \text{ feet}} = \dfrac{x \text{ inches}}{1 \text{ foot} + 6 \text{ inches}}$. Convert all measures to inches to get: $\dfrac{3 \text{ inches}}{9 \times 12 \text{ inches}} = \dfrac{x \text{ inches}}{12 \text{ inches} + 6 \text{ inches}}$. Finally, $x = \dfrac{18 \times 3}{9 \times 12} = .5$

29. **The correct answer is (B).**
$$3:4 = 3 \cdot 3 : 4 \cdot 3$$
$$= 9:12$$

30. **The correct answer is (C).** The total number of parts is $6 + 2 + 1 = 9$. Gerry receives 2 of them, so Gerry's share is $\dfrac{2}{9} \times \$72 = \$16$.

31. **The correct answer is (C).** It doesn't matter how many students there are. If 44% are boys, then 56% are girls and the ratio is $44:56 = 22:28 = 11:14$.

32. **The correct answer is (B).** An equilateral triangle is defined as having three equal sides; so one side is $\dfrac{1}{3}$ of the total.

33. **The correct answer is (B).** Let T be the capacity of the tank. Set up the equation $\dfrac{1}{3}T + 6 = \dfrac{5}{6}T$, and solve: $6 = \dfrac{5}{6}T - \dfrac{1}{3}T$
$$6 = \dfrac{3}{6}T$$
$$12 = T$$

34. **The correct answer is (A).** You can't have a fraction of a dog. (People are the same way.) Consequently, the number of dogs, d, and the number of beagles, $\dfrac{3}{8} \times \dfrac{2}{5} \times d = \dfrac{3}{20}d$ are integers. The only number less than 30 that gives an integer answer when multiplied by $\dfrac{3}{20}$ is 20.

35. **The correct answer is (D).** d dollars $= 100d$¢. The number of stamps that can be bought is the amount of dollars divided by the cost, $\dfrac{100d}{32}$.

36. **The correct answer is (2.40 or $\dfrac{12}{5}$).** A $\dfrac{1}{4}$-inch piece costs 5¢; so, a 1-inch piece costs 20¢, and 12 inches costs 12×20¢ $= 240$¢ $= \$2.40$.

37. **The correct answer is (.75 or $\frac{3}{4}$).** All of the water comes in through Channel A and out through Channels E and F. Channel B holds $\frac{5}{8}$ of the water coming in through Channel A. Three fifths of Channel B's water goes down Channel D, so the remaining $\frac{2}{5}$ of the $\frac{5}{8}$ goes down Channel E. If $\frac{2}{5} \times \frac{5}{8} = \frac{1}{4}$ of the water is leaving by Channel E, then the remaining $\frac{3}{4} = 75\%$ must be taking Channel F.

38. **The correct answer is (3).** $\dfrac{5}{x} = \dfrac{15}{9}$

$$x = \frac{5 \times 9}{15} = 3$$

39. **The correct answer is ($\frac{1}{3}$ or .333).** Remember that Joan paints $\frac{1}{2}$ of what is left, not $\frac{1}{2}$ of the fence. Jim paints $\frac{1}{3}$ of the fence, so $\frac{2}{3}$ remains. Half of $\frac{2}{3}$ is $\frac{1}{3}$.

40. **The correct answer is (100).** $\dfrac{30}{100} \times 80 = \dfrac{x}{100} \times 24$ Simplify before you multiply!

$$3 \times 10 \times 8 \times 10 = x \times 24$$
$$100 = x$$

Practice Problems in Exponents and Square Roots (pp. 183–185)

41. **The correct answer is (C).** $n^3 + n^2 = (-1)^3 + (-1)^2 = -1 + 1 = 0$

42. **The correct answer is (D).** $\dfrac{1}{y} = \sqrt{.25} = \sqrt{\dfrac{1}{4}} = \dfrac{1}{\sqrt{4}} = \dfrac{1}{2}$. Take the reciprocal of both sides of the equation to get $y = 2$.

43. **The correct answer is (E).** $4\sqrt{48} - 3\sqrt{12} = 4\sqrt{12 \times 4} - 3\sqrt{12} = 4\sqrt{4}\sqrt{12} - 3\sqrt{12}$
$$= 5\sqrt{12} = 5\sqrt{4 \times 3} = 5 \times 2 \times \sqrt{3} = 10\sqrt{3}$$

44. **The correct answer is (D).** $\left(\dfrac{1}{2}x^6\right)^2 = \left(\dfrac{1}{2}\right)^2 (x^6)^2 = \dfrac{1}{4}x^{12}$

45. **The correct answer is (E).** $\sqrt{\dfrac{x^2}{4} + \dfrac{4x^2}{9}} = \sqrt{\dfrac{9x^2}{36} + \dfrac{16x^2}{36}} = \sqrt{\dfrac{25x^2}{36}} = \dfrac{5}{6}x$

46. **The correct answer is (D).** $50{,}806 = (5 \times 10{,}000) + (8 \times 100) + 6 = 5(100)^2 + 8(100) + 6$. Consequently, $x = 100$.

47. **The correct answer is (A).** Divide both sides of the equation by 7, to get $x - y = \dfrac{20}{7}$.

48. **The correct answer is (E).** $x^2 < x$ indicates multiplying by x decreases the original value. This happens when x is a positive fraction less than 1. The statement is not true when x is negative because a negative squared is positive.

49. **The correct answer is (E).** There were 7 wives, $7 \times 7 = 7^2$ sacks, $7 \times 7 \times 7 = 7^3$ cats, and 7^4 kittens.

50. **The correct answer is (B).** A negative raised to an odd power is negative; so, you can toss out answers (A) and (E). Anything raised to the 0th power is 1. $\left(-\dfrac{1}{2}\right)^2 = \dfrac{1}{4}$, and $\left(-\dfrac{1}{2}\right)^{-2} = \dfrac{1}{\frac{1}{4}} = 4$, answer (B).

51. **The correct answer is (3).** $2^{x+2} = 32 = 2^5$. Consequently $x + 2 = 5$ and $x = 3$.

52. **The correct answer is (20).** Start with $3x - .3x = 54$ and convert the problem to fractions to get $\dfrac{30}{10}x - \dfrac{3}{10}x = 54 \Rightarrow \dfrac{27}{10}x = 54 \Rightarrow x = \dfrac{54 \times 10}{27} = 2 \times 10 = 20$. Go

    back and check whether 20 makes the original equation true.

53. **The correct answer is (.11).** $\sqrt{.0121} = \sqrt{\dfrac{121}{10,000}} = \dfrac{11}{100} = .11$. There are not enough columns to code 11/100 without first converting it to a decimal representation.

54. **The correct answer is ($\dfrac{1}{16}$ or .063).** $64^{-\frac{2}{3}} = \dfrac{1}{\left(\sqrt[3]{64}\right)^2} = \dfrac{1}{4^2} = \dfrac{1}{16}$

55. **The correct answer is (21).** The areas of the faces are 81, 49, 16 and 1, so the sides of the squares are $\sqrt{81}, \sqrt{49}, \sqrt{16}, \sqrt{1}$. The height is the sum of these values

    $$\sqrt{81} + \sqrt{49} + \sqrt{16} + \sqrt{1} = 9 + 7 + 4 + 1 = 21$$

Practice Problems in Basic Geometry (pp. 195–199)

56. **The correct answer is (B).** $2x + (x + 30) = 90$; $3x + 30 = 90$; $3x = 60$; $x = 20$.

57. **The correct answer is (D).** $m\angle ROQ + m\angle TOS = 271°$; $\angle ROQ + \angle TOS$ also equals $\angle ROS$, a straight angle, with $\angle TOQ$ counted twice; written algebraically, $m\angle ROQ + m\angle TOS = 180° + m\angle TOQ$; $271 = 180 + m\angle TOQ$; $m\angle TOQ = 271° - 180° = 91°$. $\angle TOQ$ and $\angle POV$ are vertical angles so they are equal.

58. **The correct answer is (C).** Area (ABCD) = 100 implies AB = 10; Area (PQBR) = 36 implies RB = 6; AR = AB − RB = 10 − 6 = 4. Area (TSRA) = $(AR)^2 = 4^2 = 16$.

59. **The correct answer is (E).** AB, the width of the rectangle, is given as 2. AD, the length of the rectangle, is made up of two radii of the circles; so it equals 4. The area equals the length times the width. $A = l \times w = 4 \times 2 = 8$.

60. The correct answer is (D). The side of the sheet is $(x + 4)$, so it's area is $(x + 4)^2$. You are told that another expression for the area is $x^2 + 24x$. Equating the two expressions you have $x^2 + 8x + 16 = x^2 + 24x$; which simplifies to $x = 1$. Don't stop here. $x = 1$, so the side of the sheet is $1 + 2 + 2 = 5$, and the area is 25. Don't stop here either. Each corner has area $2^2 = 4$, so the area of the sheet without the four corners is $25 - 4(4) = 9$.

61. The correct answer is (D). By adding two line segments (as below), you can greatly simplify this problem.

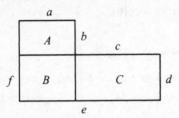

Now it is a lot easier to see that ab is the area of rectangle A and de is the area of rectangles $B + C$. All three of the smaller rectangles are accounted for, so answer (A) gives the correct area. Breaking up each of the other answers this way shows that they too give correct areas except for answer (D). In answer (D) you have af, which is the sum of rectangles A and B, and ed, which is the sum of the areas of rectangles B and C. Rectangle B is accounted for twice, so $af + ed$ is *greater* than the area of the figure.

62. The correct answer is (B). The bottom of the box is the shaded region. Its width is two sides of the square tabs, or more simply, $2s$. The length of the bottom is $3s$. When the tabs are folded up, the height of the box formed will be the height of one tab, s. The volume of the box is length times width times height, $3s \times 2s \times 1s = 6s^3$. One hint to the answer is the exponent. Length will always be given to the first power, area to the second power, and volume to the third.

63. The correct answer is (A). The length of the line drawn by the roller after one complete revolution is 4, so 4 is the circumference of the roller. The circumference equation says that $C = \pi d = 2\pi r$, Plugging 4 in for C, you have $4 = 2\pi r$, which simplifies to $r = \dfrac{2}{\pi}$.

64. The correct answer is (E). You are told the side of the square is 2. From this you know that it's diagonal is $2\sqrt{2}$. The width of the square is the diameter of the inner circle and the diagonal of the square is the diameter of the outer circle. Dividing the diameters by 2 gives their radii, $\sqrt{2}$ and 1. Plugging into the formula for the area of a circle you can compute the ratio of their areas: $(\sqrt{2})^2\pi:(1)^2\pi$. Simplifying, you're left with 2:1.

65. The correct answer is (B). Volume = length $\times$ width $\times$ depth: $24 = 8 \times 3 \times$ depth; so, depth = 1.

66. **The correct answer is (72).** Let $x = m\angle a$. Consequently, $2x = m\angle b$ and $2x = m\angle c$. You know that $m\angle a + m\angle b + m\angle c = 180°$. Substituting x for the angle measures you have $x + 2x + 2x = 180°$; $5x = 180°$; $x = 36°$. $\angle b$ and $\angle d$ are vertical angles so $m\angle d = m\angle b = 2x = 72°$.

67. **The correct answer is (20).** $(3x + 10°) + (x - 6°) = 84°$ because corresponding angles are congruent.

68. **The correct answer is (56).** Extend one of the transversals as shown below.

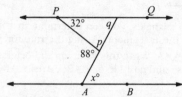

$p = 92°$ because it is supplemental to $88°$.

$q = 180° - (92° + 32°) = 56°$ because q, $92°$, and $32°$ are three angles in a triangle.

Using the rule for transversals of parallel lines, $m\angle x = m\angle q = 56°$.

69. **The correct answer is (80).** $\overline{OA}$ and $\overline{OB}$ are radii of the same circle, consequently the angles opposite them are equal. Call these angles x. The total number of degrees in a circle is 180; so, $m\angle AOB + x + x = 180$. You are told $m\angle AOB$ is $20°$, so $x = \dfrac{1}{2}(180 - 20) = 80$.

70. **The correct answer is (24).** Draw a circle around the five angles. The measures of the central angles of a circle add up to $360°$, so $x + 2x + 3x + 4x + 5x = 360$. $x = \dfrac{360}{15} = 24$.

More Practice Problems in Geometry (pp. 206–210)

71. **The correct answer is (C).** B is the midpoint of $\overline{AC}$, so AB = BC. Put a hash (/) on each of these line segments. By the same reasoning, put a double hash (//) on both $\overline{CD}$ and $\overline{DE}$. The length of $\overline{AC}$ is equal to two single hashes, while the length of $\overline{CE}$ is equal to two double hashes. These two are not necessarily equal, so C is not necessarily the midpoint of $\overline{AE}$ and Statement I is not necessarily true. Applying the same reasoning, Statement II is not necessarily true. The length of $\overline{BD}$ is a single hash plus a double hash, and the length of $\overline{AE}$ is two single hashes plus two double hashes; so, $\overline{BD}$ is half of $\overline{AE}$ and Statement III is true.

72. **The correct answer is (C).** There are several ways to proceed with this problem after you have drawn in all of the given information. The simplest approach is to say that BC and CF are both half the diagonal of the big square so they are both 4.

73. The correct answer is (A). Draw in $\overline{BE}$, where $\overline{BE}$ is perpendicular to $\overline{AC}$ and E is on $\overline{AC}$. This forms a 45-90-45 triangle and a 30-60-90 triangle. (Numbers like 30, 45, and 60 are hints that something like this is afoot.)

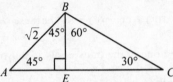

Applying the rule for 45-90-45 triangles, you can determine that AE = BE = 1. Write a '1' next to each of these segments. Using the rule for 30-60-90 you can determine that EC = $\sqrt{3}$. Write this value on the diagram. Now you know the lengths of a base and altitude of $\triangle$ABC. Area $\triangle$ABC =

$$\frac{1}{2}bh = \frac{1}{2}(1+\sqrt{3})(1) = \frac{1}{2} + \frac{\sqrt{3}}{2}$$

74. The correct answer is (B). Drawing a set of axes and marking down where each point lies can help you decide which point to test first. If you notice that (3,1) looks a lot closer to (3,4) and test it, you'll find that the distance between (3,4) and (3,1) is $\sqrt{(4-1)^2 + (3-3)^2} = 3$, not 5. Notice how when the points lie on a line parallel to an axis the distance equation becomes a lot simpler.

75. The correct answer is (B). The only quadrant in which x can not be greater than y is Quadrant II, where x is negative and y is positive.

76. The correct answer is (A). Using the formula for the midpoint would give you $(-x, -y)$ algebraically. To solve the problem graphically, put $A(x, y)$ in the first quadrant. If $(0,0)$ is the midpoint, B must be in the third quadrant. In the third quadrant x and y must *both* be negative. Hence the answer is $(-x, -y)$.

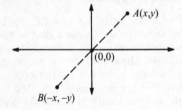

77. **The correct answer is (A).** The area of a triangle is given by the equation $A = \frac{1}{2}bh$. Call AB the base of the triangle. The corresponding altitude is then the distance from C to the *x*-axis, which is the absolute value (because distances are always positive) of point C's *y*-coordinate. Plug in 12 for A, $|y|$ for the height, and 6 for the base. What you have is $12 = \frac{1}{2}(6)(|y|)$. Solving for *y*, you get $|y| = 4$. Since C is in Quadrant III, *y* is negative; so $y = -4$.

78. **The correct answer is (C).** Call the vertices of the large triangle P(0,0), Q(0,1) and R(?, 0). Draw them on the figure along with all of the angle measures. $\triangle PQR$, $\triangle PQA$, and $\triangle PAR$ are all 30-60-90 triangles and you know that PQ = 1. Applying the rule for 30-60-90 triangles to $\triangle PQR$, you can deduce that PR = $\sqrt{3}$. Now that you know PR, apply the 30-60-90 rule a second time to deduce that PA = $\frac{\sqrt{3}}{2}$. Drop a perpendicular from A to the *x*-axis and call the point where they intersect "X". $\triangle PAX$ is a 30-60-90 triangle with hypotenuse $\frac{\sqrt{3}}{2}$, consequently its short side is $\frac{\sqrt{3}}{4}$. A and X have the same *x*-coordinate, so the *x*-coordinate of A is $\frac{\sqrt{3}}{4}$.

79. **The correct answer is (C).** The square has side $a\sqrt{2}$, so it's diagonal, which is also the circle's diameter is $2a$. A circle with diameter $2a$ has radius a and area πa^2.

80. **The correct answer is (D).** Start by drawing the picture. Owing to symmetry, the segment from the origin to the intersection point bisects the 60° angle and is the hypotenuse of two, congruent 30-60-90 triangles. The side opposite the 30° angle is a radius of the unit circle, 1, so the hypotenuse is 2.

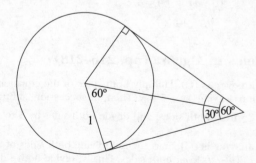

81. **The correct answer is (60).** The average is the sum divided by the number. The sum of the measures of the angles in a triangle is always 180, and there are always three angles in a triangle. The average is $180 \div 3 = 60$.

82. **The correct answer is $\left(\dfrac{7}{3} \text{ or } 2.33\right)$.** The formula for the slope of a line is $\dfrac{y_2 - y_1}{x_2 - x_1}$ for any two points on the line (x_1, y_1) and (x_2, y_2). You're told that the line passes through the origin, so let $(x_1, y_1) = (0,0)$ and $(x_2, y_2) = (3, 7)$. The slope of a line is constant so repeat the exercise with $(x_2, y_2) = (x, y)$:

$$\frac{7}{3} = \frac{y-0}{x-0} = \frac{y}{x}.$$

83. **The correct answer is (20).** The figure has already been drawn in this problem, so your next step is to fill in any information that you can. Two sides of the upper right triangle are congruent (they are both 2), so the angles opposite those two sides must also be congruent. Call these angles x. Now notice that $x°$, $x°$, and 40° make up a triangle, so their sum must be 180°. Algebraically, you have $x + x + 40 = 180$. Solving for x gives you $x = 70$. Now fill in the new information. One of the 70° angles shares a vertical angle with an angle in the lower left-hand triangle; these two angles must be equal. (Some more information to fill in.). In the lower left triangle you now have a 90° angle, a 70° angle, and a $p°$ angle. Their sum must be 180°. Solving for p gives $p = 20$.

84. **The correct answer is (130).** The figure has more information than you need. Find the triangle with angles 20°, 30°, and $r°$. As with any other triangle, their sum must be 180. $20 + 30 + r = 180$. Solve to get $r = 130$. Notice that the 100° and extra two line segments have absolutely no bearing on the problem.

85. **The correct answer is (8).** Using the formula for the distance between two points:

$$\sqrt{(9-3)^2 + (b-a)^2} = 10$$
$$36 + (b-a)^2 = 100$$
$$(b-a)^2 = 64 = 8^2$$
$$|b-a| = 8$$

Practice Problems in Algebra (pp. 216–218)

86. **The correct answer is (C).** Multiply both sides of the equation by 6 to eliminate the fraction, leaving $4x + 5 = x$. Then, in succession, subtract x from both sides, subtract 5 from both sides, and divide both sides by 3 to get $x = -\dfrac{5}{3}$

87. **The correct answer is (C).** Start by multiplying both sides of the equation by 6. Then, subtract $2(p + q)$ from both sides. Finally, divide both sides by 2.

88. **The correct answer is (A).** You don't need to know the values of a and b to evaluate $a + b - 6$, only their sum.

89. **The correct answer is (E).** Do this step by step. You are given b and c, so you can deduce a and d: $a = b - c = 4 - (-4) = 8$. $d = c - b = (-4) - 4 = -8$; alternatively, $d = -a = -8$ Finally, $d - a = -8 - 8 = -16$.

90. **The correct answer is (A).** You want to get the v isolated so you 1) Multiply both sides of the equation by uv; 2) Subtract $3v$ from both sides of the equation; 3) Distribute v out of the expression $uv - 3v$; and, 4) Divide both sides of the equation by $u - 3$.

91. **The correct answer is (D).** $\dfrac{1}{x}$ is greater than a positive number; so, x must be positive. Because you know x is positive, go ahead and multiply both sides of the inequality by $5x$ to get $5 > x$. Combine this with your original conclusion that x is positive to get $5 > x > 0$.

92. **The correct answer is (A).** Look at answer choices (A), (B) and (C). They all have the same numerator and (A) clearly has the largest denominator—it's one more than (C)'s and two more than (B)'s. Consequently, (A) is the least of these three. Likewise, (D) and (E) have the same denominator but (D)'s numerator is less, so (D) is the least of the two. Now you can plug in some very large number. $\dfrac{4}{y+1}$ becomes very small when y is large and $\dfrac{y+1}{4}$ becomes very large, so $\dfrac{4}{y+1}$ must be the least.

93. **The correct answer is (E).** Either you can do this by picking values for a and b that make every possible answer except the correct one false, or you can apply the rules for manipulating inequalities. Using $a = 2$ and $b = 1$ will cull out all of the bad answers. To manipulate the inequalities, notice that $a > b > 0$, so $\dfrac{a}{b} > 1$. And, $\dfrac{a}{b} \cdot \dfrac{a}{b}$ is greater than $1 \cdot \dfrac{a}{b}$.

94. **The correct answer is (D).** Again, this is a good place for pick and plug. Substitute -1 for x, and you get $3 > 3$, which is false; so, solution (D) contains the value that could not be x.

95. **The correct answer is (C).** This problem can be solved by plugging in values for p and q (e.g., $q = 1$ and $p = 2$) or by applying the inequality manipulations. Try to go from the given inequality to solution (C). First multiply both sides of $q < p$ by -1 and remember to reverse the inequality sign to get $-q > -p$. Then, add 5 to both sides of the inequality; $5 - q > 5 - p$. This is exactly the opposite of solution (C), so solution (C) must contain the false statement.

96. **The correct answer is (8).**
$$4(y-3)+1 = 2(y+4)-3$$
$$4y-12+1 = 2y+8-3$$
$$2y = 16$$
$$y = 8$$

97. The correct answer is (4). $4x - 6\left(3 - \dfrac{1}{2}x\right) = 10$

$$4x - 18 + 3x = 10$$
$$7x = 28$$
$$x = 4$$

98. The correct answer is any x such that $0 < x < \dfrac{1}{2}$.

$$\dfrac{1}{4} < (1-x)^2 < 1$$

$$\dfrac{1}{2} < 1 - x < 1$$

$$-\dfrac{1}{2} > x - 1 > -1$$

$$\dfrac{1}{2} > x > 0$$

99. The correct answer is (2). The remainders when 5 consecutive integers are divided by 5 are 0, 1, 2, 3, and 4. The sum of the remainders is $1 + 2 + 3 + 4 = 10$, and their average is $\dfrac{10}{5} = 2$.

100. The correct answer is any number of the form 840n + 2. You could multiply all seven numbers together and to get 201600 and add two for the answer; however, your answer wouldn't fit into the grid. Instead, notice that you need the factors $\{2^2, 3, \text{and } 5\}$ to cover the first three numbers. The next number, 6, is already accounted for because your factors include 2 and 3. To complete the minimal set of factors you need to account for all seven numbers; add a 7 and another 2 to end up with $\{2^3, 3, 5, \text{and } 7\}$. Now multiply the factors together to get 840. Any number that is two more than a multiple of 840 is a correct answer.

More Practice Problems in Algebra (pp. 225–228)

101. **The correct answer is (A).**

$$7x - 4y = 7$$

$$7\left(\frac{3}{7}y\right) - 4y = 7$$

$$-y = 7$$

$$y = -7$$

102. **The correct answer is (E).** $(x-y)^2 = x^2 - 2xy + y^2 = 25 - 2(-5) = 35$

103. **The correct answer is (A).** $x - (5 - y) = x + y - 5 = 4 - 5 = -1$

104. **The correct answer is (D).** When $x = y$, $y = \frac{5}{9}y + 8$

$$\frac{4}{9}y = 8$$

$$y = \frac{8 \times 9}{4} = 18$$

105. **The correct answer is (E).** Multiply the first equation by 2, to determine what $2c$ is in terms of b and solve: $6b - (6b - 12) = 12$. You end up with $12 = 12$. This indicates that there is more than one solution and you can't determine b.

106. **The correct answer is (C).** When Albert divided the $(x-4)$'s in step three he may have divided by 0 if $x = 4$.

107. **The correct answer is (E.)** The two equations are equivalent—take the first and multiply both sides by -1. Consequently, you have one equation with two unknowns and cannot solve for the unknowns.

108. **The correct answer is (C).**

$$(x + a)(a - x) = (a + x)(a - x) = a^2 - x^2$$

109. **The correct answer is (A).** Substitute the expression for x from the second equation into the first to get:

$$y = 3(3y + 6) + 6$$

$$y = 9y + 24$$

$$-8y = 24$$

$$y = -3$$

110. **The correct answer is (E).** $16 = (x+4)^2 - (x-4)^2$

$$= (x^2 + 8x + 16) - (x^2 - 8x + 16)$$

$$= 8x - (-8x)$$

$$= 16x$$

$$x = 1$$

111. **The correct answer is (9200).** $a^2 - b^2 = (a - b)(a + b)$

$$= (96 - 4)(96 + 4)$$

$$= 92 \times 100$$

$$= 9200$$

112. The correct answer is (3). Substitute x for y^2 to get $x^2 = 18x - 81$. Shuffling this equation around you get $0 = x^2 - 18x + 81 = (x - 9)^2$. So, $9 = x = y^2$ and $y = \pm 3$. The problem asked for a non-negative solution so the answer is 3.

113. The correct answer is (3 or 5). Start by multiplying both sides of the equation by y to get $y^2 - 8y + 15 = 0$. The factors of 15 are 3 and 5, so the polynomial easily factors to $(y - 3)(y - 5) = 0$.

114. The correct answer is (9). Call the numbers x and y. Set up the two equations: $x^2 - y^2 = 9$ and $x - y = 1$. Factor $x^2 - y^2 = 9$ into $(x - y)(x + y) = 9$. Now you can see the path to figuring out the sum: $x + y = \dfrac{(x-y)(x+y)}{x-y} = \dfrac{x^2 - y^2}{x-y} = \dfrac{9}{1} = 9$

115. The correct answer is (53). You don't need to multiply the whole polynomials, only those parts that generate a term with an x^2. These are $(3x^2 \times 9) + (2x \times x) + (6 \times 4x^2) = 27x^2 + 2x^2 + 24x^2 = 53x^2$.

Practice Problems in Word Problems and Functions (pp. 234–237)

116. The correct answer is (C). $f(x)$ takes x and returns $2x + 2$. You want something, $f^{-1}(y)$, that takes $2x + 2$ and returns x. Set up the equation $y = 2x + 2$. To find the inverse, solve for x: $x = \dfrac{1}{2}(y - 2)$. Remember that the x's and y's are just placeholders in the function so $f^{-1}(x) = \dfrac{1}{2}(x - 2) = \dfrac{1}{2}x - 1$.

117. The correct answer is (A). Let Tom's age be T. His brother's is $\dfrac{1}{3}$T and his sister's is 3T. The sum of their ages (T + $\dfrac{1}{3}$T + 3T) equals five less than twice the oldest ($2 \times$ 3T $- 5$). Solve T + $\dfrac{1}{3}$T + 3T = 6T $- 5$ to get $5 = \dfrac{5}{3}$T or T = 3.

118. The correct answer is (A). $(4, 6) \otimes (8, 2) = (4 \times 2) - (6 \times 8) = 8 - 48 = -40$.

119. The correct answer is (B). $f\left(\dfrac{3}{4}\right) = \left(\dfrac{3}{4} - 1\right)^2 = \dfrac{1}{16}$

120. The correct answer is (C). $2 \otimes (-3) = (-3)^2 - 2(2^2) = 9 - 8 = 1$.

121. The correct answer is (B). $f(x) \circ g(x) = f\left(\dfrac{1}{3}x\right) = 3(\dfrac{1}{3}x) = x$.

122. The correct answer is (B). $\lceil -2.3 \rceil + \lceil 2.3 \rceil = -3 + 2 = -1$.

123. The correct answer is (E). $3 \otimes (-2) = 3^2(-2)^3 = 9(-8) = -72$.

124. The correct answer is (A). You can't prove something is true by choosing examples, but you can disprove it with just one counter example. Let a, b, and c be 3, 2, and 1.

Property I: $a \otimes b = b \otimes a = \dfrac{5}{6}$, so it's still in the running.

Property II: $(a \otimes b) \otimes c = \dfrac{\frac{5}{6}+1}{\frac{5}{6}} = \dfrac{11}{5}$ and $a \otimes (b \otimes c) = 3 \otimes \dfrac{3}{2} = \dfrac{3+\frac{3}{2}}{\frac{9}{2}} = 1$. Since

$\dfrac{11}{5} = 1$, Property II is not always true.

Property III: $a \otimes (b + c) = 3 \otimes 3 = \dfrac{2}{3}$; and $(a \otimes b) + (a \otimes c) = \dfrac{5}{6}+\dfrac{4}{3}=\dfrac{13}{6}$.

Since $\dfrac{2}{3} \neq \dfrac{13}{6}$, Property III is not always true.

Now go back to Property I. You can prove this algebraically or you can just notice that it doesn't matter which order you do either the addition or the multiplication so it doesn't matter if you swap the order of a and b.

125. The correct answer is (B). $g(x)=\dfrac{x^2-6x+8}{x-2}=\dfrac{(x-2)(x-4)}{(x-2)}$. Because $(x-2)$ is

in the denominator $x \neq 2$. For every other case $g(x) = x - 4$. Since every number is 4 less than some other number, the only value not in $g(x)$'s range is when x is 2; $g(x)$ cannot be $2 - 4 = -2$.

126. The correct answer is (13). $f(3) = (3+1)^2 - (3-1)^2 + 1 = 16 - 4 + 1 = 13$.

127. The correct answer is (.09). $g\left(\dfrac{3}{2},\dfrac{2}{3}\right)=\left(\dfrac{\frac{3}{2}-1}{\frac{2}{3}+1}\right)^2=\left(\dfrac{\frac{1}{2}}{\frac{5}{3}}\right)^2=\left(\dfrac{3}{10}\right)^2=\dfrac{9}{100}=.09$

128. The correct answer is (200). Let S be the number of students at school:

$\dfrac{1}{4}S+\dfrac{1}{5}S+110=S$

$5S + 4S + 2200 = 20S$

$2200 = 11S$

$200 = S$

129. The correct answer is (10). Each set of a nickel, dime and quarter is worth 40¢. $\$4.00 \div 40¢ = 10$.

130. The correct answer is (12). $g(z) = \dfrac{z}{4} = 3$, so $z = 12$.

Practice Problems in Algebraic Applications (pp. 244–250)

131. **The correct answer is (E).** Let the middle integer be x so that most of the arithmetic is cancellation. The equation is $(x - 4) + (x - 2) + x + (x + 2) + (x + 4) = 3(x + 4) + 6$. This simplifies to: $5x = 3x + 18$ or $x = 9$. The sum of the integers is $5x = 45$.

132. **The correct answer is (C).**

$$\text{Average} = \frac{\text{Sum}}{\text{Number of Terms}} = \frac{2x+1+x+5+1-4x+3x+1}{4} = \frac{2x+8}{4} = \frac{1}{2}x+2$$

133. **The correct answer is (E).** The greatest average occurs when two players weigh 175 and one weighs 150. This value is $\frac{150+175+175}{3} = 166\frac{2}{3}$.

$167 > 166\frac{2}{3}$, so it cannot be the weight of the third player.

134. **The correct answer is (D).** Set up the equation $A = \frac{P + x}{2}$ and solve for x.

135. **The correct answer is (A).** All students standing in a position divisible by 4 are on Team D; so, the 52nd student is on Team D and the next, the 53rd, is on Team A.

136. **The correct answer is (E).** Each month the account *grows* by $\frac{1}{2}$% or .005.

After the first month, this can be written $x + .005x = 1.005x$. To find the amount after two months, multiply by 1.005 again to get $(1.005)(1.005)x = (1.005)^2x$. After the 120th month, the value is $(1.005)^{120}x$, where x is 1,000 for this problem.

137. **The correct answer is (C).** The elements in order are 1, 2, 2, 4, 8, 32, 256, 32×256. Without doing the multiplication, you know that the 8th element is greater than 1,000.

138. **The correct answer is (A).** Before the boys come, the cost per share is $\frac{PD}{G}$.

After the boys come, the cost is $\frac{PD}{G + B}$. The difference is

$$\frac{PD}{G} - \frac{PD}{G+B} = \frac{PDG + PDB - PDG}{G(G+B)} = \frac{PDB}{G(G+B)}$$

139. **The correct answer is (B).** You are trying to find the least score Brianne can have during the 3rd quarter and still have a 90% average overall; so, assume during the fourth quarter she had a 100% average. The equation is

$$90 = \frac{87+87+X+100}{4}.$$ Solve to get, $X = 86$.

140. **The correct answer is (C).** The medicine starts with a potency of 1. Losing half of its potency every three hours is written $\left(\frac{1}{2}\right)^{\frac{t}{3}}$. After twelve hours the medicine is all used up so you need to subtract off $\left(\frac{1}{2}\right)^{\frac{12}{3}} = \frac{1}{16}$.

141. **The correct answer is (D).** For the first 8 hours, the woman is paid $8c$ dollars. For the remaining 5 hours, she is paid $10c$ dollars for a total of $18c$.

142. **The correct answer is (E).** $\dfrac{x \text{ inches}}{y \text{ minutes}} \times \dfrac{60 \text{ minutes}}{1 \text{ hour}} \times \dfrac{1 \text{ foot}}{12 \text{ inches}} = \dfrac{5x \text{ feet}}{y \text{ hour}}$

143. **The correct answer is (D).** $\dfrac{.24}{4} = \dfrac{x}{15}$

$$x = 15 \times .06 = \$0.90$$

144. **The correct answer is (D).** $\dfrac{\text{cost}}{\text{pound}} = \dfrac{\$3.00}{\frac{3}{4} \text{lbs}} = 4 \dfrac{\text{dollars}}{\text{pound}}$

145. **The correct answer is (D).** $\dfrac{1 \text{ pool}}{8 \text{ hours}} t + \dfrac{1 \text{ pool}}{12 \text{ hours}} t = 1 \text{ pool}$

$$3t + 2t = 24 \text{ hours}$$
$$t = 4.8 \text{ hours}$$

146. **The correct answer is (16).**

1. Name the variable and set up the equation. Let the current time be t.

   Four years ago my age was half of what it will be in eight years:

   $$t - 4 = \frac{1}{2}(t + 8)$$

2. Solve the equation to get $t = 16$.

3. Check your answer: Four years ago I was twelve and in eight years I'll be 24.

147. **The correct answer is (15).**

a. $\dfrac{F + 15}{M + 15} = \dfrac{2}{1}$ and $\dfrac{F - 5}{M - 5} = \dfrac{4}{1}$

b. Manipulating the second equation you get: $F + 15 = 4M - 20 + 20 = 4M$

c. Substituting $4M$ for $F + 15$ in the first equation leaves: $\dfrac{4M}{M + 15} = \dfrac{2}{1}$

d. Solve to get $M = 15$

e. To test your answer, plug $M = 15$ into either of the original equations to get $F = 45$.

148. The correct answer is (134).
    a. List what you know:
        i. There are 10 houses with average width x.
        ii. There are 9 spaces between the houses with average width $x + 60$.
        iii. There is extra sidewalk of $60 + 60 = 120$ feet.
        iv. The total length of the sidewalk is 3206.
    b. Set up the equation $10x + 9(x + 60) + 120 = 3,206$.
    c. Solve to get the average width of a house, $x = 134$.

149. The correct answer is $\left(\dfrac{17}{8}\right)$. $\dfrac{2\frac{1}{2}+1\frac{3}{4}}{2}=\dfrac{8+2+4+3}{8}=\dfrac{17}{8}$

150. The correct answer is (10).
    a. Let x be the middle integer. Because these are even (not consecutive) integers, the largest is $x + 4$. Write: $5x = 3(x + 4)$.
    b. $5x = 3x + 12$
    c. $2x = 12$
    d. $x = 6$
    e. The greatest $= x + 4 = 10$.

151. The correct answer is $\left(\dfrac{7}{16}\right)$.

    a. Area of outer circle $= \pi(4)^2 = 16\pi$

    b. Area of third circle $= \pi(3)^2 = 9\pi$

    c. Area of band between the third and outer circles $= 16\pi - 9\pi = 7\pi$

    d. Probability of hitting the outer band $= \dfrac{7\pi}{16\pi} = \dfrac{7}{16}$.

152. The correct answer is (2.19). "The cycle is repeated..."—you are looking for a repeating series. After the first person is done, the booth has made a profit of 15¢—1¢, or 14¢. The second person loses a total of 10¢, the third 5¢; and the fourth wins 10¢. The pattern is then repeated. The net profit for every 4 people going to the booth is 14¢ + 10¢ + 5¢ − 10¢ = 19¢. After 40 people have been to the booth, the net profit is 10 × 19¢ plus the amount the booth wins from the next 3 people: 14¢, 10¢, and 5¢. The total profit is (10 × 19¢) + 14¢ + 10¢ + 5¢ = $2.19.

153. The correct answer is (8). Alex and Sam are heading apart at $35 + 45 = 80$ miles per hour. To go 640 miles it will take them $\dfrac{640 \text{ miles}}{80 \frac{\text{miles}}{\text{hour}}} = 8$ hours

154. The correct answer is $\left(\frac{1}{4} \text{ or } .25\right)$. Let s be the length of a side of the square. The area of the square is s^2. $\overline{ED}$ is a base of $\triangle BDE$ and has length $\frac{1}{2}s$ because it is the midpoint of the side of the square. The altitude corresponding to $\overline{ED}$ is $\overline{BC}$, which is also a side of the square, so it has length s. The area of $\triangle BDE =$
$$\frac{1}{2}\left(\frac{1}{2}s\right)s = \frac{1}{4}s^2.$$

155. The correct answer is ($1.50). Ellie travels 120 miles per week. When her tires are underinflated she uses 6 gallons of gas. When they are correctly inflated she uses 5 gallons of gas. The difference is one gallon at $1.50 per gallon.

Practice Problems in Graphs (pp. 257–262)

156. The correct answer is (C).
   a. In 1993 the growth rate was $\dfrac{6\text{-}5 \text{ billion}}{1999\text{-}1987} \dfrac{\text{people}}{\text{year}} = \dfrac{1 \text{ billion}}{12} \dfrac{\text{people}}{\text{year}}$.

   b. In 1880 the growth rate was roughly $\dfrac{2\text{-}1 \text{ billion}}{1930\text{-}1830} \dfrac{\text{people}}{\text{year}} = \dfrac{1 \text{ billion}}{100} \dfrac{\text{people}}{\text{year}}$.

   c. $\dfrac{1}{12} \div \dfrac{1}{100} = \dfrac{25}{3} \approx 8$

157. The correct answer is (B). As y increases, so does x, so they are proportional. As y increases, the bubble size decreases, so they are inversely proportional.

158. The correct answer is (D). The line passes close to the origin, a little above (8, 16), for a slope of 2, and below (16, 48) for a slope of 4.

159. The correct answer is (E). y does not consistently grow smaller or larger; instead it vacillates back and forth.

160. The correct answer is (C). With one hour of sleep and 8 hours of training a person reaches 60% proficiency. It takes a person with 7 hours of sleep 2 hours to reach 60% proficiency.

161. The correct answer is (D). Curves A, B, and C are $y = x^0$, $y = x^1$, and $y = x^2$ respectively. Curve D cannot have the form $y = x^n$ because when $x = -1$, y is negative implying that n is odd, but when $x = -2$, y is positive implying that n is even.

162. The correct answer is (E). The total cost is $40 plus 10¢ per date time minute, .1d.

163. The correct answer is (E). Let m be minutes. The Simplicity Plan is $10 + $0.08m$. The Per Call plan costs $0.10m$. Simplicity is better when:
   a. $10 + .08m < .1m$
   b. $10 < .02m$
   c. $1000 < 2m$
   d. $500 < m$

164. The correct answer is (A). From 1970 to 1975 apple prices doubled from 5¢ to 10¢, a 100% increase. No other period showed prices doubling.

165. The correct answer is (D). Let $f(x) = \dfrac{3x-2}{5}$ and solve for x to get

$x = \dfrac{5f(x)+2}{3}$ or $f^{-1}(x) = \dfrac{5x+2}{3}$. As a test: $f(9) = 5$ and $f^{-1}(5) = 9$.

166. The correct answer is (A). The dashed graph has the same horizontal spacing as the solid graph. Vertically, the dashed graph spans 4 units while the solid one spans 8, so it has been compressed to $\dfrac{1}{2}$ the size of the solid graph. Furthermore, the center of the dashed graph is shifted up one unit from the center of the solid graph. Taken together, these two shifts can be written $\dfrac{1}{2}f(x) + 1$—first compress the solid graph, then shift it up.

167. The correct answer is (150). 15% of $5,000 is $750; 20% savings of $750 is $150.

168. The correct answer is (25). Using the first two points, slope $= \dfrac{212-32}{100-0} = \dfrac{180}{100} = \dfrac{9}{5}$. The slope for a line is constant so $\dfrac{9}{5} = \dfrac{77-32}{x-0} = \dfrac{45}{x}$. Solving, you get $x = 25$.

169. The correct answer is (100). It takes 8 milliseconds to charge and 2 milliseconds to flash so a complete cycle requires $\dfrac{10}{1000}$ of a second. Divide 1 second by this to get $\dfrac{1}{\frac{10}{1000}} = \dfrac{1000}{10} = 100$.

170. The correct answer is (261). You can compute all of the percentages of 60 and then sum them, or you can add the percentages to get
$(90 + 75 + 95 + 90 + 85)\%$ of $60 = 435\%$ of $60 = 4.35 \times 60 = 261$.

Computing Your Score

Writing Sections 1 and 3

1. Take your written essay to an English/writing instructor to make a guesstimate of your score, based on the rubric given in this book on pages 128–129 in Unit 4.

Writing

You will receive a number from 1 to 6, based on your essay.
Write that number here: _____

2. For Section 3, multiple-choice questions on grammar, diction, idiom, and usage, *count the number you answered correctly*, and write it here: _____ Do not count any answers left blank.

3. Count the number you answered incorrectly. You will be penalized $\frac{1}{4}$ of a right answer (here shown as -2) for each wrong answer, which is traditional. Write that number of wrong answers here: _____

Writing Score Sheet

1. For showing up at the test, score 200.

2. Essay Score _____ $\times$ 37 = _____
   Actual SAT will award a sub-score ranging from 2 to 12 on the essay, as additional information for you..

3. # Correct multiple choice _____ $\times$ 7 = _____

   Subtotal 1, 2, and 3 = _____

4. Incorrect multiple choice _____ $\times$ -2 + $-$_____

   Total "Guesstimate" Score for Writing = _____
   (It's possible to total 800 here, but that will be rare. You should feel okay about a score that is 500 or above, although you should review further if you can, in order to score better.)

Critical Reading Sections 5, 7, and 8

1. Count the number of right answers in each of these 3 sections and record on the score sheet that follows. Do not count any answers left blank.

2. Count the number of wrong answers in all 3 sections. Record that number on the score sheet, where indicated.

3. Add lines 1 and 2 to obtain your subtotal, before deducting for questions answered incorrectly. [The PSAT and SAT have always deducted $\frac{1}{4}$ of a right answer (here shown as -2) for each incorrect answer.]

Critical Reading Score Sheet

1. Beginning score gift = <u>224</u>

2. All correct answers in Sections 5,
   7, and 8 = _____ $\times 8 =$ _____
   Subtotal = _____

3. All incorrect answers in Sections 5,
   7, and 8 = _____ $\times -2 = -$_____
   Guesstimate Critical Reading Score = _____

Computing Your Score

Math Sections 2, 4, and 6

1. Count the number of right answers for all multiple-choice questions in Sections 2, 4, and 6 only. All of these questions had 5 answer choices. Do not count questions with blank answer spaces—the ones you left unanswered. Record the number of right answers above Ⓐ.

2. Also for Sections 2, 4, and 6, count the wrong answers and enter the number above Ⓑ. Divide the wrong answer total by 4 and subtract the resulting number from the right answer total. And, write your answer above Ⓒ.

3. For each grid-in problem in Sections 4 and 6, count the total number of right answers. Do not count questions you left blank. Record the number of right answers above Ⓓ.

4. For each grid-in problem in Sections 4 and 6, count the wrong answers and enter the number above Ⓔ. Divide the wrong answer total by 3 and subtract the resulting number from the right answer total. Enter this value above Ⓕ. Note that you are not subtracting anything for grid-in questions that you answered incorrectly.

5. Add the two totals together to get a total raw score.

6. Multiply by 10.

7. Add 200 to get an approximate SAT score.

Math Score Sheet

$$\underline{\hspace{2cm}}_{Ⓐ} - \frac{1}{4} \times \underline{\hspace{2cm}}_{Ⓑ} = \underline{\hspace{2cm}}_{Ⓒ}$$

$$\underline{\hspace{2cm}}_{Ⓓ} - \frac{1}{3} \times \underline{\hspace{2cm}}_{Ⓔ} = \underline{\hspace{2cm}}_{Ⓕ}$$

Add the two totals together. = \underline{\hspace{2cm}}

Multiply by 10. = \underline{\hspace{2cm}}

Add 200 to get approximate SAT score. = \underline{\hspace{2cm}}

Self Evaluation for SAT Practice Test

Section 1, Essay

The scoring rubric (pp. 128–129 in Unit 4, Writing) lists which aspects of writing will be evaluated on your essay. Together with the friend, teacher, parent—or all three—who have read your essay, analyze your strengths and weaknesses, noting them here:

	Strong Point	*Needs Improvement*
Organization		
Addresses Topic Effectively		
Uses Specific Examples/Details		
Displays Sentence Variety		
Uses Correct Grammar		
Displays Strong Vocabulary		
Uses Correct Diction		
Is Logical and Clear Throughout		

Section 3, Grammar and Usage

Section 3 has 54 questions testing your grammar, diction, usage, and knowledge of effective, logical sentences and paragraphs.

List here the question number of each question that you *did not understand* or that you *missed*: _____

Questions that were correct as written were 6, 28, and 31. (On a "real test," you'll find at least two or three more that are correct as written.)

Questions on pronouns included 3, 10, 12, 13, 15, 38, 40, 47, 51, 53, and 54. If you missed any of these, or several of these, you need to study pronouns and their usage.

Questions on agreement (verb with subject, pronoun with antecedent) included 7, 8, 13 (see above), 15 (pronoun shift), 38 (see above), 40 (see above), and 48. If you missed any here, review the appropriate material in any good grammar text.

Questions on word usage or diction included 1, 9, 11, 14, 36, 39, 45, 50, and 51.

Questions involving verbs/tense of verbs/form of the verb included 4, 5, 7 (see above), 32, 41, and 46.

Questions 16 through 22 asked you to improve the prose—to edit and corrrect the given paragraphs—as you would edit your own work.

16. Lacked a clear reference for the pronoun *it*.

17. Asked you to recognize a transition word.

18. Tested your ability to revise a pair of sentences.

19. Tested your ability to see the need for a concluding sentence as a summation for the entire paragraph.

20. Asked you to fix the punctuation, in this case removing a comma that obstructed clarity.

21. Asked you to revise for clarity and logical flow.

22. Required that a word be added for parallel construction between sentence elements, in this case adding the preposition *for*.

Questions 35 through 39 asked you to edit the prose, as before.

35. Tested your ability to combine sentences to improve the opening of the paragraph.

36. Asked you to consider word choice in order to improve diction.

37. Asked you to arrange a group of sentences in the most logical order to achieve cohesion within the paragraph.

38. Required that you make "blue crab" and the referring pronoun agree in number.

39. Required you to alter one word to improve the diction in one sentence.

The remaining English grammar and usage points covered included the error of the *double negative* (2); errors in *parallel structure* (22, 23, 29, 33, and 42); the mistake of the *dangling participial phrase* (24 and 52); errors in *punctuation* (20, 25, and 30); incorrect use of *conjunction* (26, and 49); *joining subordinate clause to a main clause* (34); *lack of a verb* (32); and problems with *clarity/sentence logic* (21, 27, 34, and 37).

Okay . . . now that you know exactly what gives you trouble, you can seek help on specific aspects of English. You *can* learn this. As the saying goes, "It's not rocket science." This is *your own language*, after all. (At least it is for most of you.)

Critical Reading

	Number Right	*Number Wrong*
Section 5, Questions 1–29		
Section 7, Questions 1–27		
Section 8, Questions 1–16		

SUMMARY

1. I scored a _____ on the essay and need to review: _____

   _____

2. Of the 54 questions on the Writing, multiple-choice segment, I got _____ correct and _____ wrong. My problem areas include _____

   _____

3. Of the 72 multiple-choice Critical Reading questions, I got _____ correct and _____ wrong. When reading, I need to focus on _____

   _____

   in order to raise my score.

Math Results (Sections 2, 4, and 6)

_____ correct out of 60

Problems missed were in the areas of _____

_____

_____

Problems worked correctly were of the following types:

_____

_____

How about timing? If you are short of time on a real test, circle the more difficult problems and return to them only if time permits.

Areas needing review: _____

_____

_____

_____

Converting to Approximate SAT Score

Critical Reading Conversion

If your score was between:	Rough SAT score:
75 and 78	800
70 and 75	740 +
65 and 70	690 +
60 and 65	650 +
55 and 60	620 +
50 and 55	590 +
45 and 50	560 +
40 and 45	530 +
35 and 40	500 +
30 and 35	470 +
25 and 30	440 +
20 and 25	410 +
15 and 20	380 +
10 and 15	340 +
5 and 10	290 +
0 and 5	220 +

Math Conversion

If your score was between:	Rough SAT score:
59 and 60	800
55 and 59	720 +
50 and 55	670 +
45 and 50	620 +
40 and 45	580 +
35 and 40	550 +
30 and 35	510 +
25 and 30	480 +
20 and 25	450 +
15 and 20	410 +
10 and 15	370 +
5 and 10	320 +
0 and 5	240 +

Writing (Multiple Choice) Conversion

If your score was between:	Rough SAT score:
46 and 49	800
42 and 45	720 +
37 and 41	650 +
32 and 36	560 +
27 and 31	510 +
22 and 26	460 +

If you scored somewhat lower than you expected, fret not. These practice tests are usually harder for students than real SATs, and most people score a bit lower. A *real* test will be a treat, then, won't it? Also, now you can analyze what caused you to lose points and do something about the problem before the actual test day. Perhaps you can't "fix" as much as you'd like in the limited time left, but remember that *each correct answer is worth 8-10 points.* They all count and are worth working for.

The self evaluation will help to guide your study during further test preparation. And don't look at the columns that show what you did *wrong* as your sole evaluation. What did you do *right*? If you do certain things well, you know you can learn to do *other* things well, too.

Answers to Practice Test

Section 1
Using the scoring rubric on pages 128-129, work with your English teacher(s) to estimate a score, from 1-6.

Write that score here:_____

Section 2

1. C	11. E
2. D	12. D
3. D	13. B
4. E	14. E
5. A	15. D
6. E	16. E
7. B	17. E
8. D	18. D
9. E	19. A
10. A	20. E

Section 3

1. B	12. D	23. D	34. B	45. B
2. B	13. D	24. D	35. E	46. B
3. A	14. C	25. E	36. B	47. C
4. C	15. A	26. C	37. D	48. C
5. C	16. B	27. B	38. E	49. C
6. E	17. C	28. A	39. A	50. A
7. C	18. E	29. E	40. D	51. B
8. B	19. D	30. C	41. C	52. A
9. A	20. A	31. A	42. B	53. C
10. C	21. C	32. D	43. D	54. C
11. D	22. D	33. D	44. A	

Section 4

1. D

2. E

3. E

4. C

5. C

6. E

7. B

8. A

9. C

10. D

11. 2

12. $\frac{10}{3}$, or 3.33

13. Any x, $60 < x < 66$

14. 45

15. 9

16. $\frac{5}{4}$ or 1.25

17. $\frac{4}{5}$ or .8

18. .001

19. 36

20. $\frac{4}{3}$ or 1.33

Section 5

1. A	7. A	13. E	19. B	25. C
2. B	8. C	14. B	20. A	26. E
3. D	9. E	15. C	21. D	27. C
4. A	10. C	16. C	22. A	28. B
5. E	11. D	17. D	23. E	29. A
6. E	12. A	18. E	24. B	

Section 6

1. E	11. $\frac{5}{4}$ or 1.25
2. C	12. 667
3. D	13. 6
4. B	14. 10
5. C	15. $\frac{1}{4}$ or .25
6. A	16. 7920
7. C	17. $\frac{1}{50}$ or .02
8. E	18. Any x, $41 \leq x \leq 45$
9. C	19. $\frac{1}{2}$ or .5
10. C	20. 10

Section 7

1. C	**7.** A	**13.** D	**19.** D	**24.** E
2. B	**8.** D	**14.** E	**20.** A	**25.** A
3. B	**9.** A	**15.** D	**21.** C	**26.** D
4. D	**10.** C	**16.** C	**22.** C	**27.** E
5. C	**11.** C	**17.** C	**23.** B	
6. B	**12.** E	**18.** B		

Section 8

1. C	**5.** C	**9.** A	**13.** D
2. D	**6.** B	**10.** D	**14.** B
3. A	**7.** B	**11.** E	**15.** E
4. A	**8.** E	**12.** C	**16.** C

ANSWER SHEET FOR PRACTICE TEST

Completely darken bubbles with a No. 2 pencil.
If you make a mistake, be sure to erase mark completely. Erase all stray marks.

Start with number 1 for each new section.
If a section has fewer questions than answer spaces, leave the extra answer spaces blank.

SECTION 1

Answers will vary. If possible, ask a teacher or fellow student to review your essay and provide feedback.

SECTION 2

1 ⟨A⟩ ⟨B⟩ ⟨C⟩ ⟨D⟩ ⟨E⟩   6 ⟨A⟩ ⟨B⟩ ⟨C⟩ ⟨D⟩ ⟨E⟩   11 ⟨A⟩ ⟨B⟩ ⟨C⟩ ⟨D⟩ ⟨E⟩   16 ⟨A⟩ ⟨B⟩ ⟨C⟩ ⟨D⟩ ⟨E⟩
2 ⟨A⟩ ⟨B⟩ ⟨C⟩ ⟨D⟩ ⟨E⟩   7 ⟨A⟩ ⟨B⟩ ⟨C⟩ ⟨D⟩ ⟨E⟩   12 ⟨A⟩ ⟨B⟩ ⟨C⟩ ⟨D⟩ ⟨E⟩   17 ⟨A⟩ ⟨B⟩ ⟨C⟩ ⟨D⟩ ⟨E⟩
3 ⟨A⟩ ⟨B⟩ ⟨C⟩ ⟨D⟩ ⟨E⟩   8 ⟨A⟩ ⟨B⟩ ⟨C⟩ ⟨D⟩ ⟨E⟩   13 ⟨A⟩ ⟨B⟩ ⟨C⟩ ⟨D⟩ ⟨E⟩   18 ⟨A⟩ ⟨B⟩ ⟨C⟩ ⟨D⟩ ⟨E⟩
4 ⟨A⟩ ⟨B⟩ ⟨C⟩ ⟨D⟩ ⟨E⟩   9 ⟨A⟩ ⟨B⟩ ⟨C⟩ ⟨D⟩ ⟨E⟩   14 ⟨A⟩ ⟨B⟩ ⟨C⟩ ⟨D⟩ ⟨E⟩   19 ⟨A⟩ ⟨B⟩ ⟨C⟩ ⟨D⟩ ⟨E⟩
5 ⟨A⟩ ⟨B⟩ ⟨C⟩ ⟨D⟩ ⟨E⟩   10 ⟨A⟩ ⟨B⟩ ⟨C⟩ ⟨D⟩ ⟨E⟩   15 ⟨A⟩ ⟨B⟩ ⟨C⟩ ⟨D⟩ ⟨E⟩   20 ⟨A⟩ ⟨B⟩ ⟨C⟩ ⟨D⟩ ⟨E⟩

SECTION 3

1 ⟨A⟩ ⟨B⟩ ⟨C⟩ ⟨D⟩ ⟨E⟩   15 ⟨A⟩ ⟨B⟩ ⟨C⟩ ⟨D⟩ ⟨E⟩   29 ⟨A⟩ ⟨B⟩ ⟨C⟩ ⟨D⟩ ⟨E⟩   42 ⟨A⟩ ⟨B⟩ ⟨C⟩ ⟨D⟩ ⟨E⟩
2 ⟨A⟩ ⟨B⟩ ⟨C⟩ ⟨D⟩ ⟨E⟩   16 ⟨A⟩ ⟨B⟩ ⟨C⟩ ⟨D⟩ ⟨E⟩   30 ⟨A⟩ ⟨B⟩ ⟨C⟩ ⟨D⟩ ⟨E⟩   43 ⟨A⟩ ⟨B⟩ ⟨C⟩ ⟨D⟩ ⟨E⟩
3 ⟨A⟩ ⟨B⟩ ⟨C⟩ ⟨D⟩ ⟨E⟩   17 ⟨A⟩ ⟨B⟩ ⟨C⟩ ⟨D⟩ ⟨E⟩   31 ⟨A⟩ ⟨B⟩ ⟨C⟩ ⟨D⟩ ⟨E⟩   44 ⟨A⟩ ⟨B⟩ ⟨C⟩ ⟨D⟩ ⟨E⟩
4 ⟨A⟩ ⟨B⟩ ⟨C⟩ ⟨D⟩ ⟨E⟩   18 ⟨A⟩ ⟨B⟩ ⟨C⟩ ⟨D⟩ ⟨E⟩   32 ⟨A⟩ ⟨B⟩ ⟨C⟩ ⟨D⟩ ⟨E⟩   45 ⟨A⟩ ⟨B⟩ ⟨C⟩ ⟨D⟩ ⟨E⟩
5 ⟨A⟩ ⟨B⟩ ⟨C⟩ ⟨D⟩ ⟨E⟩   19 ⟨A⟩ ⟨B⟩ ⟨C⟩ ⟨D⟩ ⟨E⟩   33 ⟨A⟩ ⟨B⟩ ⟨C⟩ ⟨D⟩ ⟨E⟩   46 ⟨A⟩ ⟨B⟩ ⟨C⟩ ⟨D⟩ ⟨E⟩
6 ⟨A⟩ ⟨B⟩ ⟨C⟩ ⟨D⟩ ⟨E⟩   20 ⟨A⟩ ⟨B⟩ ⟨C⟩ ⟨D⟩ ⟨E⟩   34 ⟨A⟩ ⟨B⟩ ⟨C⟩ ⟨D⟩ ⟨E⟩   47 ⟨A⟩ ⟨B⟩ ⟨C⟩ ⟨D⟩ ⟨E⟩
7 ⟨A⟩ ⟨B⟩ ⟨C⟩ ⟨D⟩ ⟨E⟩   21 ⟨A⟩ ⟨B⟩ ⟨C⟩ ⟨D⟩ ⟨E⟩   35 ⟨A⟩ ⟨B⟩ ⟨C⟩ ⟨D⟩ ⟨E⟩   48 ⟨A⟩ ⟨B⟩ ⟨C⟩ ⟨D⟩ ⟨E⟩
8 ⟨A⟩ ⟨B⟩ ⟨C⟩ ⟨D⟩ ⟨E⟩   22 ⟨A⟩ ⟨B⟩ ⟨C⟩ ⟨D⟩ ⟨E⟩   36 ⟨A⟩ ⟨B⟩ ⟨C⟩ ⟨D⟩ ⟨E⟩   49 ⟨A⟩ ⟨B⟩ ⟨C⟩ ⟨D⟩ ⟨E⟩
6 ⟨A⟩ ⟨B⟩ ⟨C⟩ ⟨D⟩ ⟨E⟩   23 ⟨A⟩ ⟨B⟩ ⟨C⟩ ⟨D⟩ ⟨E⟩   37 ⟨A⟩ ⟨B⟩ ⟨C⟩ ⟨D⟩ ⟨E⟩   50 ⟨A⟩ ⟨B⟩ ⟨C⟩ ⟨D⟩ ⟨E⟩
10 ⟨A⟩ ⟨B⟩ ⟨C⟩ ⟨D⟩ ⟨E⟩   24 ⟨A⟩ ⟨B⟩ ⟨C⟩ ⟨D⟩ ⟨E⟩   38 ⟨A⟩ ⟨B⟩ ⟨C⟩ ⟨D⟩ ⟨E⟩   51 ⟨A⟩ ⟨B⟩ ⟨C⟩ ⟨D⟩ ⟨E⟩
11 ⟨A⟩ ⟨B⟩ ⟨C⟩ ⟨D⟩ ⟨E⟩   25 ⟨A⟩ ⟨B⟩ ⟨C⟩ ⟨D⟩ ⟨E⟩   39 ⟨A⟩ ⟨B⟩ ⟨C⟩ ⟨D⟩ ⟨E⟩   52 ⟨A⟩ ⟨B⟩ ⟨C⟩ ⟨D⟩ ⟨E⟩
12 ⟨A⟩ ⟨B⟩ ⟨C⟩ ⟨D⟩ ⟨E⟩   26 ⟨A⟩ ⟨B⟩ ⟨C⟩ ⟨D⟩ ⟨E⟩   40 ⟨A⟩ ⟨B⟩ ⟨C⟩ ⟨D⟩ ⟨E⟩   53 ⟨A⟩ ⟨B⟩ ⟨C⟩ ⟨D⟩ ⟨E⟩
13 ⟨A⟩ ⟨B⟩ ⟨C⟩ ⟨D⟩ ⟨E⟩   27 ⟨A⟩ ⟨B⟩ ⟨C⟩ ⟨D⟩ ⟨E⟩   41 ⟨A⟩ ⟨B⟩ ⟨C⟩ ⟨D⟩ ⟨E⟩   54 ⟨A⟩ ⟨B⟩ ⟨C⟩ ⟨D⟩ ⟨E⟩
14 ⟨A⟩ ⟨B⟩ ⟨C⟩ ⟨D⟩ ⟨E⟩   28 ⟨A⟩ ⟨B⟩ ⟨C⟩ ⟨D⟩ ⟨E⟩

ONLY ANSWERS ENTERED IN THE OVALS IN EACH GRID AREA WILL BE SCORED.
YOU WILL NOT RECEIVE CREDIT FOR ANYTHING WRITTEN IN THE BOXES ABOVE THE OVALS.

Grid-in answer bubbles for questions 11–20, each with columns for digits 0–9 and fraction/decimal markers.

Start with number 1 for each new section.
If a section has fewer questions than answer spaces, leave the extra answer spaces blank.

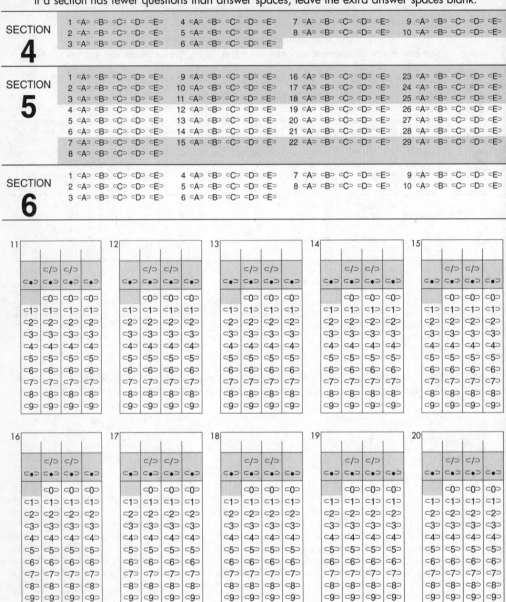

SECTION 4

1 ⟨A⟩ ⟨B⟩ ⟨C⟩ ⟨D⟩ ⟨E⟩   4 ⟨A⟩ ⟨B⟩ ⟨C⟩ ⟨D⟩ ⟨E⟩   7 ⟨A⟩ ⟨B⟩ ⟨C⟩ ⟨D⟩ ⟨E⟩   9 ⟨A⟩ ⟨B⟩ ⟨C⟩ ⟨D⟩ ⟨E⟩
2 ⟨A⟩ ⟨B⟩ ⟨C⟩ ⟨D⟩ ⟨E⟩   5 ⟨A⟩ ⟨B⟩ ⟨C⟩ ⟨D⟩ ⟨E⟩   8 ⟨A⟩ ⟨B⟩ ⟨C⟩ ⟨D⟩ ⟨E⟩   10 ⟨A⟩ ⟨B⟩ ⟨C⟩ ⟨D⟩ ⟨E⟩
3 ⟨A⟩ ⟨B⟩ ⟨C⟩ ⟨D⟩ ⟨E⟩   6 ⟨A⟩ ⟨B⟩ ⟨C⟩ ⟨D⟩ ⟨E⟩

SECTION 5

1 ⟨A⟩ ⟨B⟩ ⟨C⟩ ⟨D⟩ ⟨E⟩   9 ⟨A⟩ ⟨B⟩ ⟨C⟩ ⟨D⟩ ⟨E⟩   16 ⟨A⟩ ⟨B⟩ ⟨C⟩ ⟨D⟩ ⟨E⟩   23 ⟨A⟩ ⟨B⟩ ⟨C⟩ ⟨D⟩ ⟨E⟩
2 ⟨A⟩ ⟨B⟩ ⟨C⟩ ⟨D⟩ ⟨E⟩   10 ⟨A⟩ ⟨B⟩ ⟨C⟩ ⟨D⟩ ⟨E⟩   17 ⟨A⟩ ⟨B⟩ ⟨C⟩ ⟨D⟩ ⟨E⟩   24 ⟨A⟩ ⟨B⟩ ⟨C⟩ ⟨D⟩ ⟨E⟩
3 ⟨A⟩ ⟨B⟩ ⟨C⟩ ⟨D⟩ ⟨E⟩   11 ⟨A⟩ ⟨B⟩ ⟨C⟩ ⟨D⟩ ⟨E⟩   18 ⟨A⟩ ⟨B⟩ ⟨C⟩ ⟨D⟩ ⟨E⟩   25 ⟨A⟩ ⟨B⟩ ⟨C⟩ ⟨D⟩ ⟨E⟩
4 ⟨A⟩ ⟨B⟩ ⟨C⟩ ⟨D⟩ ⟨E⟩   12 ⟨A⟩ ⟨B⟩ ⟨C⟩ ⟨D⟩ ⟨E⟩   19 ⟨A⟩ ⟨B⟩ ⟨C⟩ ⟨D⟩ ⟨E⟩   26 ⟨A⟩ ⟨B⟩ ⟨C⟩ ⟨D⟩ ⟨E⟩
5 ⟨A⟩ ⟨B⟩ ⟨C⟩ ⟨D⟩ ⟨E⟩   13 ⟨A⟩ ⟨B⟩ ⟨C⟩ ⟨D⟩ ⟨E⟩   20 ⟨A⟩ ⟨B⟩ ⟨C⟩ ⟨D⟩ ⟨E⟩   27 ⟨A⟩ ⟨B⟩ ⟨C⟩ ⟨D⟩ ⟨E⟩
6 ⟨A⟩ ⟨B⟩ ⟨C⟩ ⟨D⟩ ⟨E⟩   14 ⟨A⟩ ⟨B⟩ ⟨C⟩ ⟨D⟩ ⟨E⟩   21 ⟨A⟩ ⟨B⟩ ⟨C⟩ ⟨D⟩ ⟨E⟩   28 ⟨A⟩ ⟨B⟩ ⟨C⟩ ⟨D⟩ ⟨E⟩
7 ⟨A⟩ ⟨B⟩ ⟨C⟩ ⟨D⟩ ⟨E⟩   15 ⟨A⟩ ⟨B⟩ ⟨C⟩ ⟨D⟩ ⟨E⟩   22 ⟨A⟩ ⟨B⟩ ⟨C⟩ ⟨D⟩ ⟨E⟩   29 ⟨A⟩ ⟨B⟩ ⟨C⟩ ⟨D⟩ ⟨E⟩
8 ⟨A⟩ ⟨B⟩ ⟨C⟩ ⟨D⟩ ⟨E⟩

SECTION 6

1 ⟨A⟩ ⟨B⟩ ⟨C⟩ ⟨D⟩ ⟨E⟩   4 ⟨A⟩ ⟨B⟩ ⟨C⟩ ⟨D⟩ ⟨E⟩   7 ⟨A⟩ ⟨B⟩ ⟨C⟩ ⟨D⟩ ⟨E⟩   9 ⟨A⟩ ⟨B⟩ ⟨C⟩ ⟨D⟩ ⟨E⟩
2 ⟨A⟩ ⟨B⟩ ⟨C⟩ ⟨D⟩ ⟨E⟩   5 ⟨A⟩ ⟨B⟩ ⟨C⟩ ⟨D⟩ ⟨E⟩   8 ⟨A⟩ ⟨B⟩ ⟨C⟩ ⟨D⟩ ⟨E⟩   10 ⟨A⟩ ⟨B⟩ ⟨C⟩ ⟨D⟩ ⟨E⟩
3 ⟨A⟩ ⟨B⟩ ⟨C⟩ ⟨D⟩ ⟨E⟩   6 ⟨A⟩ ⟨B⟩ ⟨C⟩ ⟨D⟩ ⟨E⟩

NOTES

NOTES

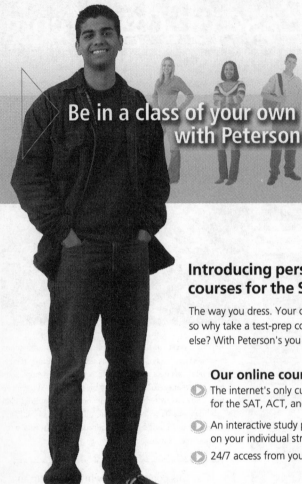